CHILTON'S Repair and Tune-Up Guide

Aspen / Volaré
1976–78

ILLUSTRATED

Prepared by the

Automotive Editorial Department

Chilton Book Company

Chilton Way
Radnor, Pa. 19089
215—687-8200

president and chief executive officer **WILLIAM A. BARBOUR;** executive vice president **RICHARD H. GROVES;** vice president and general manager **JOHN P. KUSHNERICK;** managing editor **JOHN H. WEISE, S.A.E.;** assistant managing editor **KERRY A. FREEMAN;** editor Robert F. King Jr.

CHILTON BOOK COMPANY   RADNOR, PENNSYLVANIA

Manufactured in the United States of America

234567890   654321098

Chilton's Repair & Tune-Up Guide: Aspen/Volaré
1976–78
ISBN 0-8019-6637-X pbk.

Library of Congress Catalog Card No. 77-93006

ACKNOWLEDGMENT

The Chilton Book Company expresses its appreciation to the Chrysler Corporation for technical information and illustrations contained herein.

Contents

Chapter 1

General Information and Maintenance

How to Use This Book

Chilton's Repair and Tune-Up Guide for the Aspen/Volaré is intended to give you a basic idea of how your car works and how to save money and time by servicing it yourself. The first two chapters will be the most frequently used, since they contain maintenance and tune-up information and procedures. The following eight chapters provide information and service techniques for the more complex systems of the car. Operating systems from engine through brakes are included to the extent that the average do-it-yourselfer should get involved. This book won't explain rebuilding the automatic transmission for the simple reason that the expertise required and the investment in special tools make this task uneconomical. We will tell you how to change your own brake pads and shoes, replace distributor cap and rotor, and many more jobs that will save you money, give you personal satisfaction, and help you avoid problems.

Before starting to loosen any bolts, please read through the entire section and the specific procedure. This will give you the overall view of what will be required as far as tools, supplies, and you. There is nothing more frustrating than having to walk to the bus stop on Monday morning because you were short one gasket during your Sunday afternoon repair work. So read ahead and plan ahead. Have all the necessary tools, parts, and materials assembled before you start.

The sections begin with a discussion of the system and what it involves. Adjustments and/or maintenance are then discussed, followed by removal and installation procedures and then repair or overhaul procedures where they are feasible. When repair or overhaul procedures are considered to be slightly more difficult, we tell you how to remove the part and then how to install the new or rebuilt replacement part; you at least save the labor costs of installation. Backyard repair of such components as the alternator aren't usually practical.

Two basic mechanic's rules are observed throughout. One, whenever the left side of the car is referred to, it is meant to specify the driver's side of the car. Conversely, the right side of the car means the passenger side of the car. Second, most screws and bolts are removed by turning counterclockwise and tightened by turning clockwise. Always keep safety uppermost in your mind. Stay aware of the hazards involved in working on an automobile and take the proper precautions. Use sturdy jackstands when working under a raised vehicle. Don't smoke or allow an exposed flame to come near the battery or any part of the fuel system. Use the correct tool for the job at hand. Take your time and be patient, as you gain experience you'll be able to work more quickly.

Tools and Equipment

The following list is the basic tool requirement to perform most of the procedures described in this guide. Consider tools as an investment that will more than repay their initial cost several times over.

1. A ⅜ in. drive socket set and a spark plug socket. If your car is equipped with a six cylinder engine, you'll need a ⅝ in. spark plug socket. V8 engines will require $^{13}/_{16}$ in. spark plug socket. Both of these are available just about anywhere that automotive parts are sold.

2. A set of combination wrenches (one end open and one end box) in sizes ranging from ⅜ in. to ¾ in.

3. A spark plug wire gauge.

4. Slot and phillips head screwdrivers.

5. Timing light, preferably a DC battery hook-up type.

6. Tachometer.

7. Torque wrench. This assures proper tightening of important fasteners and avoids costly stripping (too tight) or leaks (too loose).

8. Oil can filler spout.

9. Oil filter strap wrench. This tool makes removal of a tight filter much easier. Never use it to install a filter.

10. A pair of channel lock pliers.

11. Two sturdy jackstands are necessary if you plan to work under the car. Cinder blocks, bricks, and other makeshift supports are not safe.

History

The Aspen and Volaré model lines were introduced by the Chrysler Corporation in 1976 as an alternative between full or intermediate size cars and sub-compact cars. The two-door coupe is built on a 108.5 inch wheelbase, while the four-door sedan and four-door station wagon models are both built on 112.5 inch wheelbases. The station wagon model is the first compact sized wagon available from an American manufacturer since 1967 and the first from Chrysler Corporation since 1966.

Serial Number Identification

VEHICLE

The vehicle identification number is stamped on a metal plate attached to the upper left of the instrument panel. The VIN plate can easily be seen by looking through the windshield. The VIN is made up of thirteen digits. The first digit identifies the car line, the second the price class, and the third and fourth digits body style. Engine displacement is identified by the fifth digit. Model year and assembly plant are shown by the sixth and seventh digits. The last six digits are the sequential serial number.

Vehicle identification number plate

ENGINE

The engine number can contain as many as fifteen characters and digits. The first character on 225 engines designates the model year, the next three numerals are 225 (the displacement), the next one or two letters designate the model, the following four numerals the date the engine was built, and the last number the shift during which the engine was built.

On 318 and 360 engines, the first number designates model year, the next letter manufacturing plant, the next three numbers give

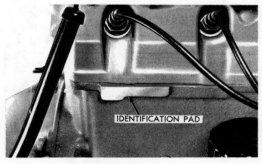

Six cylinder engine number location

Vehicle Identification Chart

Car Line	Price Class	Body Style	Engine Code	Model Year	Assembly Plant
H—Volare	G	29—2 door special (coupe)	C—225	6—1976	B—Hamtramck
N—Aspen	H	41—4 door special	G—318 2 bbl	7—1977	A—Lynch Road
	K	45—2 seat station wagon	K—360 2 bbl	8—1978	C—Jefferson
	L				D—Belvidere
	M				F—Newark
	P				G—St. Louis
	S				R—Windsor
	T				

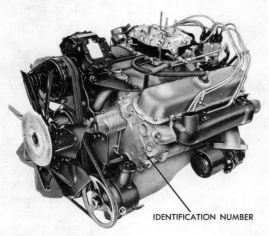

V8 engine number location

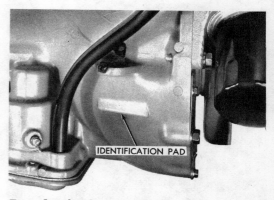

Torqueflite identification number location

Manual transmission identification number location

the displacement, the next one or two designate model, the next four numbers denote the build date, and the last four the engine sequence number.

Special information identifying an undersized crankshaft, oversized tappets, low compression, oversized cylinder bores, engine build date, and the shift is stamped on the locations shown in the illustrations.

TRANSMISSION

Manual transmission numbers are stamped on a pad located on the right side of the case. Torqueflite transmission numbers are stamped on a pad on the left side of the oil pan flange.

Routine Maintenance

AIR CLEANER

All models are equipped with a replaceable paper element in the air cleaner housing. Chrysler recommends that the filter be replaced every 30,000 miles. It should be checked more often than this, however, as a restrictive filter element will reduce fuel mileage and increase exhaust emissions. To check the filter element, unscrew the wing nut at the top of the air cleaner and lift off the lid. The filter element lifts out. If it's completely gray or black, replace it. If it's badly contaminated with oil, replace it. Before installing the new filter element, wipe out the air cleaner housing with a clean rag.

The wing nut comes off counterclockwise

If the filter is clean, leave it alone

Wipe the housing clean before installing a new filter

Six-cylinder PCV valve location

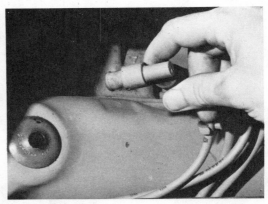

V8 PCV valve location

POSITIVE CRANKCASE VENTILATION

The positive crankcase ventilation system routes crankcase vapors to the carburetor to be burned with the air/fuel mixture. A clogged PCV system will cause poor idle and rough running. It can also create oil leaks due to increased crankcase pressure. So it pays to keep the system clear and free flowing. Once a year or every 15,000 miles (sooner if the car is only used for short trips) the system should be tested. The PCV valve should be replaced every 30,000 miles.

Testing

1. With engine running at normal idle speed, remove the PCV valve from the rocker arm cover. If the valve isn't clogged, you should hear a loud hiss and feel a strong suction when you place your finger over the valve intake.

2. Replace the PCV valve and remove the crankcase inlet air cleaner from the rocker arm cover. This is the large can located at the rear of the rocker cover on six cylinder engines and

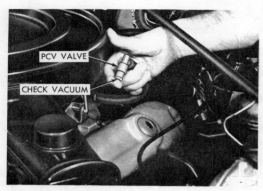

Checking PCV valve vacuum

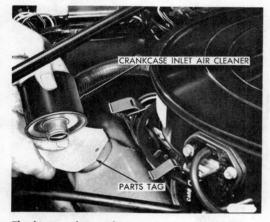

Checking crankcase inlet vacuum

the opposite rocker arm cover from the PCV valve on V8s. Hold a stiff piece of paper loosely over the hole in the rocker arm cover. After waiting a moment, you should feel the paper sucked tightly against the opening.

3. With the engine off, remove the PCV valve from the rocker arm cover and give it a good shake. If the valve is okay, you'll hear a clicking noise.

If the PCV system meets the tests, every-

thing is okay. If not replace the PCV valve. Repeat the paper test in step 2. If the results are negative, it will be necessary to clean the PCV valve hose and the passage in the bottom of the carburetor will have to be cleaned.

1. Spray carburetor solvent into the PCV valve hose and blow it dry. Don't allow the hose to remain in solvent for more than a half hour.

2. Remove the carburetor as outlined in Chapter 4. Use a ¼ in. drill rod to clean the passages in the base of the carburetor.

3. Remove the crankcase inlet air cleaner from the rocker arm cover and disconnect the hose. Clean the hose in the same manner as the PCV valve hose. Wash the crankcase inlet air cleaner in solvent. Dry it. Wet the filter by pouring a small amount of SAE 30 motor oil into it until the oil runs from the small inlet vent. Be sure that all excess oil is drained off.

PCV Valve Replacement

Be sure that you purchase the correct valve for your car. Different engines have different rates of PCV valve flow.

1. Locate the PCV valve in the rubber grommet in the rocker arm cover.

2. Pull the valve free from the rocker cover.

3. Pull the valve out of the rubber hose connected to the other end.

4. Insert the replacement valve into the hose and then push the other end into the rubber grommet on the rocker cover.

EVAPORATIVE CANISTER

This plastic canister, located in the engine compartment, stores carburetor and fuel tank vapors while the engine is off, holding them to be drawn into the engine and turned when

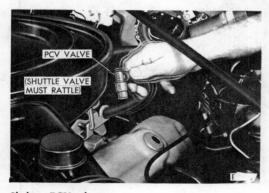

Shaking PCV valve

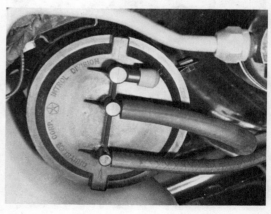

Evaporative canister

the engine is started. The filter mounted on the bottom of the canister requires replacement every 30,000 miles (15,000 miles on 1976 models).

Filter Replacement

1. Loosen the screw retaining the canister in its bracket.
2. Lift the canister out of its bracket. It's not necessary to detach the hoses from the top of the canister.

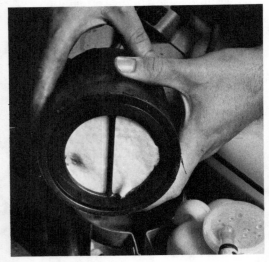

Evaporative canister filter

3. Remove the old filter from the bottom of the canister.
4. Install the replacement filter by working it into the retainers on the bottom of the canister.
5. Lower the canister back into its bracket and tighten the screw.

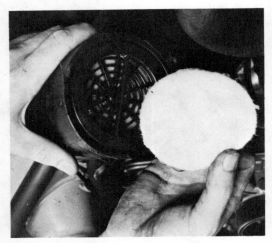

You'll have to work the new filter into place

6. Check all connecting hoses and replace any that are suspect.

DRIVE BELTS

Make it a habit to check the drive belts that run the water pump, alternator, power steering pump, air pump, and air conditioning compressor. Examine the belts for cracks which can cause the belt to break without warning. Belts which are soaked with oil or grease should also be discarded. Beside the danger of slippage, such belts will wear out quickly and can snap. Glazed belts may slip and cause an undercharged battery and/or engine overheating. After checking drive belt condition, test belt tension at the midpoint of each belt. No belt should deflect more than ⅜ in.–½ in. Adjust any belt on which deflection is greater than ½ in.

Check the belt tension about midway between the two pulleys

Belt Adjustment and Replacement

1. Loosen all retaining nuts on the accessory bracket.

Alternator adjusting bolt (arrow)

2. When replacing a belt, pry the accessory toward the engine and slip the belt from the pulleys.

3. Carefully pry the accessory out with a bar, such as a ratchet handle or broom handle, and then tighten the bracket nuts.

CAUTION: *Do not exert too much pressure on accessories such as the alternator; it's easy to damage an aluminum housing. Use just enough force to hold the accessory in place while you tighten the bracket nuts.*

4. Recheck the tension. It may be necessary to do this a few times before you get it right.

It's a good idea to carry spare belts in the trunk.

AIR CONDITIONING

No air conditioning repair or maintenance procedures except sight glass check are given; all repair work on the air conditioning system should be left to expert repairmen in that field. They are well aware of the hazards and have the proper equipment.

CAUTION: *Never open or disconnect any part of the air conditioning system. The compressed refrigerant used in the air conditioning system expands and evaporates into the atmosphere at a temperature of −21.7° F or lower. This will freeze any surface, including your eyes, that it contacts. Air conditioning refrigerant also decomposes into a poisonous gas in the presence of a flame.*

Sight Glass Check

This is the only check that should be performed by anyone not specially trained to

Air-conditioner sight glass

work on an air conditioning system. The following is a completely safe method for determining if your air conditioner requires service. The tests work best at normal temperatures (70–8° F), if the temperature is above 100° F there may be bubbles or foam in the sight glass as a part of normal operation.

1. Place the automatic transmission in Park or the manual transmission in Neutral. Put the parking brake ON.

2. Run the engine at a fast idle.

3. Set the controls for maximum cold with the blower on high position.

4. Locate the sight glass on top of the receiver-drier. This is a tall black cylinder located at the front of the engine compartment. Wipe the sight glass in the top of the receiver-drier clean with a soft rag.

5. If you see bubbles, the system must be recharged. It probably has a leak.

6. If there are no bubbles, there is either no refrigerant present in the system or it is fully charged. To check, feel the two hoses going to the compressor. If they are both at the same temperature, the system will have to be recharged. If one hose is warm (high pressure) and the other cool (low pressure), then the system is okay.

7. If the system is leaking, have it fixed as soon as possible. Leaks will eventually allow moisture to enter the system causing rust and the replacement of expensive components.

NOTE: *It's a good practice to run the air conditioner for a few minutes every so often during the cold months. This prevents the seals from drying out and the compressor possibly becoming stuck from disuse.*

FLUID LEVEL CHECKS

Engine Oil

Since the lubricating oil in the engine is the life blood of your motor, it's a good practice to keep a close watch on engine oil level. Check it at least everytime you refuel. The best time to check the engine oil level is before operating the engine or after it has been sitting for at least a few minutes in order to get an accurate reading. This allows the oil to drain back into the crankcase. To check the engine oil level, make sure that the car is resting on a level surface, remove the oil dipstick, wipe it clean and reinsert the stick firmly for an accurate reading. The oil dipstick has two marks to indicate high and low oil level. If the oil level is at or below the "add" mark on the dipstick, oil should be added as necessary to bring it up to

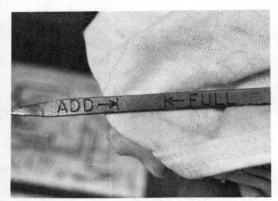

Add oil only to the full line

Sometimes its a little difficult to reach the oil filler cap through all the paraphernalia

the "full" line. The oil should be maintained in the safety margin, neither going above the "full" mark or below the "add" mark. Be sure that the dipstick is in the tube tight after checking the oil to prevent dirt from entering the oil pan.

Transmission

MANUAL

The manual transmission level should be checked twice a year, but hard use such as trailering requires more frequent checks. All manual transmissions have two square headed pipe plugs, the upper for filling and the lower for draining. Both are located on the right side of the transmission on 3-speeds. The drain plug is located on the lower left side of the 4-speed and the fill plug on the right side.

Unscrew the top plug and insert your finger to feel if the lubricant is at the level of the filler hole. If it's not, top it up with the recommended fluid discussed in fluid changes later in this chapter.

Manual transmission filler plug

AUTOMATIC

Check the automatic transmission fluid level whenever you check the engine oil. It is even more important to check the fluid level when you are pulling a trailer or subjecting the car to any other type of hard use.

Check the fluid level with the car parked on a level spot, engine warm, and the transmission lever in Neutral. The parking brake should be on.

Automatic transmission dipstick

1. Slowly move the selector lever through all the gear positions, pausing momentarily in each one. Place the lever in Neutral.
2. Open the hood and locate the automatic transmission dipstick on the right side of the car near the firewall.
3. Wipe off the top of the dipstick and around the tube to prevent dirt from falling into transmission.
4. Remove the dipstick. Fluid should be at the "Full" mark or slightly below. It should never be over the "Full" mark.

5. Add or drain fluid as necessary to bring the level to the "Full" mark. Use only automatic transmission fluid marked Dexron®. Add fluid sparingly, the difference between the "Add" and "Full" lines is only one pint. Chrysler does not recommend using any fluid additives.

Brake Master Cylinder

The master cylinder is in the left rear side of the engine compartment, on the firewall. To check the fluid level as recommended at each engine oil change interval:

1. Clean off the area around the cap. Very small particles of dirt can cause serious problems in the braking system.

2. Pry off the wire retaining clip to one side with a screwdriver. Remove the cover.

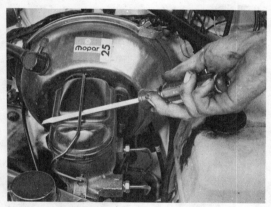

Prying off the retaining clip

3. The proper level in each of the two reservoirs is ¼ in. from the edge. Add fluid as necessary.

4. Replace the cover and snap the retaining wire back in place.

NOTE: *Use fluid marked DOT 3 or 4 only. Buy only as much fluid as you need and*

Correct fluid level

keep the cap closed tightly on the brake fluid can. The fluid attracts moisture and if water contaminated brake fluid is used in the hydraulic system it can cause real problems.

Engine Coolant

All models are equipped with a plastic expansion tank located near the radiator as part of the coolant reserve system. This prevents losing coolant when the engine is hot and the coolant expands.

Check coolant when the engine is warm and running. Observe the level in the expansion tank. It should be between the one and two quart marks. The radiator normally remains completely full, so it is not necessary to remove the radiator cap. If the system is low, add a 50% water/50% anti-freeze solution to the expansion tank.

Every two years or 30,000 miles, the coolant should be drained and the system refilled with a fresh water/anti-freeze solution. Refer to the Capacities chart for the amount of coolant you'll need and to the Anti-Freeze Chart in the Appendix for the proper solution for your average temperature.

To drain the system:

1. Open the radiator drain petcock located on the bottom of the radiator on the left side.

2. Remove the drain plugs in the sides of the cylinder block. You may have to poke a screwdriver into these if they are clogged with sediment.

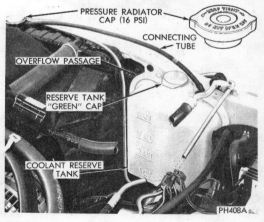

Coolant expansion tank

3. Remove the radiator cap after the coolant expansion tank is empty. Flush the system with a garden hose. If the old coolant is rusty and/or full of sediment, use a cooling system cleaning solution.

4. Close the petcock and replace the drain plugs when the system is emptied.

5. Add coolant solution to the radiator until it is completely filled. Replace the radiator cap.

6. Start the engine and run it until the top radiator hose feels warm to the touch.

7. Shut the engine off and add more coolant to the radiator if necessary.

8. Fill the expansion tank to the one quart level.

Rear Axle

It is recommended that the rear axle lubricant level be checked at each engine oil change interval. The proper lubricant is called out in the Rear Axle Lubricant Chart. The rear axle filler plug is located on the rear face of the axle on all models except the 1976 8¼ in. axle, where it is located on the right front of the housing. Plugs on 1976 models are pipe plugs and you'll need a wrench to remove them. 1977 and later models use a new rubber press-in type plug, which you can remove with your fingers. Remove the plug and insert your finger into the filler hole to feel the fluid level. It should be at the level given in the chart for that particular axle. Add lubricant as necessary to bring the level up to the correct height.

Steering Gear

The steering gear on all models is lubricated at the factory and sealed. There are no periodic services necessary on the steering gear.

Power Steering Reservoir

The power steering pump is located under the front of the engine. Check the fluid level in the reservoir at every oil change.

Filler plug—8¼ in. axle

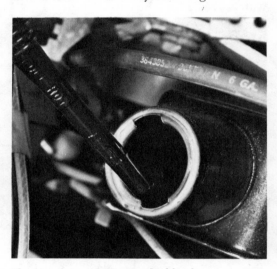

Checking the power steering fluid level

Rear Axle Identification and Lubrication Chart

Axle Size (ring gear dia)	Filler Location	Cover Bolts	Capacity (pts)	Lubricant Level
		1976		
7¼	Rear Cover	9	2.1	Bottom of filler hole to ⅝ in. below
8¼	Front Right Side	10	4.4	From ⅛ in.–¼ in. below filler hole①
		1977–78		
7¼	Cover	9	2.1	Bottom of filler hole to ⅜ in. below
8¼	Cover	10	4.4	Bottom of filler hole to ½ in. below

① Do not raise oil to bottom of filler hole as this will result in an overfill condition.

Capacities

Year	Engine No. Cyl Displacement (Cu In.)	Engine Crankcase Add 1 Qt For New Filter	TRANSMISSION Pts To Refill After Draining			Drive Axle (pts)	Gasoline Tank (gals)	COOLING SYSTEM (qts)	
			Manual					With Heater	With A/C
			3-Speed	4-Speed	Automatic				
'76–'78	6—225	4	3.5	7.0	17	2	18	13	17.5
	8—318	4	4.75	7.0	17	4.5	18	16	17.5
	8—360	4	——	——	17	4.5	18	16	16

—— Not Applicable

1. Clean off the cap and around the reservoir to prevent dirt from falling in. Foreign matter in the power steering system can cause the same problems as dirt in the brake hydraulic system.

2. Remove the cap. All models are equipped with an integral cap/dipstick.

3. Wipe the dipstick with a clean cloth and reinsert it into the reservoir. Be sure that it is firmly seated.

4. Remove the cap and check the fluid level on the dipstick. If the engine has been running, the fluid should be at the "hot" level, if not it should be at the "cold" level.

5. If it is necessary to add fluid, add only power steering fluid. Do not add automatic transmission fluid to the power steering system. Do not overfill the reservoir.

Battery

Check the electrolyte level in the battery every two months. Chrysler states that the Long Life battery need only be checked every year or 10,000 miles. Remove the cap and check that the electrolyte is at the bottom of the filler well (about ⅜ in. above the plates). Use distilled water to top up the battery.

Checking the battery electrolyte level

TIRES AND WHEELS

Buy a tire pressure gauge and keep it in the glove compartment of your car. Service station air pressure gauges are generally not working or inaccurate and should not be relied upon. The decal on the door post on the driver's side gives the recommended air pressures for the standard tires. If you are driving on replacement tires of a different type, follow the inflation recommendations of the manufacturer and never exceed the maximum pressure given on the sidewall. Always check tire pressure when the tires are cool because air pressure increases with heat and readings will go 4–6 psi higher after the tire has been run a few miles. For continued expressway driving, increase the tire pressure by a few pounds in each tire. Never mix tires of different construction on your car. When replacing tires, ensure that the new tire(s) are the same size and type as those which will be remaining on

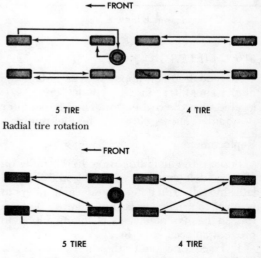

Radial tire rotation

Bias-ply tire rotation

the car. Intermixing bias ply tires with radial or bias belted tires can result in treacherous and unpredictable handling.

Rotate the tires every 10,000 miles. The rotation pattern shown will result in all tires wearing out at about the same time. If you plan on replacing the original equipment tires with duplicate types, don't use the spare and rotate only the four road wheels in the correct pattern according to the tire type. When you buy new tires, you'll only require three—the spare will be fresh and you can use a worn tire as the spare.

When removing studded snow tires in the Spring, mark them left or right with chalk so that they can be returned to the same position next Winter. Studded snow tires take a "set" and noise and wear will increase if they are installed on the opposite side from which they were removed, in addition to the possibility of losing studs. Always tighten the wheel nuts in a criss-cross pattern. Tighten them to 85 ft lbs. The accompanying chart shows the available range of tire sizes and appropriate wheel sizes for Aspen and Volare models.

Wheel and Tire Size Chart

Tire Size	Wheel Size
D78-14	4½J, 5J, 5½JJ
DR78-14	5½JJ
E78-14 °	4½J, 5J, 5½JJ, 6JJ
ER78-14 °	5½JJ, 6JJ
E70-14 °	5½JJ, 6JJ
F78-14 °	5½JJ, 6JJ
FR78-14 °	5½JJ, 6JJ
GR78-14 °	6JJ

° Chain clearance limited

FUEL FILTER

All models are equipped with an in-line fuel filter. The filter on six cylinder engines is located near the carburetor. The V8 fuel filter is mounted lower, closer to the fuel pump.

Replacement

Replace the fuel filter every 15,000 miles on 1976 models and every 30,000 on 1977 and later models. You'll need hose clamp pliers to remove the fuel line corbin clamps. Be sure the engine is cool when changing filters to prevent an accidental fire.

1. Place a rag under the filter to catch any fuel that leaks from the line.

Fuel filter (arrow)

2. Squeeze and remove the hose clamps at both ends of the filter. Remove and discard the old filter.

3. Install the replacement filter in the same manner using the new rubber hose supplied with the filter.

4. Remove the rag, start the engine, and check for leaks.

BATTERY

Operation

Many people are unaware of exactly how a battery functions and, as a result, have battery problems. There are many ways of abusing a battery and, hopefully, these will be more obvious and better understood after reading this section.

The automotive battery is essentially a hard rubber or plastic case containing a number of positive and negative lead plates immersed in a solution of sulfuric acid and water (electrolyte). The negative plates are made of sponge lead and the positive plates are largely lead dioxide. The acid reacts with these chemicals and produces electrical current. A 12 volt (V) battery consists of six 2V batteries (individual cells) separated from each other by case partitions. These partitions prevent the mixing of electrolyte from cell to cell; therefore, each cell has its own electrolyte supply. Contained in each cell is an assembly of positive and negative lead plates. To prevent electrical contact between the two plates, each positive plate is isolated from the negative by a plastic separator. The number of plates within each cell depends upon the ampere hour rating of the particular battery. The more plates that a battery has, the higher its rating. A more expensive battery, having a 70 ampere hour rating, contains six positive plates per cell while a less expensive battery, rated at 48 ampere hours, has only four positive plates per cell. The battery with a high rating can do more work before discharging than one with a lower rating. A car with many electrical accessories (air conditioning, radio, electric windows, etc.) requires a high ampere-hour battery. The cells are electrically connected in series (they are interdependent—if one cell goes bad, the battery will not work) by connections going through the cell partitions. The positive terminal of the first cell and the negative of the last are actually the posts to which the battery cables are attached.

The battery produces (it does not store) electrical energy within its case and uses this electrical energy to perform three functions: start the car; provide current for electrical components; and act as a voltage stabilizer for the system. To perform these functions, the lead plates, in effect, absorb acid and, if the battery is not recharged by the alternator, absorb all of the acid and the battery is completely discharged. Current supplied to the battery by the alternator, a charger, or another battery, reverses the chemical reaction and forces acid off the plates and returns it to the electrolyte. Returning the acid to the electrolyte restores the battery's ability to produce current. The alternator sends current into the battery and recharges it by maintaining the acid content of the electrolyte. When the acid content is low, the battery performs poorly and, so, the voltage regulator increases the alternator output in order to recharge the battery.

Maintenance

In addition to routinely checking the electrolyte level of the battery, some other minor maintenance will keep your battery in peak starting condition. Two inexpensive battery tools, a hydrometer and a post and cable cleaner, are available in most auto or hardware stores for about a dollar and more than earn back that small outlay. Besides checking the level of electrolyte, you should occasionally take a specific gravity reading to see what's going on inside the battery cells. Using your hydrometer, insert the tip into each cell and withdraw enough electrolyte to make the float ride freely. While holding the hydrometer straight up, take a reading. The specific gravity of a fully charged battery (at 80° F) is 1.270. Most commercially available hydrometers also have colored sections to save you reading the scale and these will clearly tell you your battery cell is (a) charged, (b) bor-

Battery post and cable cleaner

derline—should be recharged, or (c) dead. Repeat the specific gravity for each cell.

NOTE: *Battery electrolyte or "acid" is very caustic and will dissolve skin and paintwork with equal relish, so be careful. Readings should be taken in as normal a room temperature atmosphere as possible. If the temperature varies from the 80° F standard above, add or subtract four (0.004) points for every 10° above (+) or below (−) the standard.*

The most completely charged battery will do you no good on a cold, rainy evening if the cables and posts are caked with corrosion. This is where your little wire brush cleaner comes in. Loosen and remove the cable clamps from the battery posts. Using the pointed end of the brush, give the inside surface of the clamp a good cleaning until it shines. Next take the other end and place it over the post. Clean the post with a rotating

Battery cable removal

motion until you achieve a shiny post. This done, install the clamps and retighten.

Keep the top of the battery clean, as a film of dirt can sometimes completely discharge a battery. A solution of baking soda and water may be used to clean the top surface, but be careful to flush this off with clear water and that none of the solution enters the filler holes.

Lubrication

FUEL AND OIL RECOMMENDATIONS

Unleaded gasoline should be used in all Aspens and Volares except for 1976 models equipped with the 318 cu. in. V8, Torqueflite transmission, and air pump which were ordered without the catalytic converter system. All other cars must use unleaded fuel. Using leaded gasoline in a converter equipped car will render the system inoperative. Cars with the converter system will have unleaded fuel markings on the instrument panel and near the gas cap. Most importantly, converter cars have the narrow filler tube which permits only the smaller unleaded nozzles to be used.

The fuel used must have a minimum anti-knock rating of 87, gasoline classification number of 2, or a 91 Research Octane Number. The anti-knock rating is marked on most gas pumps throughout the country and is obtained by adding the Motor Octane and the Research Octane numbers and then dividing by two. Look for the 87 anti-knock rating.

Cars which are equipped with the catalytic converter system should not use any gasoline additives, such as fuel system cleaners. Fuel system additives may have a detrimental effect on the converter.

Engine oil should be selected with regard to the anticipated temperatures during the period before the next oil change. Using the chart, select the oil viscosity for the lowest expected temperature and you will be assured of easy cold starting and adequate engine protection. The oil you pour into your engine should have the designation SE marked on the top or side of its container. Under the classification system adopted by the American Petroleum Institute (API) in May, 1970, SE is the highest designation for passenger car use. The S stands for passenger car and the second letter denotes a more specific application. E means

the most complete variety of additives to improve the performance of the oil, making it suitable for the most rigorous passenger car use.

Recommended SAE Viscosity Grades

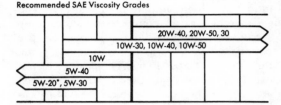

*SAE 5W-20 Not recommended for sustained high speed vehicle operation.

LUBRICANT CHANGES

Engine Oil and Filter

In order to maintain adequate engine protection and performance, the oil must be changed at least every 6 months or 7500 miles (5000 miles for 1976 models). The manufacturer recommends that the oil filter be changed at the first oil change and every other one after that. It may be a better idea to change the filter every time you drain the oil. The filter holds one quart of dirty oil and the expense of a new filter is more than outweighed by increased engine protection.

The recommended oil change interval is only for cars driven normally. If your automobile is being used under extremely dusty conditions, change the oil and filter sooner. The same thing goes for cars which are constantly driven in stop and go city traffic, extended idling can cause an acid and sludge buildup problem. Always drain the oil after the engine has been run long enough to bring it to normal operating temperature. Hot oil will flow more easily and more contaminants will be removed with the oil than if it were drained cold. A large capacity drain pan (5 or 6 quarts), oil filter, strap wrench, oil can spout, and a wrench to fit the oil pan drain plug are the only necessary tools. These are readily available at any automotive parts store or most large discount stores. These tools will more than pay for themselves after a few do-it-yourself oil changes. One other necessity is containers for the used oil. You will find that plastic bleach containers make excellent storage bottles. Two ecologically desirable solutions to the used oil problem are to take it to a service station and ask permission to dump it into their sump tank or keep it and use it around the yard as a preservative for exposed wood such as fence posts.

To change your oil and filter:

1. Run the engine until it reaches normal operating temperature. Jack up the front of the car and support it on jackstands or use drive-on ramps.

2. Slide a drain pan under the oil pan drain plug. Be sure that it holds at least 5 quarts.

3. Loosen the drain plug with a wrench and then turn it out by hand. If you maintain a slight pressure on it with your hand, you can prevent hot oil from squirting onto your fingers.

4. Remove the plug and allow the oil to drain into the pan.

Oil filter removal

5. When all oil has drained from the engine, clean the plug and install it in the pan. Don't overtighten it.

6. Move the drain pan under the oil filter. The filter is located on the lower right side of six cylinder engines, almost in the center. The V8 oil filter is located at the right rear of the engine.

7. Install the oil filter strap wrench on the filter and turn it slowly off, allowing the oil to drain into the pan. This can be done from the top on six cylinder engines.

8. Completely remove and discard the old oil filter. Use a clean rag to wipe off the filter mounting base on the engine.

9. Wipe a small amount of fresh oil onto the rubber gasket of the replacement filter.

10. Spin the filter into place by hand. When the gasket is flush with the mounting on the engine, give it another ½ to ¾ of a turn. If you overtighten the filter, it will probably leak and will surely be difficult to remove for the next oil change.

NOTE: *If you cannot remove an old filter that someone has overtightened, drive a*

Coat the gasket with oil

punch or screwdriver through the filter and use it to turn the filter off.

11. Clean up the area around the filter. Oil invariably drips onto the V8 exhaust pipe and the side of the six cylinder engine.

12. Remove the oil filler cap and add five quarts of fresh oil (only four if you didn't change the filter). An oil can spout is handy for this, but you can use a can opener and a funnel if you don't have one.

13. Check the oil level with the dipstick, it should be at "full." Replace the oil filler cap.

14. Start the engine. The oil pressure warning light should go out in a few seconds. If it doesn't, stop the engine and check for the problem. Perhaps you forgot to replace the drain plug and lost your oil.

15. With the engine running and the oil light out, check for leaks at the filter and drain plug.

16. Stop the engine, wait a few minutes, and then check the oil level again.

Transmission

Manual

Chrysler doesn't specifically recommend manual transmission lubricant changes, but it is suggested that it be changed at regular intervals on cars which see heavy duty use such as trailer towing. It might be a good idea to change the manual transmission lube if you have just purchased the car from a previous owner.

To drain the lubricant, remove the plug from the transmission (right side on 3-speeds, left side on 4-speeds) and allow the lube to drain into a pan. Replace the drain plug. Remove the filler plug and fill the transmission with Dexron® automatic transmission fluid up to the level of the filler hole. Transmission capacity is given in the Capacities Chart.

NOTE: *If gear rattle at idle speeds or under light acceleration has been a problem, fill the transmission with SAE 90 gear lubricant. This should eliminate any objectionable noise.*

Occasional greasing of the shift linkage will ease gear shifting. On column shift models, lubricate the linkage at the lower end of the steering column with multi-purpose chassis grease. On 3-speed floor shift models, the shift mechanism has a grease nipple which can be reached from under the car. With the shifter in neutral, grease the nipple until lubricant appears on the operating levers wich are covered with a rubber boot. On 4-speed transmissions, remove the shift boot bezel and pull the boot up to expose the shifter. Apply grease to the sliding surfaces of the mechanism, while moving the shifter back and forth through the gears.

AUTOMATIC

Chrysler recommends that the automatic transmission fluid and filter be changed at 24,000 mile intervals on cars used for trailer towing. It doesn't specifically recommend fluid and filter changes for vehicles in normal use, but it might not be a bad idea to do it if you purchased the car used. 1976 models and 1977 models built before January 10, 1977 have a torque converter drain plug which allows draining the complete transmission. Models manufactured after that date do not have the drain plug, so that only the transmission pan can be drained. To change the transmission fluid and filter you'll need a new filter, pan gasket, and sufficient fluid to refill the transmission. Two quarts are enough for the later models, 9 quarts will be needed if you're draining the complete transmission on earlier models with the torque converter drain plug. All models use Dexron® or Type A automatic transmission fluid.

1. Run the engine until it reaches normal operating temperature.

2. Jack up the front of the car and support it on jackstands or use drive-on ramps. Be sure to block the rear wheels.

3. Place a large container under the transmission oil pan. If you are draining the torque converter, it will have to hold 9 quarts.

4. Loosen the rear pan bolts first to allow the fluid to drain into the pan without making a mess on the garage floor. Remove the pan and discard the gasket.

Converter drain plug

5. If you're draining the converter, remove the access plate at the front of the torque converter housing. If you can't see the drain plug, turn the engine clockwise with a wrench on the crankshaft pulley until you can. Remove the drain plug and allow the fluid to empty into the pan.

6. Install the drain plug. Tightening torque is 90 in. lbs. Don't overtighten it. Install the access plate.

7. Unscrew and discard the old transmission filter.

8. Install a new filter. Don't overtighten the retaining screws.

9. Clean the oil pan in solvent and allow it to dry. Make sure that you don't leave any lint in the pan.

10. Install the oil pan using a new gasket. Tighten the bolts in a criss-cross pattern. Tightening torque on the bolts is only 150 in. lbs (about 12 ft lbs), so don't overtighten them. The transmission case is aluminum.

11. If the torque converter has been drained, pour six quarts of Dexron® automatic transmission fluid down the dipstick tube. If only the pan has been drained, add two quarts of transmission fluid. A long neck funnel is handy for this job.

12. Start the engine and let it idle for about two minutes.

13. With the parking brake on, move the transmission selector through each of the gear positions. Stop in Neutral.

14. Add enough fluid to bring the level up to the "add one pint" line. Check the fluid as described earlier in this chapter. Add only enough fluid to bring the level up to "Full". Never overfill the automatic transmission, this can cause foaming and leakage.

Rear Axle

Chrysler recommends that the rear axle lubricant need not be changed except for cars used in severe service. Trailer towing is in that category, and if you frequently pull a trailer the rear axle lubricant should be changed at 36,000 mile intervals. If the car has been purchased used or the rear axle submerged on a boat ramp, it is also a good idea to change the lubricant. You'll need sufficient lubricant of the viscosity called for in the Rear Axle Lubricant Chart and a suction gun, since there's no drain plug.

In lieu of a suction gun to drain the rear axle lubricant, the cover can also be removed.

To drain the lube by removing the cover:

1. Jack the rear of the car and support the axle housing with jackstands. Position a drain pan.

2. Gradually loosen the cover bolts until lubricant begins to seep out past the gasket. It may be necessary to pry the cover loose from the housing.

3. When all the lubricant has drained, scrape away all traces of the old gasket and thoroughly clean the surface.

4. Apply a $1/16$ in. bead of MOPAR Silicone Rubber Sealant (Part No. 3683829) or an equivalent gasket forming substitute, along the bolt circle of the cover.

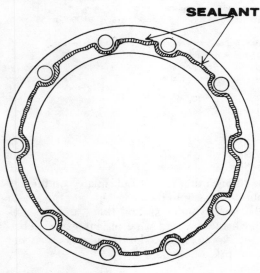

Rear axle sealant application

5. Allow the sealant to cure while you clean the housing cover and dry it.

6. Install the cover. Install the ratio identification tag beneath one of the bolts.

NOTE: *If for any reason, the cover is not installed within 20 minutes of applying the sealant, the old sealant should be removed and a new bead installed.*

7. Fill the rear axle with the proper type and quantity of lubricant, selected from the Rear Axle Lubricant Chart.

To remove the lubricant by suction gun:

1. Jack up the rear of the car and support the axle housing with jackstands.

2. Remove the filler plug and siphon the lubricant out with a suction gun.

3. Fill the rear axle to the level specified in the Rear Axle Lubricant Chart.

4. Replace the filler plug and lower the car.

CHASSIS GREASING

Upper and lower ball joints (four in all) the pitman arm, and the tie-rod ends (four) require greasing every three years or 30,000 miles. Halve that interval for cars driven regularly over unpaved back roads or used for other severe service. You'll need a cartridge of #2 chassis lubricant rated EP and a hand grease gun.

1. Jack up the front of the car and support it at the lower control arms with jack stands.

2. Locate the grease fittings and wipe them clean.

3. Push the grease gun over the grease fitting and pump the lubricant in until grease flows freely from the bottom of the seal or when the seal begins to balloon.

4. Wipe off any excess grease and lower the car.

HEAT RISER

Every 30,000 miles, the heat riser valve should be checked for free operation and lubricated with penetrating oil. The valve is located on the exhaust manifold near the point that the exhaust pipe attaches to the manifold. Try to turn the valve counterweight by hand. If it's stuck, tap the end of the shaft a few times with a hammer. Apply penetrating oil to the shaft ends and work the valve back and forth a few times. If the valve is still stuck and can't be loosened with oil and/or heat, it will have to be replaced.

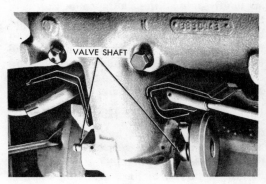

V8 heat riser

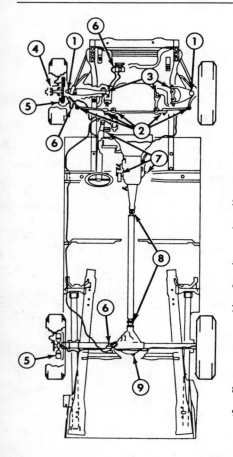

1. Suspension ball joints—every 6 months, inspect seals—replace if damaged or leaking.
2. Steering linkage joints—every 3 years or 30,000 miles relubricate with P/N 2525035 or equivalent.
3. Upper and lower control arm bushings—inspect for deterioration every oil change.
4. Front wheel bearings—inspect, clean, relubricate with P/N 3837794 or equivalent AT LEAST every 22,500 miles or whenever brakes are serviced.
5. Brake linings—inspect every 15,000 miles and/or during wheel bearing service.
6. Brake and power steering hoses—every 6 months inspect for deterioration and leaks.
7. Transmission—Manual—every 6 months check fluid level. Maintain fluid level at bottom of filler plug hole with DEXRON automatic transmission fluid.
   Shift mechanisms—lubricate with P/N 2932524 or equivalent. Column (3 speed) as required. Floor, 3 speed (through fitting) every 7,500 miles, 4 speed (pack) every 10,000 miles or 6 months.
8. Universal joint seals—every 6 months inspect for leakage, replace joint if leakage is evident.
9. Rear axle—lubricant, no periodic level check required. Examine for leakage during engine oil change, use P/N 3744994 or equivalent, if required.

Lubrication points

BODY LUBRICATION

An occasional cleaning and lubrication of body parts will keep them operating smoothly and quietly and prevent rusting.

Hood Lock, Release Mechanism, and Safety Catch

Use chassis grease on these parts. Sparingly apply grease to all the sliding contact areas of the latch and release lever and to the ends of the hood lock release links (on models with an inside hood release). Work lubricant into the lock mechanism until all rubbing surfaces are coated. Apply a film of grease to the pivot contact areas of the safety catch.

Hood Hinges and Door Hinges

Use engine oil on all link or hinge pivots and Lubriplate® to the gear teeth and sliding contact areas. Use engine oil on the door hinges. Apply oil to the lower hinge spring ends and contact areas.

Locks

Apply a thin film of Lubriplate® on the key and insert it into the lock. Operate the key in the lock cylinder several times and then remove the key and wipe off any excess lubricant. Apply engine oil to the door lock ratchet and striker bolt.

Station Wagon Liftgate

Sparingly apply engine oil to the liftgate hinge pivot pins. Do not lubricate the hydraulic lift props. Use a stainless wax lubricant on the liftgate latch striker plate and bolt.

FRONT WHEEL BEARINGS

The front wheel bearings should be checked when replacing brake pads or removing the brake disc for any service. They should be repacked every 22,500 miles regardless of any other required service. Rear wheel bearings require no attention. The front wheel bearings should be removed, cleaned, and

Lubrication and Maintenance Schedules

			Mileage Intervals Mileage in Thousands					
			7.5	15	22.5	30	37.5	45
Automatic choke	Check and adjust as required	AT				•		
Carburetor choke shaft	Apply solvent every six months	OR		•	•		•	•
Carburetor air filter	Replace	AT				•		
Cooling system	Check and service as required every 12 months	OR		•			•	
Crankcase inlet air cleaner	Clean	AT				•		
Engine oil	Change every six months	OR		•	•		•	•
Engine oil filter	Replace at initial oil change and every 2nd oil change thereafter	OR						
Fast idle cam and pivot pin	Apply solvent every six months	OR		•	•		•	•
Fuel filter	Replace	AT				•		
Idle speed and air-fuel mixture	Check and adjust as required	AT				•		
Ignition cables	Check and replace as required at time of spark plug replacement							
Manifold heat control valve	Apply solvent	AT				•		
Positive crankcase vent valve	Check operation and replace if necessary				•		•	
Positive crankcase vent valve	Replace	AT				•		
Spark plugs (without cat. conv.)	Replace	AT			•			•
Spark plugs (with cat. conv.)	Replace	AT				•		

Lubrication and Maintenance Schedules (cont.)

Mileage Intervals Mileage in Thousands

Component	Service	7.5	15	22.5	30	37.5	45	Interval
Tappet adjustment 6 cyl. eng.	Check and adjust as required	•		•		•		AT
Underhood rubber and plastic components (emission hoses)	Inspect and replace if necessary	•		•				AT
Vapor storage canister filter element	Replace			•				AT
Power steering	Check fluid level							Every oil change
Exhaust system	Check for leaks, missing or damaged parts							Every 6 months
Brake master cylinder	Inspect fluid level							Every 6 months
Transmission	Inspect fluid level							Every 6 months
Brake & power steering hoses	Check for deterioration or leaks							Every 6 months
Air conditioned cars	Check belts, sight glass & operation of controls							Every 6 months
Ball joints, steering linkage, and universal joints	Inspect seals							Every 6 months
Hood lock, rel. mech. & safety catch	Lubricate							Every 6 months
Drive belts	Check condition & tension							Every oil change
Upper and lower control arm bushings	Inspect							Every oil change
Tires	Rotate							Every 10,000 miles

Cooling system	Drain, flush & refill	At 24 months or 30,000 miles and every 12 months or 15,000 miles thereafter
Brake linings	Inspect	Every 15,000 miles
Front wheel bearings *①	Inspect	Every 22,500 miles
Automatic transmission—severe usage only	Change fluid & filter, adjust bands	Every 24,000 miles
Ball joints & tie rod ends	Lubricate	Every 3 years of 30,000 miles

NOTE: *Local driving conditions, or special equipment such as high performance or heavy duty options may require special service recommendations.*

* Inspect the front wheel bearings whenever the brake drums or rotors are removed to inspect or service the brake system.

① Severe usage such as police or taxi service involving frequent or continuous brake application: Lubricate every 9,000 miles.

packed with a grease recommended for disc brake service. Wheel bearing packing and adjustment are covered in Chapter 9.

Pushing, Towing, and Jump Starting

Cars with automatic transmission may not be started by pushing or towing. Manual transmission cars may be started by pushing. The car need not be pushed very fast to start.

To push start a manual transmission car:

1. Make sure that the bumpers of the two cars align so as not to damage either one. It might be a good idea to put an old tire between the two bumpers.

2. Turn on the ignition switch in the pushed car. Place the transmission in Second or Third gear and hold down the clutch pedal.

3. Have the car pushed to a speed of 10–15 mph.

4. Ease up on the clutch and press down on the accelerator slightly at the same time. If the clutch is engaged abruptly, damage to the push vehicle may result.

The car should not be towed to start, since there is a chance of the towed vehicle ramming the tow car.

These cars should not be towed farther than 15 miles or faster than 30 mph. If these limits must be exceeded, remove the driveshaft to prevent transmission damage.

Jump starting is the only way to start an automatic transmission car with a weak battery, and is the best method for a manual transmission car.

CAUTION: *Do not attempt this procedure on a frozen battery. It may explode.*

1. Turn off all electrical equipment. Place the automatic transmission in Park or the manual in Neutral. Set the parking brake.

2. Make sure that the two vehicles are not touching. It is a good idea to keep the engine running in the booster vehicle.

3. Remove the caps from both batteries and cover the openings with cloths.

4. Attach one end of a jumper cable to the positive (+) terminal of the booster battery. The red cable is usually positive. Attach the other end to the positive terminal of the discharged battery.

CAUTION: *Be very careful about these connections. An alternator and regulator can be destroyed in a remarkably short time if battery, polarity is reversed.*

5. Attach one end of the other cable (the black one) to the negative (−) terminal of the booster battery. Attach the other end to a ground point on the engine of the car being started. Do not connect it to the battery.

CAUTION: *Don't lean over the battery while making this last connection.*

6. If the engine will not start, disconnect the batteries as soon as possible. If this is not done, the two batteries will soon reach a state of equilibrium, with both too weak to start an engine. This is no problem if the engine of the booster vehicle is running fast enough to keep up the charge. Lengthy cranking can also damage the starter.

7. Reverse the procedure exactly to remove the jumper cables. Discard the rags, because they may have acid on them.

Jacking and Hoisting

The jack supplied with the car should never be used for any service operation other than tire changing. NEVER get under the car while it is supported only by the jack. They often slip or topple over. Always block the wheels when changing tires.

Some of the service operations in this book require that one or both ends of the car be raised and supported safely. It is understood that hydraulic lifts are not often found in the home garage, but there are reasonable and safe substitutes. Small hydraulic, screw, or scissors jacks are satisfactory for raising the car.

Heavy wooden blocks or adjustable jack-stands should be used to support the car while it is being worked on. Drive-on trestles, or ramps, are also a handy and safe way to raise the car. These can be bought or constructed from suitable heavy timbers or steel.

In any case, it is always best to spend a little extra time to make sure that the car is lifted and supported safely.

CAUTION: *Concrete blocks are not recommended. They may break if the load is not evenly distributed. Boxes and milk crates of any description should not be used.*

Chapter 2

Tune-Up and Troubleshooting

Tune-Up Procedures

An automotive tune-up is an orderly process of inspection, diagnosis, testing, and adjustment that may be needed to maintain peak engine performance or restore the engine to original operating efficiency.

Tests by the Champion Spark Plug Company showed that an average 11.36% improvement in gas economy could be expected after a tune-up. A change to new spark plugs alone provided a 3.44% decrease in fuel use. As for emissions, significantly lower emissions were recorded at idle after a complete tune-up on a car needing service. An average 45.37% reduction of CO emissions was recorded at idle after a complete tune-up, HC emissions were cut 55.5%.

The tune-up is also a good opportunity to perform a general preventive maintenance check-out on everything in the engine compartment. Look for failed or about to fail components such as loose or damaged wiring, leaking fuel lines, cracked coolant hoses, and frayed fan belts.

Chrysler recommends replacing spark plugs at 30,000 mile intervals on cars equipped with catalytic converters and 15,000 mile intervals on non-converter cars. It would be a good idea to check the spark plugs and ignition system before those mileage readings as a preventive maintenance measure. If you are experiencing

starting problems or below average fuel economy you will, of course, want to tune the car before those intervals. Each step of the tune-up should be followed in the order given. If any of the specifications on the emission control sticker under your hood differ from those given in the "Tune-Up Specifications" chart, use the figures from the sticker. Running changes made by the manufacturer are often incorporated into the sticker. When you decide on a tune-up schedule for your car, follow it religiously. A regular tune-up will head off winter no-starts and summer stalling. A small investment in time and parts pays off in improved gas mileage and engine performance. The procedures given here are tailored specifically for your Volare or Aspen.

SPARK PLUGS

A typical spark plug consists of a metal shell surrounding a ceramic insulator. A metal electrode extends downward through the center of the insulator and protrudes a small distance. Located at the end of the plug and attached to the side of the outer metal shell is the side electrode. The side electrode bends in at 90° so its tip is even with, and parallel to, the tip of the center electrode. The distance between these two electrodes (measured in thousandths of an inch) is called the spark plug gap. The spark plug in no way produces a spark but merely provides a gap across which the current can arc. The coil produces over 30,000 volts, which travels to the distributor

Tune-Up Specifications

Year	Engine No. Cyl Displacement (cu in.)	SPARK PLUGS		IGNITION TIMING		IDLE SPEED	
		Type	Gap (in.)	Manual Trans (deg)	Auto Trans (deg)	Manual Trans (rpm)	Auto Trans (rpm)
1976	6—225 1 bbl	RBL-13Y	0.035	6B	2B	750	750
1976	6—225 1 bbl Calif	RBL-13Y	0.035	4B	2B	800	750
1976	8—318 2 bbl	RN-12Y	0.035	2B	2B	750	750
1976	8—318 2 bbl Calif	RN-12Y	0.035	2B	TDC	750	750
1976	8—318 2 bbl Fed Air Pump	RN-12Y	0.035	——	2A	——	900
1976	8—360	RN-12Y	0.035	——	2B	——	800
1977	6—225 1 bbl	RBL-15Y	0.035	12B	12B	700	700
1977	6—225 1 bbl High Alt and Calif	RBL-15Y	0.035	8B	8B	750	750
1977	6—225 2 bbl	RBL-15Y	0.035	12B	12B	750	750
1977	6—225 2 bbl Calif	RBL-13Y	0.035	4B	4B	850	850
1977	8—318 2 bbl	RN-12Y	0.035	8B	8B	700	700
1977	8—318 2 bbl High Alt and Calif	RN-12Y	0.035	TDC	TDC	850	850
1977	8—360 2 bbl	RN-12Y	0.035	——	10B	——	700
1978	6—225 1 bbl	RBL-16Y	0.035	12BTDC	12BTDC	700	700
1978	6—225 2 bbl	RBL-16Y	0.035	12BTDC	12BTDC	700	700

Tune-Up Specifications (cont.)

Year	Engine No. Cyl. Displacement (cu in.)	SPARK PLUGS		IGNITION TIMING		IDLE SPEED	
		Type	Gap (in.)	Manual Trans (deg)	Auto Trans (deg)	Manual Trans (rpm)	Auto Trans (rpm)
1978	6—225 1 bbl Calif	RBL-16Y	0.035	8BTDC	8BTDC	750	750
1978	6—225 2 bbl Calif	RBL-16Y	0.035	10BTDC	10BTDC	750	750
1978	8—318 2 bbl	RN-12Y	0.035	16BTDC	16BTDC	700 (750-Calif)	700 (750-Calif)
1978	8—318 4 bbl	RN-12Y	0.035	16BTDC	16BTDC	700 (750-Calif)	700 (750-Calif)
1978	8—360 2 bbl	RN-12Y	0.035	——	20BTDC	700 (750-Calif)	700 (750-Calif)
1978	8—360 4 bbl	RN-12Y	0.035	——	16BTDC	700 (750-Calif)	700 (750-Calif)

—— Not Applicable
Calif—California
Fed—Federal (49 States)
   Due to ongoing production line changes, the above information may conflict with the tune-up information shown on the underhood emissions control sticker. In the event there are differences, use the information on the underhood sticker.

where it is distributed through the spark plug wires to the plugs. The current passes along the center electrode and jumps the gap to the side electrode and, in so doing, ignites the air/fuel mixture in the combustion chamber. All plugs have a resistor built into the center electrode to reduce interference to any nearby radio and television receivers. The resistor also cuts down on the erosion of plug electrodes caused by excessively long sparking. Resistor spark plug wiring is original equipment on all models.

   Spark plug life and efficiency depend upon the condition of the engine and the temperatures to which the plug is exposed. Combustion chamber temperatures are affected by many factors such as compression ratio of the engine, fuel/air mixtures, exhaust emission equipment, and the type of driving you do. Spark plugs are designed and classified by number according to the heat range at which they will operate most efficiently. The amount of heat that the plug absorbs is determined by the length of the lower insulator. The longer the insulator (it extends farther into the engine), the hotter the plug will operate; the shorter it is, the cooler it will operate. A plug that absorbs little heat and remains too cool will quickly accumulate deposits of oil and carbon since it is not hot enough to burn them off. This leads to plug fouling and consequently to misfiring. A plug that absorbs too much heat will have no deposits but, due to the excessive heat, the electrodes will burn away quickly and, in some instances, pre-ignition may result. Pre-ignition takes place when plug tips get so hot that they glow sufficiently to ignite the fuel/air mixture before the spark does. This early ignition will usually cause a pinging (sounding much like castanets) during low speeds and heavy loads. In severe cases, the heat may become high enough to start the fuel/air mixture burning throughout the combustion chamber rather than just to the front of the plug as in normal operation. At this time, the piston is rising in the cylinder making its compression stroke. The burning mass is compressed and an explosion results forcing the piston and rod assembly down in the cylinder while it is still trying to go up. Something has to give, and it does-pistons are often damaged. Obviously, this detonation (explosion) is a destructive condition that can be avoided by installing a spark plug designed and specified for your particular engine.

A set of spark plugs usually requires replacement after 15,000 to 20,000 miles depending on the type of driving. The electrode on a new spark plug has a sharp edge but, with use, this edge becomes rounded by erosion causing the plug gap to increase. In normal operation, plug gap increases about 0.001 in. for every 1,000–2,000 miles. As the gap increases, the plug's voltage requirement also increases. It requires a greater voltage to jump the wider gap and about two to three times as much voltage to fire a plug at high speeds and acceleration than a idle.

The higher voltage produced by the electronic ignition is one of the primary reasons for the prolonged replacement interval for spark plugs in later cars. A consistently hotter spark prevents the fouling of plugs for much longer than could normally be expected; this spark is also able to jump across a larger gap more efficiently than a spark from a conventional system. However, even plugs used with the electronic ignition system wear after time in the engine.

In addition to performing their primary function of igniting the air/fuel mixture, spark plugs can also serve as very useful diagnostic tools. Once removed, compare your spark plugs with the samples in the "Troubleshooting" section at the end of this chapter. Typical plug conditions are illustrated along with their causes and remedies. Plugs which exhibit only normal wear and deposits can be cleaned, gapped, and reinstalled. However, it is a good practice to replace the spark plugs at each tune-up.

Spark Plug Replacement

Tools needed for spark plug replacement include a ratchet handle, short extension, spark plug socket ($^{13}/_{16}$ in. for V8s, $^5/_8$ in. for sixes), combination spark plug gap gauge and bending tool, and a can of penetrating oil. A torque wrench makes for more accurate spark plug tightening, but is not absolutely necessary. Check the "Tune-Up Specifications" chart for the correct spark plugs for your engine before rushing out to the parts store.

When you're removing spark plugs, you should work on one at a time. Don't start by removing the plug wires all at once, because unless you number them, they may become

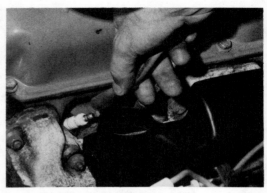

Twist the boot to remove the plug wire

mixed up. Take a minute before you begin and number the wires with tape. The best location for numbering is near where the wires come out of the distributor cap.

1. Twist the spark plug boot and remove the boot and wire from the plug. Do not pull on the wire itself.

2. Once the wire is removed, use a brush or rag to clean the area around the spark plug. Make sure that all dirt is removed so that none will enter the cylinder after the plug is removed.

3. Remove the spark plug using the proper size socket. V8s require a $^{13}/_{16}$ in. socket. Six cylinder engines use tapered seat spark plugs and require the smaller $^5/_8$ in. socket. Turn the socket counterclockwise to remove the plug. On six cylinder engines, the spark plug tube will sometimes also come out. Wipe it clean before replacing it.

4. If the spark plug is stubborn, squirt some penetrating oil onto the plug threads. Give the oil a minute to work and then remove the plug. Be sure to hold the socket straight on the spark plug. This is sometimes difficult, but you can crack the insulator or

Keep the socket straight on the plug to avoid breaking it

Checking spark plug gap

round off the hex on the plug if the socket isn't held straight.

5. Once the plug is out, check it against those shown in section 4.6 of the "Troubleshooting" section at the end of the chapter.

6. Most new spark plugs come pre-gapped, but the factory setting sometimes changes in shipping and should be checked. Use a wire feeler gauge. Flat feeler gauges are not accurate when used on spark plugs. The correct size feeler gauge should pass through the electrode gap with a slight drag. If you're in doubt, try one size smaller and one larger. The smaller gauge should go through easily, while the larger one shouldn't fit at all. If the gap is incorrect, use the electrode bending tool on the end of the gauge to adjust the gap. When adjusting the gap, always bend the side electrode. Never bend or try to adjust the center electrode.

7. Squirt a drop of penetrating oil on the threads of the new plug and install it. Don't heavily oil the threads. Turn the plug in clockwise by hand.

8. When the spark plug is finger tight, tighten it with a wrench. If a torque wrench is available, tighten the spark plug to 30 ft. lbs. (V8) or 10 ft. lbs. (six). If you don't have a torque wrench, give the plug about ⅛ of turn with the wrench after it's finger tight. Don't overtighten the spark plug.

9. Install the spark plug boot firmly over the plug. Proceed to remove the remaining plugs in the same manner. Should the wires become mixed up, refer to the firing order illustration in the beginning of Chapter 3.

Checking and Replacing Spark Plug Cables

Visually inspect the spark plug cables for burns, cuts, or breaks in the insulation. Check the spark plug boots and the nipples on the distributor cap and the coil. Replace any damaged wiring. If no physical damage is obvious, the wires can be checked with an ohmmeter for excessive resistance. Remove the distributor cap and leave the wires connected to the cap. Connect one lead of the ohmmeter to the corresponding electrode inside the cap and the other lead to the spark plug terminal (remove it from the spark plug for the test). Replace any wire which shows over 50,000 ohms. Test the coil wire by connecting the ohmmeter between the center contact in the cap and either of the primary terminals at the coil. If the total resistance of the coil and cable is more than 25,000 ohms, remove the cable from the coil and check the resistance of the cable. If the resistance is higher than 15,000 ohms, replace the cable. If resistance is less, check the coil for a loose connection or for a bad coil. Check the top of the coil for cracks or carbon tracking.

Replace spark plug cables one at a time when installing a new set, this way there can be no mix-ups. Refer to the firing order illustration in Chapter 3 if you do become confused. Start by replacing the longest cable first. Install the boot firmly over the spark plug. Route the wire exactly the same as the original. Insert the nipple firmly into the tower on the distributor cap. Repeat the process for each cable.

ELECTRONIC IGNITION SYSTEM

Chrysler Corporation has been using this system on all of its cars since 1973. The system consists of a magnetic pulse distributor, electronic control unit, dual element ballast resistor, and special ignition coil. The distributor outwardly resembles a standard breaker point unit, but is internally quite different. The usual breaker points, cam, and condenser are replaced with a reluctor and pick-up unit.

The ignition primary circuit is connected from the battery, through the ignition switch, through the primary side of the ignition coil, to the control unit where it is grounded. The secondary circuit is the same as in a conventional ignition system: the secondary side of the coil, the coil wire to the distributor, the rotor, the spark plug wires, and the spark plugs.

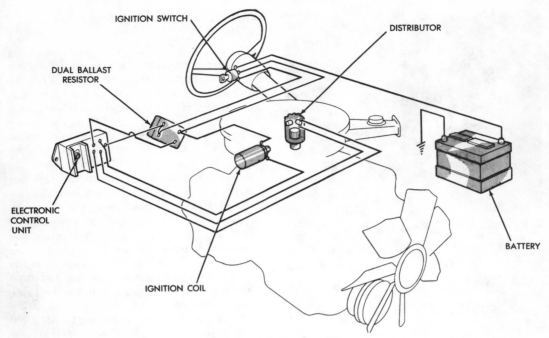

Electronic ignition schematic

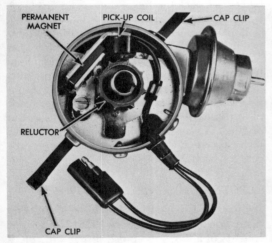

Electronic ignition distributor—cap removed

Electronic control unit. Don't touch it with the engine running unless you want a healthy shock

The magnetic pulse distributor is also connected to the control unit. As the distributor shaft turns, the reluctor rotates past the pick-up unit. As the reluctor turns by the pick-up unit, each of the six or eight teeth on the reluctor pass near the pick-up unit once during each distributor revolution (two crankshaft revolutions since the distributor turns at one half crankshaft speed). As the reluctor teeth move close to the pick-up unit, the rotating reluctor induces voltage into the magnetic pick-up unit. When the pulse enters the control unit, it signals the control unit to interrupt the ignition primary circuit. This causes the primary circuit to collapse and begins the induction of the magnetic lines of force from the primary side of the coil into the secondary side of the coil. This induction provides the required voltage to fire the spark plugs.

The advantages of this system are that the transistors in the control unit can make or break the primary ignition circuit much faster than the conventional ignition points can, and higher primary voltage can be utilized, since this system can be made to handle higher volt-

Dual ballast resistor (arrow)

Check the inside of the cap for any defects

age without adverse effects, where standard breaker points would quickly burn. The quicker switching time of this system allows longer coil primary circuit saturation time and longer induction time when the primary circuit collapses. This increased time allows the primary circuit to build up more current and the secondary circuit to discharge more current.

Inspection

The electronic ignition system is practically maintenance free and should require very little attention, but an inspection at tune-up intervals is advised to prevent problems.

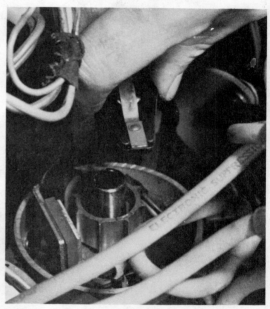

The rotor only goes on and off one way

Prying the retainer clips from the distributor cap

Check the ignition wires as previously discussed. Ignition wire condition is more critical on electronic ignition systems than on conventional breaker point systems. Using either your finger or a screwdriver, pry the two retaining clips from the distributor cap. Lift the cap off the distributor and check the outside of the cap for cracks or other damage. Examine the inside of the cap for carbon tracking. Check each of the contacts for erosion or chipping. Replace the cap if damage or excessive erosion of the contacts is present. Pull straight up on the rotor to remove it. Check the tip of the rotor for pitting or erosion, replace if necessary.

Troubleshooting Electronic Ignition

Condition	Possible Cause	Correction
ENGINE WILL NOT START (Fuel and carburetion known to be OK)	a) Dual Ballast Resistor	Check resistance of each section: Compensating resistance: .50–.60 ohms @ 70°–80° F Auxiliary Ballast: 4.75–5.75 ohms Replace if faulty. Check wire positions.
	b) Faulty Ignition Coil	Check for carbonized tower. Check primary and secondary resistances: Primary: 1.41–1.79 ohms @ 70°–80° F Secondary: 9,200–11,700 ohms @ 70°–80° F Check in coil tester.
	c) Faulty Pickup or Improper Pickup Air Gap	Check pickup coil resistance: 400–600 ohms Check pickup gap: .010 in. *nonmagnetic* feeler gauge should not slip between pickup coil core and an aligned reluctor blade. No evidence of pickup core striking reluctor blades should be visible. To reset gap, tighten pickup adjustment screw with a .008 in. *nonmagnetic* feeler gauge held between pickup core and an aligned reluctor blade. After resetting gap, run distributor on test stand and apply vacuum advance, making sure that the pickup core does not strike the reluctor blades.

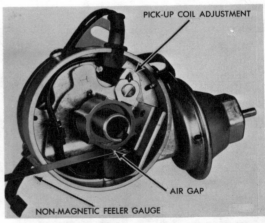

Checking the distributor air gap. Use a brass gauge

	d) Faulty Wiring	Visually inspect wiring for brittle insulation. Inspect connectors. Molded connectors should be inspected for rubber inside female terminals.
	e) Faulty Control Unit	Replace if all of the above checks are negative. Whenever the control unit or dual ballast is replaced, make sure the dual ballast wires are correctly inserted in the keyed molded connector.
ENGINE SURGES SEVERELY (Not Lean Carburetor)	a) Wiring	Inspect for loose connection and/or broken conductors in harness.
	b) Faulty Pickup Leads	Disconnect vacuum advance. If surging stops, replace pickup.

Troubleshooting Electronic Ignition (cont.)

Condition	Possible Cause	Correction
	c) Ignition Coil	Check for intermittent primary.
ENGINE MISSES (Carburetion OK)	a) Spark Plugs	Check plugs. Clean and regap if necessary.
	b) Secondary Cable	Check cables with an ohmmeter.
	c) Ignition Coil	Check for carbonized tower. Check in coil tester.
	d) Wiring	Check for loose or dirty connections.
	e) Faulty Pickup Lead	Disconnect vacuum advance. If miss stops, replace pickup.
	f) Control Unit	Replace if the above checks are negative.

IGNITION TIMING

Timing should be checked at each tune-up. The timing marks consist of a notch on the rim of the crankshaft pulley or vibration damper and a graduated scale attached to the engine front (timing) cover. A stroboscopic flash (dynamic) timing light must be used, as a static light is too inaccurate for emission controlled engines.

There are three basic types of timing light available. The first is a simple neon bulb with two wire connections. One wire connects to the spark plug terminal and the other plugs into the end of the spark plug wire for the No. 1 cylinder, thus connecting the light in series with the spark plug. This type of light is pretty dim and must be held very closely to the timing marks to be seen. Sometimes a dark corner has to be sought out to see the flash at all. This type of light is very inexpensive. The second type operates from the car battery— two alligator clips connect to the battery terminals, while an adapter enables a third clip to be connected to the No. 1 spark plug and wire. This type is a bit more expensive, but it provides a nice bright flash that you can see even in bright sunlight. It is the type most often seen in professional shops. The third type replaces the battery power source with 110 volt current.

To check and adjust the timing:

1. Warm up the engine to normal operating temperature. Stop the engine and connect the timing light to the No. 1 (left front on V8, front on six) spark plug wire. Clean off the timing marks and mark the pulley or damper notch and timing scale with white chalk.

2. Disconnect and plug the vacuum line at the distributor. This is done to prevent any distributor vacuum advance.

3. Start the engine and adjust the idle speed to that specified in the "Tune-Up Specifications" chart.

V8 timing marks

Six-cylinder timing marks

4. Aim the timing light at the point marks. Be careful not to touch the fan, because it may appear to be standing still. If the pulley or damper notch isn't aligned with the proper timing mark (see the "Tune-Up Specifications" chart), the timing will have to be adjusted.

NOTE: *TDC or Top Dead Center corresponds to 0 degrees. B, or BTDC, or Before Top Dead Center may be shown as BEFORE. A, or ATDC, or After Top Dead Center may be shown as AFTER.*

Using the timing light

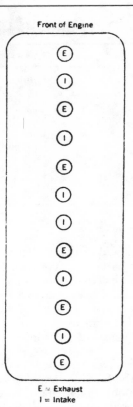

Front of Engine

E = Exhaust
I = Intake

Valve location—slant six

5. Loosen the distributor base clamp lock-nut. You can buy trick wrenches which make this task a lot easier. Turn the distributor slowly to adjust the timing, holding it by the body and not the cap. Turn the distributor in the direction of rotor rotation (found in the "firing Order" illustration in Chapter 3) to re-tard, and against the direction of rotation to advance.

6. Tighten the locknut. Check the timing again, in case the distributor moved slightly as you tightened it.

7. Replace the distributor vacuum line. Correct the idle speed if it changed.

8. Stop the engine and disconnect the timing light.

VALVE LASH

This adjustment is required only on the six-cylinder; it should be done at every tune-up or whenever there is excessive noise from the valve mechanism.

NOTE: *Do not set the valve lash closer than specified in an attempt to quiet the valve mechanism. This will result in burned valves.*

The valves can be adjusted with the engine running, but the amateur will have better luck with the following procedure.

1. The engine must be at normal operating temperature. Mark the crankshaft pulley into three equal 120° segments, starting at the timing mark.

2. Remove the valve (rocker) cover and the distributor cap.

3. Set the engine at TDC on the No. 1 cylinder by aligning the mark on the crankshaft pulley with the 0° mark on the timing cover pointer. The distributor rotor should point at the position of the No. 1 spark plug wire in the distributor cap. Both rocker arms on the No. 1

cylinder should be free to move slightly. If all this isn't the case, you have No. 6 cylinder at TDC and will have to turn the engine 360° in the normal direction of rotation.

4. The cylinders are numbered from front to rear. The intake and exhaust valves are in the following sequence, starting at the front: E-I, E-I, E-I, I-E, I-E, I-E. Note that intake and exhaust valves have different settings.

5. The lash is measured between the rocker arm and the end of the valve.

6. To check the lash, insert the correct size feeler gauge between the rocker arm and the valve. Press down lightly on the other end of the rocker arm. If the gauge cannot be inserted, loosen the self-locking adjustment nut on top of the rocker arm. Tighten the nut until the gauge can just be inserted and withdrawn without buckling.

7. After both valves for the No. 1 cylinder are adjusted, turn the engine so that the pulley turns 120° in the normal direction of rotation (clockwise). The distributor rotor will turn 60°, since it turns at half engine speed.

8. Check that the rocker arms are free and adjust the valves for the next cylinder in the firing order, 5. The firing order is 1-5-3-6-2-4.

9. Turn the engine 120° to adjust each of the remaining cylinders in the firing order. When you are done the engine will have made two complete revolutions (720°) and the rotor one complete revolution (360°).

10. Replace the rocker cover with a new gasket. Replace the distributor cap. Start the engine and check for leaks.

CARBURETOR ADJUSTMENTS

NOTE: *The following are basic carburetor adjustments which are performed as part of the engine tune-up procedure, for more complete adjustment procedures, see Chapter 4, "Emission Controls and Fuel System".*

Idle Speed/Mixture

To adjust the idle speed and mixture, it is best to use an exhaust gas analyzer. This will insure that the proper level of emissions is maintained. However, if you do not have an exhaust gas analyzer, use the following procedure and eliminate those steps which pertain to the exhaust gas analyzer. When you have adjusted the carburetor it would be wise to have it checked with an exhaust gas analyzer.

1. Leave the air cleaner installed.

2. Run the engine at fast idle speed to stabilize the entire temperature.

3. Make sure the choke plate is fully released.

4. Connect a tachometer to the engine, following the manufacturer's instructions.

5. Connect an exhaust gas analyzer and insert the probe as far into the tailpipe as possible.

6. Check the ignition timing and set it to specification if necessary.

7. If equipped with air conditioning, turn the air conditioner off.

8. Put the transmission in Neutral. Make sure the hot idle compensator valve is fully seated.

9. If equipped with a distributor vacuum control valve, place a clamp on the line between the valve and the intake manifold.

10. Turn the engine idle speed adjusting screw in or out to adjust the idle speed to specification. If the carburetor is equipped with an electric solenoid throttle positioner, turn the solenoid adjusting screw in or out to obtain the specified rpm.

CAUTION: *On engines equipped with catalytic converters, be careful not to adjust the idle speed with the catalyst protection system solenoid; a dangerous engine overspeed*

Curb idle speed adjustment screw

condition could result. See Chapter 4 for a description of this system.

11. Adjust the curb idle speed screw until it just touches the stop on the carburetor body. Back the curb idle speed screw out 1 full turn.

12. Turn each idle mixture adjustment screw 1/16 turn richer (counterclockwise). Wait 10 seconds and observe the reading on the exhaust gas analyzer. Continue this procedure until the meter indicates a definite increase in the richness of the mixture.

NOTE: *This step is very important when using an exhaust gas analyzer. A carburetor that is set too lean will cause a false reading from the analyzer, indicating a rich mixture. Because of this, the carburetor must first be*

Idle mixture screw (arrow). The one on the other side is hidden

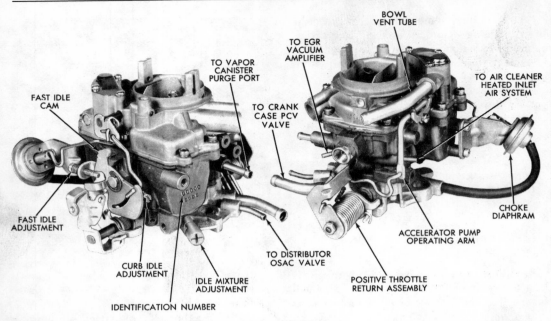

Holley one-bbl carburetor adjustment points

known to have a rich mixture to verify the reading on the analyzer.

13. After verifying the reading on the meter, adjust the mixture screws to obtain an air-fuel ratio of 14.2 Turn the mixture screws clockwise (leaner) to raise the meter reading or counterclockwise (richer) to lower the meter reading.

14. If the idle speed changes as the mixture screws are adjusted, adjust the speed to specification (see Step 10) and readjust the mixture so that the specified air/fuel ratio is maintained at the specified idle speed.

If the idle is rough, the screws may be adjusted independently provided that the 14.2 air/fuel ratio is maintained.

15. Remove the analyzer, the tachometer, and the clamp on the vacuum line.

Trouble-shooting

The following section is designed to aid in the rapid diagnosis of engine problems. The systematic format is used to diagnose problems ranging from engine starting difficulties to the need for engine overhaul. It is assumed that the user is equipped with basic hand tools and test equipment (tach-dwell meter, timing light, voltmeter, and ohmmeter).

Troubleshooting is divided into two sections. The first, *General Diagnosis*, is used to locate the problem area. In the second, *Specific Diagnosis*, the problem is systematically evaluated.

General Diagnosis

PROBLEM: Symptom	Begin diagnosis at Section Two, Number ———
Engine won't start:	
Starter doesn't turn	1.1, 2.1
Starter turns, engine doesn't	2.1
Starter turns engine very slowly	1.1, 2.4
Starter turns engine normally	3.1, 4.1
Starter turns engine very quickly	6.1
Engine fires intermittently	4.1
Engine fires consistently	5.1, 6.1
Engine runs poorly:	
Hard starting	3.1, 4.1, 5.1, 8.1
Rough idle	4.1, 5.1, 8.1
Stalling	3.1, 4.1, 5.1, 8.1
Engine dies at high speeds	4.1, 5.1
Hesitation (on acceleration from standing stop)	5.1, 8.1
Poor pickup	4.1, 5.1, 8.1
Lack of power	3.1, 4.1, 5.1, 8.1
Backfire through the carburetor	4.1, 8.1, 9.1
Backfire through the exhaust	4.1, 8.1, 9.1
Blue exhaust gases	6.1, 7.1
Black exhaust gases	5.1
Running on (after the ignition is shut off)	3.1, 8.1
Susceptible to moisture	4.1
Engine misfires under load	4.1, 7.1, 8.4, 9.1
Engine misfires at speed	4.1, 8.4
Engine misfires at idle	3.1, 4.1, 5.1, 7.1, 8.4

PROBLEM: Symptom	Probable Cause
Engine noises: ①	
Metallic grind while starting	Starter drive not engaging completely
Constant grind or rumble	*Starter drive not releasing, worn main bearings
Constant knock	Worn connecting rod bearings
Knock under load	Fuel octane too low, worn connecting rod bearings
Double knock	Loose piston pin
Metallic tap	*Collapsed or sticky valve lifter, excessive valve clearance, excessive end play in a rotating shaft
Scrape	*Fan belt contacting a stationary surface
Tick while starting	S.U. electric fuel pump (normal), starter brushes
Constant tick	*Generator brushes, shreaded fan belt
Squeal	*Improperly tensioned fan belt
Hiss or roar	*Steam escaping through a leak in the cooling system or the radiator overflow vent
Whistle	*Vacuum leak
Wheeze	Loose or cracked spark plug

① —It is extremely difficult to evaluate vehicle noises. While the above are general definitions of engine noises, those starred (*) should be considered as possibly originating elsewhere in the car. To aid diagnosis, the following list considers other potential sources of these sounds.

Metallic grind:
Throwout bearing; transmission gears, bearings, or synchronizers; differential bearings, gears; something metallic in contact with brake drum or disc.

Metallic tap:
U-joints; fan-to-radiator (or shroud) contact.

Scrape:
Brake shoe or pad dragging; tire to body contact; suspension contacting undercarriage or exhaust; something non-metallic contacting brake shoe or drum.

Tick:
Transmission gears; differential gears; lack of radio suppression; resonant vibration of body panels; windshield wiper motor or transmission; heater motor and blower.

Squeal:
Brake shoe or pad not fully releasing; tires (excessive wear, uneven wear, improper inflation); front or rear wheel alignment (most commonly due to improper toe-in).

Hiss or whistle:
Wind leaks (body or window); heater motor and blower fan.

Roar:
Wheel bearings; wind leaks (body and window).

Specific Diagnosis

This section is arranged so that following each test, instructions are given to proceed to another, until a problem is diagnosed.

INDEX

Group		Topic
1	*	Battery
2	*	Cranking system
3	*	Primary electrical system
4	*	Secondary electrical system
5	*	Fuel system
6	*	Engine compression
7	**	Engine vacuum
8	**	Secondary electrical system
9	**	Valve train
10	**	Exhaust system
11	**	Cooling system
12	**	Engine lubrication

*—The engine need not be running.
**—The engine must be running.

SAMPLE SECTION

Test and Procedure	Results and Indications	Proceed to
4.1—Check for spark: Hold each spark plug wire approximately ¼″ from ground with gloves or a heavy, dry rag. Crank the engine and observe the spark.	→ If no spark is evident:	4.2
	→ If spark is good in some cases:	4.3
	→ If spark is good in all cases:	4.6

DIAGNOSIS

1.1—Inspect the battery visually for case condition (corrosion, cracks) and water level.	If case is cracked, replace battery:	1.4
	If the case is intact, remove corrosion with a solution of baking soda and water (CAUTION: *do not get the solution into the battery*), and fill with water:	1.2
1.2—Check the battery cable connections: Insert a screwdriver between the battery post and the cable clamp. Turn the headlights on high beam, and observe them as the screwdriver is gently twisted to ensure good metal to metal contact. **Testing battery cable connections using a screwdriver**	If the lights brighten, remove and clean the clamp and post; coat the post with petroleum jelly, install and tighten the clamp:	1.4
	If no improvement is noted:	1.3

1.3—Test the state of charge of the battery using an individual cell tester or hydrometer.		If indicated, charge the battery. NOTE: *If no obvious reason exists for the low state of charge (i.e., battery age, prolonged storage), the charging system should be tested:*	1.4

Spec. Grav. Reading	Charged Condition
1.260-1.280	Fully Charged
1.230-1.250	Three Quarter Charged
1.200-1.220	One Half Charged
1.170-1.190	One Quarter Charged
1.140-1.160	Just About Flat
1.110-1.130	All The Way Down

State of battery charge

Electrolyte temperature (°F)	Specific gravity correction
+120	+.016
+100	+.012
	+.008 ADD
+80	+.004 to reading
	no correction
+60	−.004
	−.008
+40	−.012
	−.016
+20	−.020
	−.024 SUBTRACT
0	−.028 from reading
	−.032
−20	−.036
	−.040

The effect of temperature on the specific gravity of battery electrolyte

Test and Procedure	Results and Indications	Proceed to
1.4—Visually inspect battery cables for cracking, bad connection to ground, or bad connection to starter.	If necessary, tighten connections or replace the cables:	2.1

Tests in Group 2 are performed with coil high tension lead disconnected to prevent accidental starting.

Test and Procedure	Results and Indications	Proceed to
2.1—Test the starter motor and solenoid: Connect a jumper from the battery post of the solenoid (or relay) to the starter post of the solenoid (or relay).	If starter turns the engine normally:	2.2
	If the starter buzzes, or turns the engine very slowly:	2.4
	If no response, replace the solenoid (or relay).	3.1
	If the starter turns, but the engine doesn't, ensure that the flywheel ring gear is intact. If the gear is undamaged, replace the starter drive.	3.1
2.2—Determine whether ignition override switches are functioning properly (clutch start switch, neutral safety switch), by connecting a jumper across the switch(es), and turning the ignition switch to "start".	If starter operates, adjust or replace switch:	3.1
	If the starter doesn't operate:	2.3
2.3—Check the ignition switch "start" position: Connect a 12V test lamp between the starter post of the solenoid (or relay) and ground. Turn the ignition switch to the "start" position, and jiggle the key.	If the lamp doesn't light when the switch is turned, check the ignition switch for loose connections, cracked insulation, or broken wires. Repair or replace as necessary:	3.1
	If the lamp flickers when the key is jiggled, replace the ignition switch.	3.3

Checking the ignition switch "start" position

Test and Procedure	Results and Indications	Proceed to
2.4—Remove and bench test the starter, according to specifications in the car section.	If the starter does not meet specifications, repair or replace as needed:	3.1
	If the starter is operating properly:	2.5
2.5—Determine whether the engine can turn freely: Remove the spark plugs, and check for water in the cylinders. Check for water on the dipstick, or oil in the radiator. Attempt to turn the engine using an 18" flex drive and socket on the crankshaft pulley nut or bolt.	If the engine will turn freely only with the spark plugs out, and hydrostatic lock (water in the cylinders) is ruled out, check valve timing:	9.2
	If engine will not turn freely, and it is known that the clutch and transmission are free, the engine must be disassembled for further evaluation:	Next Chapter

Tests and Procedures	Results and Indications	Proceed to
3.1—Check the ignition switch "on" position: Connect a jumper wire between the distributor side of the coil and ground, and a 12V test lamp between the switch side of the coil and ground. Remove the high tension lead from the coil. Turn the ignition switch on and jiggle the key.	If the lamp lights:	3.2
	If the lamp flickers when the key is jiggled, replace the ignition switch:	3.3
	If the lamp doesn't light, check for loose or open connections. If none are found, remove the ignition switch and check for continuity. If the switch is faulty, replace it:	3.3

(To distributor)   COIL   BATTERY

Checking the ignition switch "on" position

3.2—Check the ballast resistor with an ohmmeter (low scale). With the engine at operating temperature and the ignition switch off, disconnect the four leads on the resistor. Connect the ohmmeter to the auxiliary (molded) resistor terminals one and two. The reading should be between 4.75 and 5.75 ohms. Next, connect the ohmmeter to the compensating (wire wound) resistor terminals three and four. The reading should be 0.5 to 0.6 ohms.	If readings differ from these, replace the ballast resistor.	
3.3—Test the coil primary resistance. Connect an ohmmeter between the battery (+) terminal and the negative (−) terminal of the coil. Resistance should be between 1.0 and 1.79 ohms.	If readings differ from these, check the coil secondary resistance before replacing the coil, or perform a coil substitution test.	4.1

Testing the coil primary resistance

Test and Procedure	Results and Indications	Proceed to
4.1—Check for spark: Hold each spark plug wire approximately ¼″ from ground with gloves or a heavy, dry rag. Crank the engine, and observe the spark.	If no spark is evident:	4.2
	If spark is good in some cylinders:	4.3
	If spark is good in all cylinders:	4.6
4.2—Check for spark at the coil high tension lead: Remove the coil high tension lead from the distributor and position it approximately ¼″ from ground. Crank the engine and observe spark. CAUTION: *This test should not be performed on cars equipped with transistorized ignition.*	If the spark is good and consistent:	4.3
	If the spark is good but intermittent, test the primary electrical system starting at 3.3:	3.3
	If the spark is weak or non-existent, replace the coil high tension lead, clean and tighten all connections and retest. If no improvement is noted:	4.4
4.3—Visually inspect the distributor cap and rotor for burned or corroded contacts, cracks, carbon tracks, or moisture. Also check the fit of the rotor on the distributor shaft (where applicable).	If moisture is present, dry thoroughly, and retest per 4.1:	4.1
	If burned or excessively corroded contacts, cracks, or carbon tracks are noted, replace the defective part(s) and retest per 4.1:	4.1
	If the rotor and cap appear intact, or are only slightly corroded, clean the contacts thoroughly (including the cap towers and spark plug wire ends) and retest per 4.1: If the spark is good in all cases: If the spark is poor in all cases:	4.6 4.5
4.4—Check the coil secondary resistance: Connect an ohmmeter between the coil battery (+) terminal and the coil tower. Resistance should be between 9,400 and 11,700 ohms.	If readings differ from these, perform a coil substitution test, and retest per 4.1.	

Testing the coil secondary resistance

Test and Procedure	Results and Indications	Proceed to
4.5—Visually inspect the spark plug wires for cracking or brittleness. Ensure that no two wires are positioned so as to cause induction firing (adjacent and parallel). Remove each wire, one by one, and check resistance with an ohmmeter.	Replace any cracked or brittle wires. If any of the wires are defective, replace the entire set. Replace any wires with excessive resistance (over 8000Ω per foot for suppression wire), and separate any wires that might cause induction firing.	4.6
4.6—Remove the spark plugs, noting the cylinders from which they were removed, and evaluate according to the chart below.	See below.	See below.

	Condition	Cause	Remedy	Proceed to
	Electrodes eroded, light brown deposits.	Normal wear. Normal wear is indicated by approximately .001″ wear per 1000 miles.	Clean and regap the spark plug if wear is not excessive: Replace the spark plug if excessively worn:	4.7
	Carbon fouling (black, dry, fluffy deposits).	If present on one or two plugs:		
		Faulty high tension lead(s).	Test the high tension leads:	4.5
		Burnt or sticking valve(s).	Check the valve train: (Clean and regap the plugs in either case.)	9.1
		If present on most or all plugs: Overly rich fuel mixture, due to restricted air filter, improper carburetor adjustment, improper choke or heat riser adjustment or operation.	Check the fuel system:	5.1
	Oil fouling (wet black deposits)	Worn engine components. NOTE: *Oil fouling may occur in new or recently rebuilt engines until broken in.*	Check engine vacuum and compression: Replace with new spark plug	6.1
	Lead fouling (gray, black, tan, or yellow deposits, which appear glazed or cinderlike).	Combustion by-products.	Clean and regap the plugs: (Use plugs of a different heat range if the problem recurs.)	4.7

	Condition	Cause	Remedy	Proceed to
	Gap bridging (deposits lodged between the electrodes).	Incomplete combustion, or transfer of deposits from the combustion chamber.	Replace the spark plugs:	4.7
	Overheating (burnt electrodes, and extremely white insulator with small black spots).	Ignition timing advanced too far.	Adjust timing to specifications:	8.2
		Overly lean fuel mixture.	Check the fuel system:	5.1
		Spark plugs not seated properly.	Clean spark plug seat and install a new gasket washer: (Replace the spark plugs in all cases.)	4.7
	Fused spot deposits on the insulator.	Combustion chamber blow-by.	Clean and regap the spark plugs:	4.7
	Pre-ignition (melted or severely burned electrodes, blistered or cracked insulators, or metallic deposits on the insulator).	Incorrect spark plug heat range.	Replace with plugs of the proper heat range:	4.7
		Ignition timing advanced too far.	Adjust timing to specifications:	8.2
		Spark plugs not being cooled efficiently.	Clean the spark plug seat, and check the cooling system:	11.1
		Fuel mixture too lean.	Check the fuel system:	5.1
		Poor compression.	Check compression:	6.1
		Fuel grade too low.	Use higher octane fuel:	4.7

Test and Procedure	Results and Indications	Proceed to
4.7—Determine the static ignition timing: Using the flywheel or crankshaft pulley timing marks as a guide, locate top dead center on the *compression* stroke of the No. 1 cylinder. Remove the distributor cap.	Adjust the distributor so that the rotor points toward the No. 1 tower in the distributor cap, and the points are just opening:	4.8
4.8—Check coil polarity: Connect a voltmeter negative lead to the coil high tension lead, and the positive lead to ground (NOTE: *reverse the hook-up for positive ground cars*). Crank the engine momentarily. **Checking coil polarity**	If the voltmeter reads up-scale, the polarity is correct:	5.1
	If the voltmeter reads down-scale, reverse the coil polarity (switch the primary leads):	5.1

Test and Procedure	*Results and Indications*	*Proceed to*
5.1—Determine that the air filter is functioning efficiently: Hold paper elements up to a strong light, and attempt to see light through the filter.	Clean permanent air filters in gasoline (or manufacturer's recommendation), and allow to dry. Replace paper elements through which light cannot be seen:	5.2
5.2—Determine whether a flooding condition exists: Flooding is identified by a strong gasoline odor, and excessive gasoline present in the throttle bore(s) of the carburetor.	If flooding is not evident:	5.3
	If flooding is evident, permit the gasoline to dry for a few moments and restart.	
	If flooding doesn't recur:	5.6
	If flooding is persistant:	5.5
5.3—Check that fuel is reaching the carburetor: Detach the fuel line at the carburetor inlet. Hold the end of the line in a cup (not styrofoam), and crank the engine.	If fuel flows smoothly:	5.6
	If fuel doesn't flow (NOTE: *Make sure that there is fuel in the tank*), or flows erratically:	5.4
5.4—Test the fuel pump: Disconnect all fuel lines from the fuel pump. Hold a finger over the input fitting, crank the engine (with electric pump, turn the ignition or pump on); and feel for suction.	If suction is evident, blow out the fuel line to the tank with low pressure compressed air until bubbling is heard from the fuel filler neck. Also blow out the carburetor fuel line (both ends disconnected):	5.6
	If no suction is evident, replace or repair the fuel pump:	5.6
	NOTE: *Repeated oil fouling of the spark plugs, or a no-start condition, could be the result of a ruptured vacuum booster pump diaphragm, through which oil or gasoline is being drawn into the intake manifold (where applicable).*	
5.5—Check the needle and seat: Tap the carburetor in the area of the needle and seat.	If flooding stops, a gasoline additive (e.g., Gumout) will often cure the problem:	5.6
	If flooding continues, check the fuel pump for excessive pressure at the carburetor (according to specifications). If the pressure is normal, the needle and seat must be removed and checked, and/or the float level adjusted:	5.6
5.6—Test the accelerator pump by looking into the throttle bores while operating the throttle.	If the accelerator pump appears to be operating normally:	5.7
	If the accelerator pump is not operating, the pump must be reconditioned. Where possible, service the pump with the carburetor(s) installed on the engine. If necessary, remove the carburetor. Prior to removal:	5.7
5.7—Determine whether the carburetor main fuel system is functioning: Spray a commercial starting fluid into the carburetor while attempting to start the engine.	If the engine starts, runs for a few seconds, and dies:	5.8
	If the engine doesn't start:	6.1

Test and Procedures	*Results and Indications*	*Proceed to*
5.8—Uncommon fuel system malfunctions: See below:	If the problem is solved: If the problem remains, remove and recondition the carburetor.	6.1

Condition	*Indication*	*Test*	*Usual Weather Conditions*	*Remedy*
Vapor lock	Car will not re-start shortly after running.	Cool the components of the fuel system until the engine starts.	Hot to very hot	Ensure that the exhaust manifold heat control valve is operating. Check with the vehicle manufacturer for the recommended solution to vapor lock on the model in question.
Carburetor icing	Car will not idle, stalls at low speeds.	Visually inspect the throttle plate area of the throttle bores for frost.	High humidity, 32-40° F.	Ensure that the exhaust manifold heat control valve is operating, and that the intake manifold heat riser is not blocked.
Water in the fuel	Engine sputters and stalls; may not start.	Pump a small amount of fuel into a glass jar. Allow to stand, and inspect for droplets or a layer of water.	High humidity, extreme temperature changes.	For droplets, use one or two cans of commercial gas dryer (Dry Gas) For a layer of water, the tank must be drained, and the fuel lines blown out with compressed air.

Test and Procedure	*Results and Indications*	*Proceed to*
6.1—Test engine compression: Remove all spark plugs. Insert a compression gauge into a spark plug port, crank the engine to obtain the maximum reading, and record.	If compression is within limits on all cylinders:	7.1
	If gauge reading is extremely low on all cylinders:	6.2
	If gauge reading is low on one or two cylinders:	6.2
	(If gauge readings are identical and low on two or more adjacent cylinders, the head gasket must be replaced.)	

Testing compression
(© Chevrolet Div. G.M. Corp.)

Compression pressure limits
(© Buick Div. G.M. Corp.)

Maxi. Press. Lbs. Sq. In.	*Min. Press. Lbs. Sq. In.*	*Maxi. Press. Lbs. Sq. In.*	*Min. Press. Lbs. Sq. In.*	*Max. Press. Lbs. Sq. In.*	*Min. Press. Lbs. Sq. In.*	*Max. Press. Lbs. Sq. In.*	*Min. Press. Lbs. Sq. In.*
134	101	162	121	188	141	214	160
136	102	164	123	190	142	216	162
138	104	166	124	192	144	218	163
140	105	168	126	194	145	220	165
142	107	170	127	196	147	222	166
146	110	172	129	198	148	224	168
148	111	174	131	200	150	226	169
150	113	176	132	202	151	228	171
152	114	178	133	204	153	230	172
154	115	180	135	206	154	232	174
156	117	182	136	208	156	234	175
158	118	184	138	210	157	236	177
160	120	186	140	212	158	238	178

Test and Procedure	Results and Indications	Proceed to
6.2—Test engine compression (wet): Squirt approximately 30 cc. of engine oil into each cylinder, and retest per 6.1.	If the readings improve, worn or cracked rings or broken pistons are indicated:	Next Chapter
	If the readings do not improve, burned or excessively carboned valves or a jumped timing chain are indicated:	7.1
	NOTE: *A jumped timing chain is often indicated by difficult cranking.*	
7.1—Perform a vacuum check of the engine: Attach a vacuum gauge to the intake manifold beyond the throttle plate. Start the engine, and observe the action of the needle over the range of engine speeds.	See below.	See below

	Reading	Indications	Proceed to
	Steady, from 17-22 in. Hg.	Normal.	8.1
	Low and steady.	Late ignition or valve timing, or low compression:	6.1
	Very low	Vacuum leak:	7.2
	Needle fluctuates as engine speed increases.	Ignition miss, blown cylinder head gasket, leaking valve or weak valve spring:	6.1, 8.3
	Gradual drop in reading at idle.	Excessive back pressure in the exhaust system:	10.1
	Intermittent fluctuation at idle.	Ignition miss, sticking valve:	8.3, 9.1
	Drifting needle.	Improper idle mixture adjustment, carburetors not synchronized (where applicable), or minor intake leak. Synchronize the carburetors, adjust the idle, and retest. If the condition persists:	7.2
	High and steady.	Early ignition timing:	8.2

Test and Procedure	Results and Indications	Proceed to
7.2—Attach a vacuum gauge per 7.1, and test for an intake manifold leak. Squirt a small amount of oil around the intake manifold gaskets, carburetor gaskets, plugs and fittings. Observe the action of the vacuum gauge.	If the reading improves, replace the indicated gasket, or seal the indicated fitting or plug: If the reading remains low:	8.1 7.3
7.3—Test all vacuum hoses and accessories for leaks as described in 7.2. Also check the carburetor body (dashpots, automatic choke mechanism, throttle shafts) for leaks in the same manner.	If the reading improves, service or replace the offending part(s): If the reading remains low:	8.1 6.1
8.1—Check the point dwell angle: Connect a dwell meter between the distributor primary wire and ground. Start the engine, and observe the dwell angle from idle to 3000 rpm.	If necessary, adjust the dwell angle. NOTE: *Increasing the point gap reduces the dwell angle and vice-versa.* If the dwell angle moves outside specifications as engine speed increases, the distributor should be removed and checked for cam accuracy, shaft end-play and concentricity, bushing wear, and adequate point arm tension (NOTE: *Most of these items may be checked with the distributor installed in the engine, using an oscilloscope*):	8.2
8.2—Connect a timing light (per manufacturer's recommendation) and check the dynamic ignition timing. Disconnect and plug the vacuum hose(s) to the distributor if specified, start the engine, and observe the timing marks at the specified engine speed.	If the timing is not correct, adjust to specifications by rotating the distributor in the engine: (Advance timing by rotating distributor opposite normal direction of rotor rotation, retard timing by rotating distributor in same direction as rotor rotation.)	8.3
8.3—Check the operation of the distributor advance mechanism(s): To test the mechanical advance, disconnect all but the mechanical advance, and observe the timing marks with a timing light as the engine speed is increased from idle. If the mark moves smoothly, without hesitation, it may be assumed that the mechanical advance is functioning properly. To test vacuum advance and/or retard systems, alternately crimp and release the vacuum line, and observe the timing mark for movement. If movement is noted, the system is operating.	If the systems are functioning: If the systems are not functioning, remove the distributor, and test on a distributor tester:	8.4 8.4
8.4—Locate an ignition miss: With the engine running, remove each spark plug wire, one by one, until one is found that doesn't cause the engine to roughen and slow down.	When the missing cylinder is identified:	4.1

Test and Procedure	Results and Indications	Proceed to
9.1—Evaluate the valve train: Remove the valve cover, and ensure that the valves are adjusted to specifications. A mechanic's stethoscope may be used to aid in the diagnosis of the valve train. By pushing the probe on or near push rods or rockers, valve noise often can be isolated. A timing light also may be used to diagnose valve problems. Connect the light according to manufacturer's recommendations, and start the engine. Vary the firing moment of the light by increasing the engine speed (and therefore the ignition advance), and moving the trigger from cylinder to cylinder. Observe the movement of each valve.	See below	See below

Observation	Probable Cause	Remedy	Proceed to
Metallic tap heard through the stethoscope.	Sticking hydraulic lifter or excessive valve clearance.	Adjust valve. If tap persists, remove and replace the lifter:	10.1
Metallic tap through the stethoscope, able to push the rocker arm (lifter side) down by hand.	Collapsed valve lifter.	Remove and replace the lifter:	10.1
Erratic, irregular motion of the valve stem.*	Sticking valve, burned valve.	Recondition the valve and/or valve guide:	Next Chapter
Eccentric motion of the pushrod at the rocker arm.*	Bent pushrod.	Replace the pushrod:	10.1
Valve retainer bounces as the valve closes.*	Weak valve spring or damper.	Remove and test the spring and damper. Replace if necessary:	10.1

*—When observed with a timing light.

Test and Procedure	Results and Indications	Proceed to
9.2—Check the valve timing: Locate top dead center of the No. 1 piston, and install a degree wheel or tape on the crankshaft pulley or damper with zero corresponding to an index mark on the engine. Rotate the crankshaft in its direction of rotation, and observe the opening of the No. 1 cylinder intake valve. The opening should correspond with the correct mark on the degree wheel according to specifications.	If the timing is not correct, the timing cover must be removed for further investigation:	

Test and Procedure	Results and Indications	Proceed to
10.1—Determine whether the exhaust manifold heat control valve is operating: Operate the valve by hand to determine whether it is free to move. If the valve is free, run the engine to operating temperature and observe the action of the valve, to ensure that it is opening.	If the valve sticks, spray it with a suitable solvent, open and close the valve to free it, and retest. If the valve functions properly: If the valve does not free, or does not operate, replace the valve:	 10.2 10.2
10.2—Ensure that there are no exhaust restrictions: Visually inspect the exhaust system for kinks, dents, or crushing. Also note that gasses are flowing freely from the tailpipe at all engine speeds, indicating no restriction in the muffler or resonator.	Replace any damaged portion of the system:	11.1
11.1—Visually inspect the fan belt for glazing, cracks, and fraying, and replace if necessary. Tighten the belt so that the longest span has approximately ½″ play at its midpoint under thumb pressure. **Checking the fan belt tension** (© Nissan Motor Co. Ltd.)	Replace or tighten the fan belt as necessary:	11.2
11.2—Check the fluid level of the cooling system.	If full or slightly low, fill as necessary: If extremely low:	11.5 11.3
11.3—Visually inspect the external portions of the cooling system (radiator, radiator hoses, thermostat elbow, water pump seals, heater hoses, etc.) for leaks. If none are found, pressurize the cooling system to 14-15 psi.	If cooling system holds the pressure: If cooling system loses pressure rapidly, reinspect external parts of the system for leaks under pressure. If none are found, check dipstick for coolant in crankcase. If no coolant is present, but pressure loss continues: If coolant is evident in crankcase, remove cylinder head(s), and check gasket(s). If gaskets are intact, block and cylinder head(s) should be checked for cracks or holes. If the gasket(s) is blown, replace, and purge the crankcase of coolant: NOTE: *Occasionally, due to atmospheric and driving conditions, condensation of water can occur in the crankcase. This causes the oil to appear milky white. To remedy, run the engine until hot, and change the oil and oil filter.*	11.5 11.4 12.6

Test and Procedure	Results and Indication	Proceed to
11.4—Check for combustion leaks into the cooling system: Pressurize the cooling system as above. Start the engine, and observe the pressure gauge. If the needle fluctuates, remove each spark plug wire, one by one, noting which cylinder(s) reduce or eliminate the fluctuation. **Radiator pressure tester** (© American Motors Corp.)	Cylinders which reduce or eliminate the fluctuation, when the spark plug wire is removed, are leaking into the cooling system. Replace the head gasket on the affected cylinder bank(s).	
11.5—Check the radiator pressure cap: Attach a radiator pressure tester to the radiator cap (wet the seal prior to installation). Quickly pump up the pressure, noting the point at which the cap releases. **Testing the radiator pressure cap** (© American Motors Corp.)	If the cap releases within ± 1 psi of the specified rating, it is operating properly: If the cap releases at more than ± 1 psi of the specified rating, it should be replaced:	11.6 11.6
11.6—Test the thermostat: Start the engine cold, remove the radiator cap, and insert a thermometer into the radiator. Allow the engine to idle. After a short while, there will be a sudden, rapid increase in coolant temperature. The temperature at which this sharp rise stops is the thermostat opening temperature.	If the thermostat opens at or about the specified temperature: If the temperature doesn't increase: (If the temperature increases slowly and gradually, replace the thermostat.)	11.7 11.7
11.7—Check the water pump: Remove the thermostat elbow and the thermostat, disconnect the coil high tension lead (to prevent starting), and crank the engine momentarily.	If coolant flows, replace the thermostat and retest per 11.6: If coolant doesn't flow, reverse flush the cooling system to alleviate any blockage that might exist. If system is not blocked, and coolant will not flow, recondition the water pump.	11.6 —
12.1—Check the oil pressure gauge or warning light: If the gauge shows low pressure, or the light is on, for no obvious reason, remove the oil pressure sender. Install an accurate oil pressure gauge and run the engine momentarily.	If oil pressure builds normally, run engine for a few moments to determine that it is functioning normally, and replace the sender. If the pressure remains low: If the pressure surges: If the oil pressure is zero:	— 12.2 12.3 12.3

Test and Procedure	Results and Indications	Proceed to
12.2—Visually inspect the oil: If the oil is watery or very thin, milky, or foamy, replace the oil and oil filter.	If the oil is normal:	12.3
	If after replacing oil the pressure remains low:	12.3
	If after replacing oil the pressure becomes normal:	—
12.3—Inspect the oil pressure relief valve and spring, to ensure that it is not sticking or stuck. Remove and thoroughly clean the valve, spring, and the valve body.	If the oil pressure improves:	—
	If no improvement is noted:	12.4

Oil pressure relief valve
(© British Leyland Motors)

Test and Procedure	Results and Indications	Proceed to
12.4—Check to ensure that the oil pump is not cavitating (sucking air instead of oil): See that the crankcase is neither over nor underfull, and that the pickup in the sump is in the proper position and free from sludge.	Fill or drain the crankcase to the proper capacity, and clean the pickup screen in solvent if necessary. If no improvement is noted:	12.5
12.5—Inspect the oil pump drive and the oil pump:	If the pump drive or the oil pump appear to be defective, service as necessary and retest per 12.1:	12.1
	If the pump drive and pump appear to be operating normally, the engine should be disassembled to determine where blockage exists:	Next Chapter
12.6—Purge the engine of ethylene glycol coolant: Completely drain the crankcase and the oil filter. Obtain a commercial butyl cellosolve base solvent, designated for this purpose, and follow the instructions precisely. Following this, install a new oil filter and refill the crankcase with the proper weight oil. The next oil and filter change should follow shortly thereafter (1000 miles).		

Chapter 3

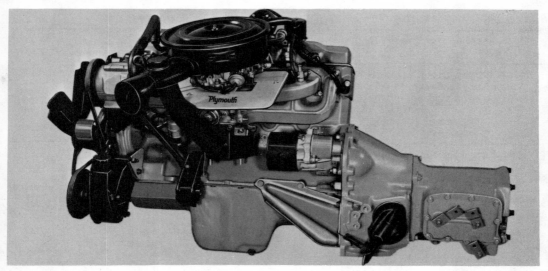

Engine and Engine Rebuilding

Engine Electrical

DISTRIBUTOR

Removal

1. Disconnect the vacuum advance line at the distributor.

2. Disconnect the primary wire at the coil. On electronic ignition, disconnect the lead wire at the harness connector.

3. Unfasten the distributor cap retaining clips and lift off the cap.

4. Mark the distributor body and the engine block to indicate the position of the body in the block. Scribe a mark on the edge of the distributor housing to indicate the position of the rotor on the distributor. These marks can be used as guides when installing the distributor.

5. Remove the distributor hold-down clamp screw and clamp.

6. Carefully lift the distributor out of the block. Note the slight rotation of the distributor shaft on a six as the distributor is removed. When installing the distributor the rotor must be in this position as the distributor is inserted into the block.

Installation
(Engine Has Not Been Rotated)

1. Install a new seal in the groove of the distributor shaft and carefully lower the distributor into the distributor bore.

2. With the rotor positioned slightly to the side of the mark on the distributor body, engage the distributor drive gear with the camshaft drive gear on a six. As the distributor slides into place the rotor will rotate slightly and align with the mark on the body. On a V8, engage the distributor shaft tongue with the oil pump drive gear slot.

3. Install the distributor hold-down clamp and bolt. Do not tighten.

4. Install the distributor cap and coil primary wire or lead wire.

5. Set the point gap where necessary and time the engine.

6. Tighten the distributor hold-down clamp and install the vacuum advance hose.

Installation
(Engine Has Been Rotated)

If the crankshaft has been rotated or otherwise disturbed (as during engine rebuilding) after the distributor was removed, proceed as follows to install the distributor.

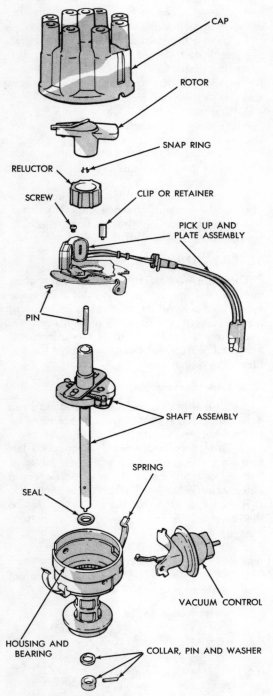

V8 distributor disassembled

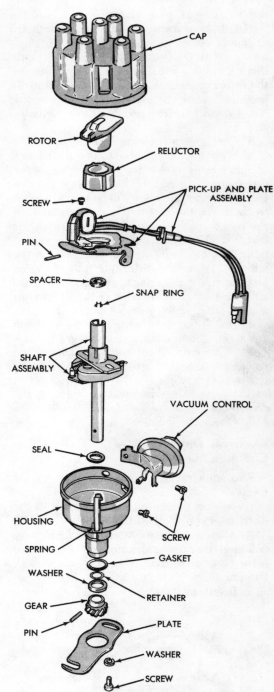

Six-cylinder distributor disassembled

1. Bring the No. 1 piston to TDC by removing the No. 1 spark plug and inserting a finger over the hole while rotating the crankshaft. The compression pressure can be felt as the No. 1 piston approaches TDC on the compression stroke. The TDC timing mark on the crankshaft vibration damper should now be opposite the indicator on the timing chain case.

2. *For six-cylinder engines:* Align the distributor so that the rotor will be in position *just ahead* of the distributor cap terminal for

the No. 1 spark plug when the distributor is installed. Now lower the distributor into its engine block opening, engaging the distributor gear with the camshaft drive gear. Be sure that the rubber O-ring seal is in the groove in the distributor shank. When the distributor is properly seated, the rotor should be under the No. 1 distributor cap terminal. Proceed with step 4.

3. *For eight-cylinder engines:* Clean the top of the engine block around the distributor opening to ensure a good seal between the distributor base and the block. Align the distributor so that the rotor will be in position *directly under* the distributor cap terminal for the No. 1 spark plug when the distributor is installed. The slot in the drive gear should point to the first intake manifold bolt on the left side. Lower the distributor into its engine block opening, engaging the tongue of the distributor shaft with the slot in the distributor and oil pump drive gear.

4. Install the distributor hold-down clamp and tighten its retaining screw finger tight.

5. Replace the distributor cap. Connect the primary wire to the coil or the lead wire to the harness.

6. Connect the vacuum advance line to the distributor.

7. Check the ignition timing.

Electronic Distributor Air Gap Adjustment

This adjustment is not required at regular intervals.

1. Release the spring clips and remove the distributor cap. Pull off the rotor.

2. Align one reluctor tooth with the pick-up coil tooth by turning the engine. The reluctor is the six or eight-toothed ring around the distributor shaft.

3. Insert an 0.008 in. *nonmagnetic* (brass)

feeler gauge between the reluctor tooth and the pick-up coil tooth.

4. Loosen the hold-down screw and adjust the gap using the screwdriver slot in the mounting plate. Contact should be made between the reluctor tooth, the feeler gauge, and the pick-up coil tooth.

5. Tighten the hold-down screw.

6. Remove the feeler gauge. No force should be required.

7. Check the gap with a 0.010 in. *nonmagnetic* feeler gauge. It should not fit; don't force it into the gap.

8. Turn the distributor shaft and apply vacuum to the vacuum advance unit. If it is adjusted properly and nothing is bent, the pick-up coil tooth will not hit the reluctor teeth.

ALTERNATOR

The alternator is basically an alternating current (AC) generator with solid state rectifiers which convert AC current to DC current (direct current) for charging the battery.

Be sure to read and follow the "Alternator Service Precautions" before servicing the vehicle charging system.

Alternator Service Precautions

Because alternator (AC) systems differ from generator (DC) systems, special care must be taken when servicing the charging system.

1. Battery polarity should be checked before any connections, such as jumper cables or battery charger leads, are made. Reversed battery connections will damage the rectifiers. It is recommended that the battery cables be disconnected before connecting a battery charger.

2. The battery must *never* be disconnected while the alternator is running.

3. Always disconnect the battery ground lead before replacing the alternator.

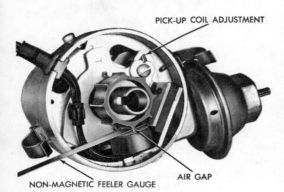

Air gap adjustment

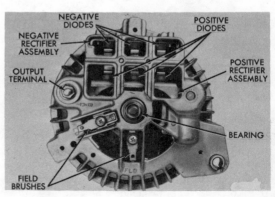

Alternator rear view

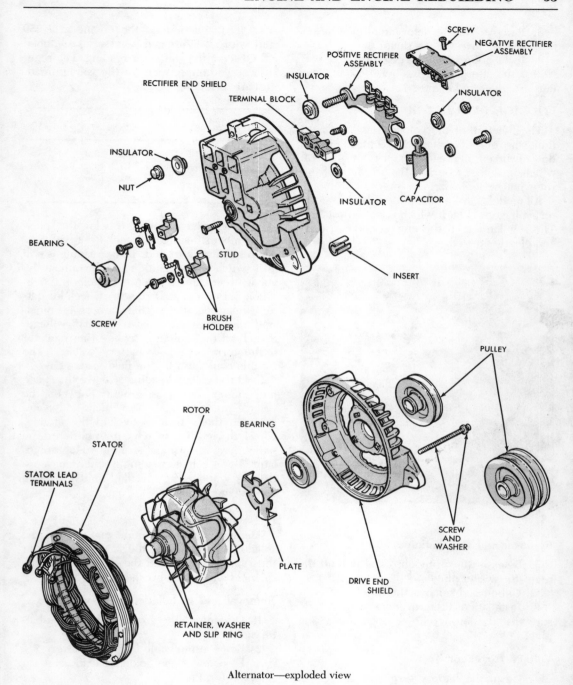

Alternator—exploded view

4. Do not attempt to polarize an alternator, or the regulator of an alternator equipped car.

5. Do not short across or ground any alternator terminals.

6. Always disconnect the battery ground lead before removing the alternator output cable, whether the engine is running or not.

7. If electric arc welding has to be done on the car, first disconnect the battery and alternator cables. Never start the car with the welding unit attached.

Removal and Installation

1. Disconnect both battery cables at the battery terminals.

2. Disconnect the alternator output (BAT) and field (FLD) leads, and disconnect the ground wire.

3. Remove the alternator mounting bracket bolts and remove the alternator.

4. Installation is the reverse of the above. Adjust the alternator drive belt tension. Details are given in Chapter 1.

VOLTAGE REGULATOR

The function of the voltage regulator is to limit the output voltage by controlling the flow of current in the alternator rotor field coil which, in effect, controls the strength of the rotor magnetic field.

All models have a solid-state (silicon transistor) voltage regulator which is not adjustable. The regulator is in the engine compartment and clearly labeled.

Voltage regulator (arrow)

Removal and Installation

1. Release the spring clips and pull off the regulator wiring plug.

2. Unbolt and remove the regulator.

3. Installation is the reverse of removal. Be sure that the spring clips engage the wiring plug.

Voltage Regulator Test

1. Clean the battery terminals and check the specific gravity of the battery electrolyte. If the specific gravity is below 1.200, charge the battery before performing the voltage regulator test as it must be above 1.200 to allow a prompt, regulated voltage check.

2. Connect the positive lead of the test voltmeter to the positive lead to the positive battery terminal.

3. Connect the voltmeter negative lead to a good body ground.

4. Start and operate the engine at 1,250 rpm with all lights and accessories switched off. Observe the voltmeter reading. The regulator is working properly if the voltage readings are as follows:

Ambient Temp Near Regulator	Voltage Range
Below 20° F	14.9–15.9
80° F	13.9–14.6
140° F	13.3–13.9
Above 140° F	Less than 13.6

5. If the voltage reading is below the specified limits or fluctuates, check for a bad voltage regulator or ground. If the reading is still low, switch off the ignition and disconnect the voltage regulator connector. Switch on the ignition but do not start the car. Check for battery voltage at the wiring harness terminal. Both leads should have battery voltage. Switch off the ignition. Replace the regulator if the terminals show battery voltage. The trouble could also be the field-loads relay.

6. If the voltage reading is above the specified limits, check the ground between the voltage regulator and the vehicle body, and between the vehicle body and the engine. Check the ignition switch circuit between the switch battery terminal and the voltage regulator. If the voltage reading is still high (more than ½ V above the specified limits), replace the voltage regulator.

STARTER

All models use a reduction gear starter. The solenoid is mounted on the starter. The starter must be removed from the car to service the solenoid and motor brushes.

Removal and Installation

1. Disconnect the ground cable at the battery.

2. Remove the cable from the starter.

3. Disconnect the solenoid leads at their solenoid terminals.

4. Remove the starter securing bolt and stud nut and remove the starter from the engine flywheel housing. On some models with automatic transmissions, the oil cooler tube bracket will interfere with starter removal. In this case, remove the starter securing bolt and stud nut, slide the cooler tube bracket off the stud, then remove the starter.

5. Installation is the reverse of the above. Be sure that the starter and flywheel housing

mating surfaces are free of dirt and oil. When tightening the bolt and nut, hold the starter away from the engine to ensure proper alignment.

Starter Overhaul

SOLENOID AND BRUSH SERVICE

1. Remove the starter from the car and support the starter gear housing in a vise with soft jaws.

2. Remove the two thru-bolts and the starter end assembly.

3. Carefully pull the armature up and out of the gear housing and the starter frame and field assembly.

4. Carefully pull the frame and field assembly up just enough to expose the terminal screw (which connects the series field coils to one pair of motor brushes) and support it with two blocks.

5. Support the terminal by placing a finger behind the terminal and remove the terminal screw.

6. Unwrap the shunt field coil lead from the other starter brush terminal. Unwrap the solenoid lead wire from the brush terminals.

7. Remove the steel and fiber thrust washer.

8. Remove the nut, steel washer, and insulating washer from the solenoid terminal.

9. Straighten the solenoid wire and re-

TERMINAL SCREW

Removing the starter terminal screw

Unwinding the solenoid lead wire

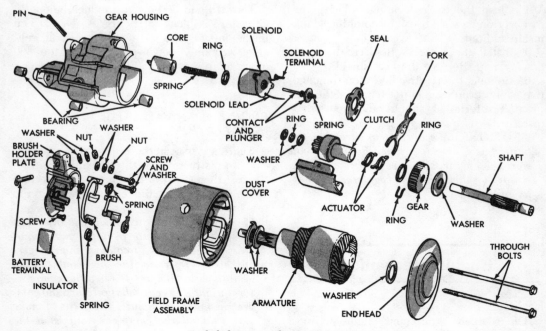

Exploded view—reduction gear starter

move the brush holder plate with the brushes and solenoid as an assembly.

10. Inspect the starter brushes. Brushes that are worn more than one-half the length of new brushes or are oil-soaked, should be replaced.

11. Assemble the starter using the reverse of the above procedure. When resoldering the shunt field and solenoid leads, make a strong, low-resistance connection using a high-temperature solder and resin flux.

CAUTION: *Do not break the shunt field wire units when removing and installing the brushes.*

BATTERY

Refer to Chapter 1 for details on the battery.

Removal and Installation

1. Disconnect the negative (ground) cable terminal and then the positive cable terminal. Special pullers are available to remove battery terminals. Remove the heat shield.

NOTE: *Always disconnect the battery ground cable first, and connect it last.*

2. Remove the hold-down clamp.

3. Remove the battery, being careful not to spill the acid.

NOTE: *Spilled acid can be neutralized with a baking soda/water solution. If you somehow get acid into your eyes, flush with lots of water and visit a doctor.*

4. Clean the cable terminals of any corrosion, using a wire brush or an old jackknife inside and out.

5. Install the battery. Replace the hold-down clamp. Replace the heat shield.

6. Connect the positive and then the negative cable terminal. Do not hammer them in place. The terminals should be coated lightly (externally) with grease to prevent corrosion.

CAUTION: *Make absolutely sure that the battery is connected properly before you start the engine. Reversed polarity can destroy your alternator and regulator in a matter of seconds.*

Engine Mechanical

DESIGN

The standard equipment engine in most models is the 225 cu in. slant-six. Although

Firing Order

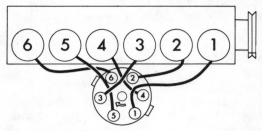

Six cylinder firing order

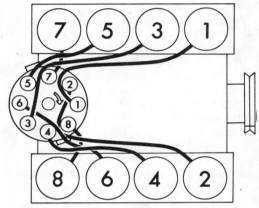

V8 firing order

this engine has a long stroke by modern standards, it presents a low profile because the block is canted 30° to the right.

The 318 and 360 cu in. engines belong to Chrysler's A block series of V8s. The 318 cu in. engine answers the need for a small, reliable, economy power-plant, while the 360 offers more power.

ENGINE REMOVAL AND INSTALLATION

There are two methods of engine removal. The first is to remove the transmission from the car, then take out the engine. The second is to remove only the engine, leaving the transmission in place.

CAUTION: *If the car has air conditioning, detach the compressor from the engine and set it aside. Do not disconnect any refrigerant lines—refer to the air conditioning "Caution" in Chapter 1. Keep the compressor upright. On reinstallation, turn the compressor pulley by hand a few turns to make sure that all the compressor oil is in the sump.*

General Engine Specifications

Year	Engine No. Cyl Displacement (Cu In.)	Carburetor Type	Horsepower @ rpm ■	Torque @ rpm (ft lbs) ■	Bore x Stroke (in.)	Compression Ratio	Oil Pressure @ 2000 rpm
'76–'78	6—225	1 bbl	100 @ 3600	170 @ 1600	3.406 x 4.125	8.4 : 1	55
	6—225 Calif	1 bbl	90 @ 3600	165 @ 1600	3.406 x 4.125	8.4 : 1	55
	6—225	2 bbl	110 @ 3600	180 @ 2000	3.406 x 4.125	8.4 : 1	55
	8—318	2 bbl	150 @ 4000	225 @ 1600	3.910 x 3.310	8.5 : 1	55
	8—318 Calif	2 bbl	140 @ 3600	250 @ 2000	3.910 x 3.310	8.5 : 1	55
	8—360	2 bbl	170 @ 4000	280 @ 2400	4.000 x 3.580	8.4 : 1	55
	8—360	4 bbl	175 @ 4000	270 @ 2400	4.000 x 3.580	8.0 : 1	55
	8—318	4 bbl	①	①	3.910 x 3.310	8.5 : 1	55

① Horsepower and torque figures not available at time of printing

Crankshaft and Connecting Rod Specifications
All measurements are given in inches

Year	Engine No. Cyl Displacement (Cu in.)	CRANKSHAFT				CONNECTING ROD		
		Main Brg Journal Dia	Main Brg Oil Clearance	Shaft End-Play	Thrust on No.	Journal Diameter	Oil Clearance	Side Clearance
'76–'78	6—225	2.7495–2.7505	.0005–.0015	.002–.007	3	2.1865–2.1875	.0005–.0015	.006–.012
	8—318	2.4495–2.5005	.0005–.0015	.002–.007	3	2.124–2.125	.0005–.0025	.006–.014
	8—360	2.8095–2.8105	.0005–.0020	.002–.007	3	2.124–2.125	.0005–.0020	.006–.014

Ring Gap
All measurements are given in inches

Year	Engine No. Cyl Displacement (Cu in.)	Top Compression	Bottom Compression	Oil Control
'76–'78	All	.010–.020	.010–.020	.015–.055

Ring Side Clearance
All measurements are given in inches

Year	Engine No. Cyl Displacement (Cu in.)	Top Compression	Bottom Compression	Oil Control
'76–'78	All engines	.0015–.0030	.0015–.0030	.0002–.0050

Valve Specifications

Year	Engine No. Cyl Displacement (Cu in.)	Seat Angle (deg)	Face Angle (deg)	Spring Test Pressure (lbs @ in.)	Spring Installed Height (in.)	STEM TO GUIDE Clearance (in.)		STEM Diameter (in.)	
						Intake	Exhaust	Intake	Exhaust
'76–'78	6—225	45	45	143 @ 1.31	1²¹⁄₃₂	.0010–.0030	.0020–.0040	.3725	.3715
	8—318	45	①	177 @ 1.31	1²¹⁄₃₂	.0010–.0030	.0020–.0040	.3725	.3715
	8—360	45	①	182 @ 1.31	1²¹⁄₃₂	.0010–.0030	.0020–.0040	.3725	.3715

① Intake 45°, Exhaust 43°

Torque Specifications
All readings in ft lbs

Year	Engine No. Cyl Displacement (Cu in.)	Cylinder Head Bolts	Rod Bearing Bolts	Main Bearing Bolts	Crankshaft Pulley Bolt	Flywheel to Crankshaft Bolts	MANIFOLD	
							Intake	Exhaust
'76–'78	6—225	70	45	85	Press fit	55	10①	10
	8—318	95	45	85	100	55	35	15/20②
	8—360	95	45	85	100	55	35	15/20②

① Intake to exhaust manifold bolts—20 ft lbs studs—30 ft lbs
② Nuts/screws

Removal of Transmission and Engine

1. Scribe the outline of the hood hinge brackets on the bottom of the hood and remove the hood.

2. Drain the cooling system. Remove the radiator.

3. Remove and plug the fuel lines from the pump. Remove the air cleaner.

4. Being sure to take note of their positions, remove all wires and hoses which attach to the engine (except air conditioning hoses). Remove all emission control equipment which may be damaged by the engine removal pro-

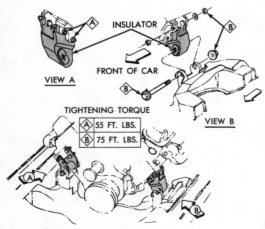

Front motor mounts

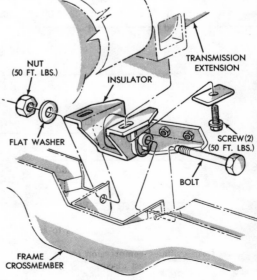

Rear engine mounts

cedure. Remove the emission canister, coolant reservoir, and any other interfering items.

5. If the vehicle is equipped with air conditioning and/or power steering, remove the unit from the engine and position it out of the way without disconnecting the lines.

6. On six-cylinder models, attach a lifting sling to the engine cylinder head. On V8 models remove the carburetor and attach the engine lifting fixture to the carburetor flange studs on the intake manifold.

7. Raise the vehicle support the rear of the engine with a jack.

8. On automatic transmission models, drain the transmission and torque converter. On standard transmission models, disconnect the clutch torque shaft from the engine.

9. Disconnect the exhaust pipe/s from the exhaust manifold/s.

10. Remove the driveshaft.

11. Disconnect the transmission linkage and any wiring or cables which attach to the transmission.

12. Remove the engine rear support crossmember and remove the transmission.

13. Remove the bolts which attach the motor mounts to the chassis.

14. Lower the vehicle and attach a chain hoist or other lifting device to the engine.

15. Raise the engine and carefully remove it from the vehicle.

16. Reverse above procedure to install.

Removal of Engine Alone

It is possible to remove the engine without removing the transmission. If this is to be done, care must be taken not to allow the weight of the engine to rest on the torque converter hub (automatic transmission) or transmission input shaft (standard transmission).

Perform Steps 1–7 and 10 of the "Removal of Transmission and Engine" operation. If the car has an automatic transmission, attach a remote starter switch to the engine, remove the inspection plate from the bellhousing, crank the engine to gain access to the torque converter-to-drive-plate attaching nuts and remove the nuts. Remove the starter. If the car has a manual transmission, disconnect the clutch torque shaft from the engine block and the clutch linkage from the adjustment rod. Remove the bolt which attaches the transmission filler tube to the engine (automatic transmission). Support the transmission and remove the bolts which attach the transmission to the engine or clutch bellhousing. When removing the engine, place a block of wood on

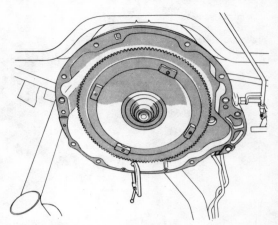

Holding torque converter with clamp

the lifting point of a floor jack and position the jack under the transmission. As the engine is removed from the vehicle, raise and lower the jack as required so that the angle of the transmission duplicates as nearly as possible the angle of the engine. Use a clamp so that the torque converter doesn't fall out of the transmission.

When installing the engine into a vehicle with an automatic transmission, keep in mind that the crankshaft flange bolt circle, the inner and outer circle of holes in the driveplate, and the four tapped holes in the front face of the converter all have one hole offset. To ensure proper engine-torque converter balance, the torque converter must be mounted to the driveplate in the same location in which it was originally installed.

When installing the engine into a vehicle with a manual transmission, it may be necessary to disconnect the driveshaft, and turn the transmission output shaft, with the transmission in gear, to get the transmission input shaft splines to mesh with the inner hub on the clutch disc.

CYLINDER HEAD

Removal and Installation

CAUTION: *Don't loosen the head bolts until the engine is thoroughly cool, to prevent warping.*

Six-Cylinder

1. Disconnect the battery.

2. The entire cooling system must be drained by opening the drain cock in the radiator and removing the drain plug on the right-side of the engine block.

3. Remove the vacuum line at the carbu-

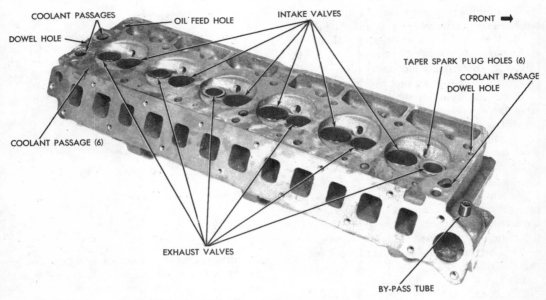

COOLANT PASSAGES — OIL FEED HOLE — INTAKE VALVES — FRONT ➡

DOWEL HOLE

TAPER SPARK PLUG HOLES (6)

COOLANT PASSAGE
DOWEL HOLE

COOLANT PASSAGE (6)

EXHAUST VALVES

BY-PASS TUBE

Cylinder head—slant six engine

retor and distributor. Remove the air cleaner and fuel line.

4. Disconnect the accelerator linkage.

5. Remove the spark plug wires at the plugs.

6. Disconnect the heater hoses.

7. Disconnect the temperature sending wire.

8. Disconnect the exhaust pipe at the exhaust manifold flange.

9. Disconnect the diverter valve vacuum line at the intake manifold and take the air tube assembly from the cylinder head.

10. Remove the PCV and evaporative control system connections.

11. Remove the intake/exhaust manifold and carburetor as an assembly. Remove the valve cover.

12. Remove the rocker arm and shaft assembly.

13. Remove the pushrods, being sure to mark them so they may be installed in their original location.

14. Remove the 14 head bolts and the cylinder head. If the head sticks, operate the starter to loosen it by compression or rap it upward with a soft hammer. Do not force anything between the head and block.

15. Clean the gasket surfaces of both the head and the block. Remove the carbon deposits from the top of each piston and from the combustion chambers.

16. Check the head for warpage as detailed in the "Engine Rebuilding" section.

Installation of the cylinder head is as follows:

17. Use a new head gasket and coat both of its sides with sealer.

18. Tighten the head bolts in three stages and the sequence illustrated to the proper torque specification.

The bolts should be retorqued after the first 500 miles or so, unless a special gasket is used.

19. The rest of installation is the reverse of removal. Refill the cooling system when completed.

V8s

1. Drain the cooling system and disconnect the battery ground cable.

2. Remove the alternator, air cleaner, and fuel line.

3. Disconnect the accelerator linkage.

4. Remove the vacuum advance line from between the carburetor and the distributor.

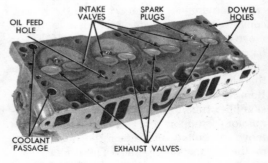

INTAKE VALVES — SPARK PLUGS — DOWEL HOLES

OIL FEED HOLE

COOLANT PASSAGE — EXHAUST VALVES

V8 cylinder head

Six cylinder head torque sequence

5. Remove the distributor cap and wires as an assembly.

6. Disconnect the coil wires, water temperature sending unit, heater hoses, and by-pass hose.

7. Remove the closed ventilation system, the evaporative control system (if so equipped), and the valve covers.

8. Remove the intake manifold, ignition coil, and carburetor as an assembly. Remove the tappet chamber cover.

9. Remove the exhaust manifolds.

10. Remove the rocker and shaft assemblies.

11. Remove the pushrods and keep them in order to ensure installation in their original location.

12. Remove the head bolts from each cylinder head and remove the cylinder heads. If the head sticks, operate the starter to loosen it by compression or rap it upward with a soft hammer. Do not force anything between the head and the block.

To install the cylinder heads, proceed as follows:

13. Clean all the gasket surfaces of the engine block and the cylinder heads. Remove the carbon deposits from the top of each piston and from the combustion chambers.

V8 head torque sequence

14. Check the head for warpage as detailed in the "Engine Rebuilding" section.

15. Coat new cylinder head gaskets with sealer, install the gaskets, and replace the cylinder heads.

16. Tighten the head bolts in the sequence shown in three stages until the specified torque is reached. The bolts should be retorqued after the first 500 miles or so unless special gaskets are used. The special gaskets don't require retorquing.

17. The rest of the installation procedure is the reverse of removal. The last step is to refill the cooling system.

Valve Guides

These engines do not have removable valve guides. 0.005, 0.015, and 0.030 in. oversize valves (stem diameter) are available. To use these, ream the worn guides to the smallest oversize which will clean up wear. Always start with the smallest reamer and proceed in steps to the largest, as this maintains the concentricity of the guide with the valve seat.

As an alternate procedure, some automotive machine shops bore out the stock guides and replace them with bronze or cast iron guides which are of stock internal dimensions.

Overhaul

See the "Engine Rebuilding" section at the end of this chapter for details on a valve job or cylinder head overhaul. This section should be consulted for checking head warpage, even if no other work is to be done on the head.

ROCKER SHAFTS

Removal and Installation

Six-Cylinder

1. Remove the closed ventilation system.
2. Remove the evaporative control system (if so equipped).
3. Remove the valve cover with its gasket.
4. Take out the rocker arm and shaft assembly securing bolts and remove the rocker arm and shaft.
5. Reverse the above for installation. The oil hole on the end of the shaft must be on the top and point toward the front of the engine to provide proper lubrication to the rocker arms. The special bolt goes to the rear. Torque the rocker arm bolts to 25 ft lbs and be sure to adjust the valves.

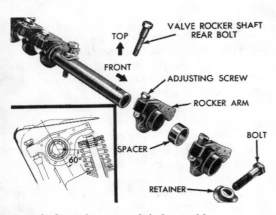

Six-cylinder rocker arm and shaft assembly

V8s

The stamped steel rocker arms are arranged on one rocker arm shaft per cylinder head. To remove the rocker arms and shaft:

1. Disconnect the spark plug wires.
2. Disconnect the closed ventilation and evaporative control system (if so equipped).

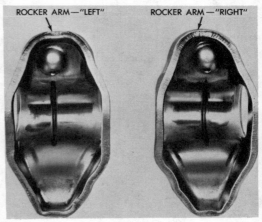

V8 rocker arm identification

3. Remove the valve covers with their gaskets.
4. Remove the rocker shaft bolts and retainers, and lift off the rocker arm assembly.
5. Reverse the above procedure to install. The notch on the end of both rocker shafts should point to the engine centerline and toward the front of the engine on the left cylinder head, or toward the rear on the right cylinder head. Torque the rocker shaft bolts to 17 ft lbs.

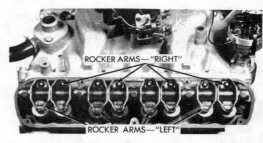

Rocker arm location on shaft—V8

INTAKE MANIFOLD

Removal and Installation

Six-Cylinder Combination Manifold

1. Remove the air cleaner and the fuel line from the carburetor.
2. Disconnect the accelerator linkage. De-

tach the vacuum lines, crankcase vent hose, carburetor vent line, carburetor air heater, and automatic choke rod.

3. Disconnect the exhaust pipe at the exhaust manifold flange. Remove the carburetor.

4. Remove the manifold assembly-to-cylinder head nuts and washers and remove the intake and exhaust manifolds as a single unit. The manifolds may be separated by removing the three bolts which hold them together.

5. Installation is the reverse of the removal procedure. When installing the manifold assembly, use new gaskets and a good commercial sealer. Loosen the three bolts which secure the intake manifold to the exhaust manifold to maintain proper alignment in relation to each other and the block. Torque these three bolts to 20 ft lbs in this sequence: inner bolts first, then the outer two bolts. Torque the manifold assembly to cylinder head nuts to 10 ft lbs.

V8s

1. Drain the cooling system and disconnect the battery.

2. Remove the air cleaner and fuel line from the carburetor. Disconnect any interfering air pump system components.

3. Disconnect the accelerator linkage.

4. Remove the vacuum control line between the carburetor and distributor.

5. Remove the distributor cap and wires.

6. Disconnect the coil wires, temperature sending unit wires, and heater and by-pass hoses.

7. Remove the intake manifold securing bolts and remove the manifold and carburetor as an assembly.

8. To install the manifold, reverse the removal procedure. Be sure to torque the mani-

V8 intake manifold—torque sequence

fold in three steps and remember to use a good commercial sealer on new manifold gaskets.

EXHAUST MANIFOLD
Removal and Installation
SIX-CYLINDER

The intake and exhaust manifolds are combined in one unit on this engine. Refer to the intake manifold removal procedure.

V8

1. Disconnect the exhaust manifold at the flange where it mates to the exhaust pipe.

2. If the vehicle is equipped with air injection and/or a carburetor-heated air stove, remove them.

V8 exhaust manifold

3. Remove the exhaust manifold by removing the securing bolts and washers. To reach these bolts, it may be necessary to jack the engine slightly off its front mounts. When the exhaust manifold is removed, sometimes the securing studs will screw out with the nuts. If this occurs, the studs must be replaced with the aid of sealing compound on the coarse thread ends. If this is not done, water leaks may develop at the studs. To install the exhaust manifold, reverse the removal procedure. No conical washers are used on the center branch.

TIMING COVER AND CHAIN

NOTE: *Check the slack in the chain after installation.*

Removal and Intallation
SIX-CYLINDER

1. Drain the cooling system and disconnect the battery.

2. Remove the radiator and fan.

3. With a puller, remove the vibration damper.

4. Loosen the oil pan bolts to allow clear-

Removing the vibration damper

Removing V8 vibration damper

ance, and remove the timing case cover and gasket.

5. Slide the crankshaft oil slinger off the front of the crankshaft.

6. Remove the camshaft sprocket bolt.

7. Remove the timing chain with the camshaft sprocket.

8. On installation: Turn the crankshaft to line up the timing mark on the crankshaft sprocket with the centerline of the camshaft (without the chain).

Timing mark alignment—6 cylinder

9. Install the camshaft sprocket and chain. Align the timing marks.

10. Torque the camshaft sprocket bolt to 35 ft lbs.

11. Replace the oil slinger.

12. Reinstall the timing case cover with a new gasket and torque the bolts to 17 ft lbs. Retighten the engine oil pan to 17 ft lbs.

13. Press the vibration damper back on.

14. Replace the radiator and hoses.

15. Refill the cooling system.

V8

1. Disconnect the battery and drain the cooling system.

2. Remove the vibration damper pulley. Unbolt and remove the vibration damper with a puller. Remove the fuel lines and fuel pump, then loosen the oil pan bolts and remove the front bolt on each side.

3. Remove the timing gear cover and the crankshaft oil slinger.

4. Remove the camshaft sprocket lockbolt, securing cup washer, and fuel pump eccentric. Remove the timing chain with both sprockets.

5. To begin the installation procedure, place the camshaft and crankshaft sprockets on a flat surface with the timing indicators on an imaginary centerline through both sprocket bores. Place the timing chain around both sprockets. Be sure that the timing marks are in alignment.

CAUTION: *When installing the timing chain, have an assistant support the camshaft with a screwdriver to prevent it from contacting the freeze plug in the rear of the engine block. Remove the distributor and the oil pump/distributor drive gear. Position the screwdriver against the rear side of the cam gear and be careful not to damage the cam lobes.*

6. Turn the crankshaft and camshaft to align them with the keyway location in the crankshaft sprocket and the keyway or dowel hole in the camshaft sprocket.

V8 timing mark alignment

7. Lift the sprockets and timing chain while keeping the sprockets tight against the chain in the correct position. Slide both sprockets evenly onto their respective shafts.

8. Use a straightedge to measure the alignment of the sprocket timing marks. They must be perfectly aligned.

9. Install the fuel pump eccentric, cup washer, and camshaft sprocket lockbolt, and torque to 35 ft lbs. If camshaft end play exceeds 0.010 in., install a new thrust plate. It should be 0.002–0.006 in. with the new plate.

Checking Timing Chain Slack

1. Position a scale next to the timing chain to detect any movement in the chain.

Checking timing chain slack—six cylinder

2. Place a torque wrench and socket on the camshaft sprocket attaching bolt. Apply either 30 ft lbs (if the cylinder heads are installed on the engine) or 15 ft lbs (cylinder heads removed) of force to the bolt and rotate the bolt in the direction of crankshaft rotation in order to remove all slack from the chain.

3. While applying torque to the camshaft sprocket bolt, the crankshaft should not be allowed to rotate. It may be necessary to block the crankshaft to prevent rotation.

4. Position the scale over the edge of a timing chain link and apply an equal amount of torque in the opposite direction. If the move-

Checking timing chain slack—V8

ment of the chain exceeds ⅛ in., replace the chain.

**Timing Gear Cover
Seal Replacement**

NOTE: *A seal remover and installer tool is required to prevent seal damage.*

Inspecting seal for proper seating

1. Using a seal puller, separate the seal from the retainer.

2. Pull the seal from the case.

3. To install the seal place it face down in the case with the seal lips downward.

4. Seat the seal tightly against the cover face. There should be a maximum clearance of .0014 in. between the seal and the cover. Be careful not to overcompress the seal.

CAMSHAFT

Removal and Installation

SIX-CYLINDER

1. Remove the cylinder head, timing gear cover, camshaft sprocket, and timing chain.

2. Remove the valve tappets, keeping them in order to ensure intallation in their original locations.

3. Remove the crankshaft sprocket.

4. Remove the distributor and oil pump.

5. Remove the fuel pump.

6. Install a long bolt into the front of the camshaft to facilitate its removal.

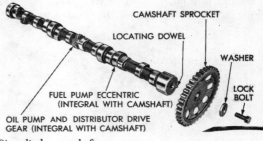

Six-cylinder camshaft

Camshaft removal

7. Remove the camshaft, being careful not to damage the cam bearings with the cam lobes.

8. Lubricate the camshaft lobes and bearing journals. It is recommended that 1 pt of Chrysler Crankcase Conditioner be added to the initial crankcase oil fill.

9. Install the camshaft in the engine block. From this point, reverse the removal procedure.

V8

1. Remove the cylinder heads. Remove the timing gear cover, the camshaft and crankshaft sprocket, and the timing chain.

2. Remove the valve tappets, keeping them in order to ensure installation in their original location.

3. Remove the distributor and lift out the oil pump and distributor driveshaft.

4. Remove the camshaft thrust plate.

5. Install a long bolt into the front of the camshaft and remove the camshaft, being careful not to damage the cam bearings with the cam lobes.

6. Lubricate the camshaft lobes and bearing journals. It is recommended that 1 pt. of Chrysler Crankcase Conditioner be added to the initial crankcase oil fill. Insert the camshaft into the engine block within 2 in. of its final position in the block.

7. Have an assistant support the camshaft with a screwdriver to prevent the camshaft from contacting the freeze plug in the rear of the engine block. Remove the distributor and the oil pump/distributor drive gear. Position the screwdriver against the rear side of the

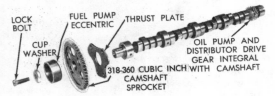

V8 camshaft

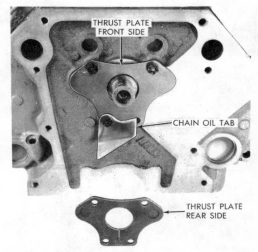

V8 timing chain oil tab installation

Positioning the distributor drive gear

cam gear and be careful not to damage the cam lobes.

8. Replace the camshaft thrust plate. If camshaft end play exceeds 0.010 in., install a new thrust plate. It should be 0.002–0.006 in. with the new plate.

9. Install the oil pump and distributor driveshaft. Install the distributor.

10. Inspect the crown of all the tappet faces with a straightedge. Replace any tappets which have dished or worn surfaces. Install the tappets.

11. Install the timing gear, gear cover, and the cylinder heads.

PISTON AND CONNECTING RODS

The following are specific instructions for all Aspen/Volare engines. For more detailed instructions, see the "Engine Rebuilding" section at the end of this chapter.

The notch on the top of each piston must face the front of the engine.

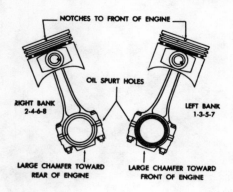

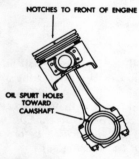

Piston and connecting rod positioning

To position the connecting rod correctly, the oil squirt hole should point to the right-side on all six-cylinder engines. On all V8 engines, the larger chamfer of the lower connecting rod bore must face toward the crankpin journal fillet.

Engine Lubrication

OIL PAN

Removal and Installation

SIX-CYLINDER

1. Drain the radiator, disconnect the radiator hoses, disconnect the battery, and remove the oil dipstick. Remove the fan shroud attaching screws, and loop the shroud rearward over the engine. Jack up the vehicle and drain the oil.

2. Remove the steering arm center link. Disconnect the idler arm ball joints.

3. Disconnect the exhaust pipe from the manifold and secure it out of the way.

4. Support the block with a jack and wooden block. Remove the front engine mounts and raise the engine 1½ to 2 inches. Take out the oil pan attaching bolts. Rotate

the engine crankshaft in order to clear the counterweights. Remove the oil pan.

5. To install the pan, reverse the removal procedure. Torque the pan bolts to 200 in. lbs. Use a new gasket.

V8

1. Disconnect the battery and remove the dipstick.

2. Jack up the vehicle and drain the oil. remove the torque converter-to-engine left housing strut.

3. Remove the idler arms and steering linkage ball joints from the center link.

4. Disconnect the exhaust pipe(s) from the manifold and move it out of the way.

5. Place a jack under the transmission and remove transmission-to-rear engine mount bolts. Raise the transmission to clear the oil-pan. Remove the oil pan bolts and the oil pan.

6. To install the pan, be sure that the oil strainer will touch the bottom of the pan.

7. Using a new gasket, install the oil pan. Torque the bolts to 200 in. lbs. On 360 engines, be certain that the notches on the side gaskets overlap the rear seal.

8. Install the engine-to-converter housing strut.

9. From this point, reverse the removal procedure.

REAR MAIN BEARING OIL SEAL

Replacement oil seals are the split rubber type. Both halves of the seal must be replaced at the same time.

Oil pan gasket installation

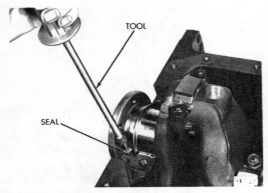

Removing upper seal—six cylinder

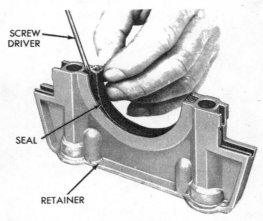

Removing lower seal—six cylinder

1. Remove the oil pan. On V8 engines, remove the oil pump.

2. Remove the rear main bearing cap and seal retainer.

3. Remove the lower half rope seal from the bearing cap. Remove the upper half by driving on either exposed end with a short piece of $3/16$ in. brazing wire. As the end of the seal becomes exposed, grasp it with a pair of pliers and pull it gently from the block.

4. Loosen the crankshaft main bearing caps just enough to allow the crankshaft to drop $1/16$ in. Do not allow the crankshaft to drop enough to permit the main bearings to become displaced.

5. Wipe the crankshaft clean and lightly oil the crankshaft and new seal before installation.

6. Hold the seal tightly against the crankshaft (with the paint stripe to the rear) and install the upper seal half into its groove. If necessary, rotate the crankshaft as the seal is pushed in place.

7. Install the lower seal half into the rear main bearing cap, with the paint stripe to the rear.

8. Install the rear main bearing cap. CAUTION: *Make sure that all main bearings are properly located before tightening the rest of the bearing caps.*

9. Tighten the rest of the bearing caps.

10. Install the oil pump, if removed, and oil pan.

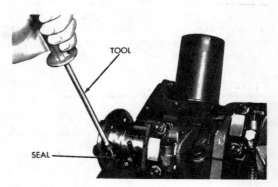

Removing upper seal—V8

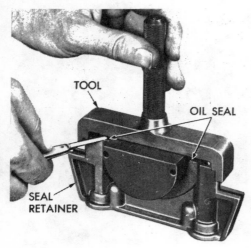

Trimming oil seal

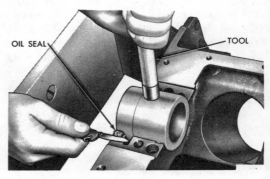

Trimming V8 rear main seal

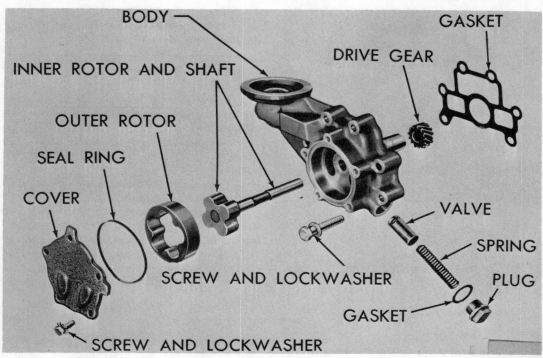

Six cylinder oil pump—exploded view

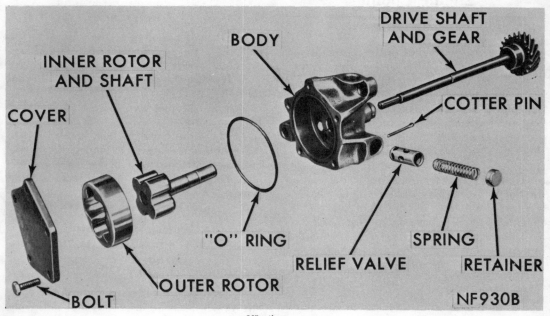

V8 oil pump

OIL PUMP

Removal and Installation

SIX-CYLINDER

1. Drain the radiator, disconnect its upper and lower hoses, and remove the fan shroud.

2. Raise the vehicle and remove the front engine mounting bolts. Jack the engine up 2 in. under the right front corner of the oil pan.

3. Remove the oil filter, oil pump attaching bolts, and pump assembly.

4. Installation is the reverse of the removal

STRAIGHT
EDGE

FEELER GAUGE

Measuring rotor clearance

procedures. Always use a new O-ring and gaskets. Torque the bolts to 200 in. lbs.

V8s

1. Remove the oil pan.
2. Remove the oil pump from the rear main bearing cap.
3. Reverse the above steps to install. Torque the bolts to 30 ft lbs.

Engine Cooling

Refer to Chapter 1 for the coolant level checking procedure and to the Appendix for "Antifreeze" charts. The coolant should periodically be drained and the system flushed with clean water, at the intervals specified in Chapter 1. Service stations have reverse flushing equipment available; there are also permanently-installed do-it-yourself reverse flushing attachments available at a reasonable price.

There is a coolant drain cock at the bottom of the radiator. Six-cylinder engines have a coolant drain plug on the right side of the engine block; V8s have one on each side.

The coolant should always be maintained at a minimum of −20° F freezing protection, regardless of the prevailing temperature. This concentration assures rust protection and the highest possible boiling point. It also prevents the heater core from freezing on air-conditioned cars.

Certain simple modifications can be made to the cooling system for improved performance under severe conditions. The fan can be replaced with either a high-output unit or a clutch type designed for air conditioned cars or a flextype. The flex unit flattens out at high rpm, moving less air and reducing the horsepower required to drive it.

RADIATOR

Removal and Installation

1. Drain the cooling system. Detach and plug the oil cooling lines for the automatic transmission.
2. Disconnect the hose clamps and remove the upper and lower radiator hoses from the radiator.
3. Remove the fan shroud. Slide the shroud rearward over the fan and rest it on the engine.
4. Remove the radiator attaching bolts and lift the radiator out of the car.
5. Reverse the above steps to install. On automatic transmission cars, check the fluid level. Fill the cooling system with the proper mixture of anti-freeze and water. Run the engine with the heater on and the radiator cap off for about 10 minutes, checking the level frequently.

WATER PUMP

Removal and Installation

SIX-CYLINDER WITHOUT AIR CONDITIONING AND/OR AIR PUMP

1. Drain the cooling system. Remove the battery. If the engine has a fan shroud, remove and swing it back over the engine.
2. Remove the power steering and alternator belts.
3. Take off the fan, spacer, pulley, and bolts as a unit.
4. Move the lower by-pass hose clamp to the center of the hose. Disconnect the heater hose and the lower hose of the water pump.
5. Remove the water pump bolts and the pump.
6. Reverse the procedure for installation.

SIX-CYLINDER WITH AIR CONDITIONING AND/OR AIR PUMP

1. Remove the battery and drain the cooling system. Remove the fan shroud and swing it back over the engine.
2. Disconnect the transmission oil cooler lines (if automatic transmission) and remove the lower radiator hoses. Cap the openings to prevent the entry of dirt and excessive fluid loss.
3. Remove the radiator.
4. Loosen the alternator, power steering pump, idler pulley, and air pump.

5. Take off the fan, spacer, pulley, and bolts as an assembly. Remove all the belts.

6. Remove the compressor and/or air pump bracket and secure it out of way.

7. Move the lower by-pass hose clamp to the center of the hose. Disconnect the heater hose.

8. Remove the water pump bolts and the pump.

9. Reverse the procedure for installation.

V8

1. Drain the cooling system and move the fan shroud out of the way.

2. Disconnect the transmission oil cooler lines (automatic) and all radiator hoses. Cap the openings to prevent the entry of dirt or excessive fluid loss.

3. Remove the radiator, if necessary.

4. Loosen the alternator adjusting strap bolts. Remove the belts.

5. On engines with no air conditioning, remove the alternator bracket bolts from the water pump. Swing the alternator out of the way and tighten the pivot bolt. On engines with air conditioning, remove the idler pulley assembly and alternator with the adjusting bracket.

6. Remove the fan, spacer/fluid drive, pulley, and bolts as an assembly.

CAUTION: *Do not let fluid drain into the fan-drive bearing.*

7. Disconnect the heater and all by-pass hoses.

8. Remove the compressor-to-front mounting bracket bolts.

9. Remove the water pump attaching bolts and the water pump.

10. Carefully lift the compressor out of the way.

On installation:

11. Install the by-pass hose and position the clamp in the center of the hose.

12. Install the pump with a new gasket and torque it to 30 ft lbs. Be sure that the pump turns freely.

13. Install the heater hose and route it near the by-pass hose clamps.

14. On V8s with air conditioning, install the front bracket on the compressor. Torque the bracket bolts to 50 ft lbs. Torque the pump bolts to 30 ft lbs.

15. Replace the alternator, bracket, and idler pulley assembly. Torque to 30 ft lbs.

16. Install the compressor clutch assembly (if applicable).

17. Install the fan assembly. Check and adjust all belts.

18. Install the radiator, hoses, and transmission cooling lines.

19. Install the fan shroud and fill the cooling system. Check the fluid level in the transmission.

THERMOSTAT

The thermostat is located in the engine water outlet housing at the front of the engine, connected to the upper radiator hose. Poor heater output is often caused by a thermostat stuck in the open position; occasionally a thermostat sticks shut causing overheating.

V8 thermostat housing

CAUTION: *Do not attempt to correct an overheating condition by permanently removing the thermostat. This will result in the coolant flowing through the radiator too fast to be cooled properly or in coolant loss. Thermostat flow restriction is designed into the system.*

Removal and Installation

1. Partially drain the cooling system to a level slightly below the thermostat. The thermostat is at the engine end of the upper radiator hose.

2. Remove the upper radiator hose from the thermostat housing.

3. Remove the thermostat housing bolts. Remove the housing.

4. Remove the thermostat from the block.

5. To install, reverse the above steps. Use a new gasket and gasket sealer. Always place the thermostat with the temperature sensing end facing into the block. On the six, the vent hole must be up.

Engine Rebuilding

This section describes, in detail, the procedures involved in rebuilding a typical engine. The procedures specifically refer to an inline engine, however, they are basically identical to those used in rebuilding engines of nearly all design and configurations. Procedures for servicing atypical engines (i.e., horizontally opposed) are described in the appropriate section, although in most cases, cylinder head reconditioning procedures described in this chapter will apply.

The section is divided into two sections. The first, Cylinder Head Reconditioning, assumes that the cylinder head is removed from the engine, all manifolds are removed, and the cylinder head is on a workbench. The camshaft should be removed from overhead cam cylinder heads. The second section, Cylinder Block Reconditioning, covers the block, pistons, connecting rods and crankshaft. It is assumed that the engine is mounted on a work stand, and the cylinder head and all accessories are removed.

Procedures are identified as follows:

Unmarked—Basic procedures that must be performed in order to successfully complete the rebuilding process.

Starred (*)—Procedures that should be performed to ensure maximum performance and engine life.

Double starred (**)—Procedures that may be performed to increase engine performance and reliability. These procedures are usually reserved for extremely heavy-duty or competition usage.

In many cases, a choice of methods is also provided. Methods are identified in the same manner as procedures. The choice of method for a procedure is at the discretion of the user.

The tools required for the basic rebuilding procedure should, with minor exceptions, be those

TORQUE (ft. lbs.) *

U.S.

Bolt Diameter (inches)	Bolt Grade (SAE)				Wrench Size (inches)	
	1 and 2	5	6	8	Bolt	Nut
1/4	5	7	10	10.5	3/8	7/16
5/16	9	14	19	22	1/2	9/16
3/8	15	25	34	37	9/16	5/8
7/16	24	40	55	60	5/8	3/4
1/2	37	60	85	92	3/4	13/16
9/16	53	88	120	132	7/8	7/8
5/8	74	120	167	180	15/16	1
3/4	120	200	280	296	1-1/8	1-1/8
7/8	190	302	440	473	1-5/16	1-5/16
1	282	466	660	714	1-1/2	1-1/2

Metric

Bolt Diameter (mm)	Bolt Grade				Wrench Size (mm) Bolt and Nut
	5D	8G	10K	12K	
6	5	6	8	10	10
8	10	16	22	27	14
10	19	31	40	49	17
12	34	54	70	86	19
14	55	89	117	137	22
16	83	132	175	208	24
18	111	182	236	283	27
22	182	284	394	464	32
24	261	419	570	689	36

*—Torque values are for lightly oiled bolts. CAUTION: Bolts threaded into aluminum require much less torque.

General Torque Specifications

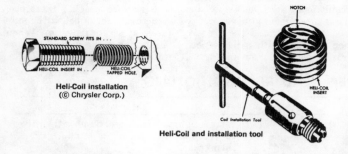

Heli-Coil installation
(© Chrysler Corp.)

Heli-Coil and installation tool

Heli-Coil Insert			Drill	Tap	Insert. Tool	Extracting Tool
Thread Size	Part No.	Insert Length (In.)	Size	Part No.	Part No.	Part No.
1/2 -20	1185-4	3/8	17/64(.266)	4 CPB	528-4N	1227-6
5/16-18	1185-5	15/32	Q(.332)	5 CPB	528-5N	1227-6
3/8 -16	1185-6	9/16	X(.397)	6 CPB	528-6N	1227-6
7/16-14	1185-7	21/32	29/64(.453)	7 CPB	528-7N	1227-16
1/2 -13	1185-8	3/4	33/64(.516)	8 CPB	528-8N	1227-16

Heli-Coil Specifications

included in a mechanic's tool kit. An accurate torque wrench, and a dial indicator (reading in thousandths) mounted on a universal base should be available. Bolts and nuts with no torque specification should be tightened according to size (see chart). Special tools, where required, all are readily available from the major tool suppliers (i.e., Craftsman, Snap-On, K-D). The services of a competent automotive machine shop must also be readily available.

When assembling the engine, any parts that will be in frictional contact must be pre-lubricated, to provide protection on initial start-up. Vortex Pre-Lube, STP, or any product specifically formulated for this purpose may be used. NOTE: *Do not use engine oil.* Where semi-permanent (locked but removable) installation of bolts or nuts is desired, threads should be cleaned and coated with Loctite. Studs may be permanently installed using Loctite Stud and Bearing Mount.

Aluminum has become increasingly popular for use in engines, due to its low weight and excellent heat transfer characteristics. The following precautions

must be observed when handling aluminum engine parts:
—Never hot-tank aluminum parts.
—Remove all aluminum parts (identification tags, etc.) from engine parts before hot-tanking (otherwise they will be removed during the process).
—Always coat threads lightly with engine oil or anti-seize compounds before installation, to prevent seizure.
—Never over-torque bolts or spark plugs in aluminum threads. Should stripping occur, threads can be restored according to the following procedure, using Heli-Coil thread inserts:

Tap drill the hole with the stripped threads to the specified size (see chart). Using the specified tap (NOTE: *Heli-Coil tap sizes refer to the size thread being replaced, rather than the actual tap size*), tap the hole for the Heli-Coil. Place the insert on the proper installation tool (see chart). Apply pressure on the insert while winding it clockwise into the hole, until the top of the insert is one turn below the surface. Remove the installation tool, and break the installation tang from the bottom of the in-

sert by moving it up and down. If the Heli-Coil must be removed, tap the removal tool firmly into the hole, so that it engages the top thread, and turn the tool counter-clockwise to extract the insert.

Snapped bolts or studs may be removed, using a stud extractor (unthreaded) or Vise-Grip pliers (threaded). Penetrating oil (e.g., Liquid Wrench) will often aid in breaking frozen threads. In cases where the stud or bolt is flush with, or below the surface, proceed as follows:

Drill a hole in the broken stud or bolt, approximately 1/2 its diameter. Select a screw extractor (e.g., Easy-Out) of the proper size, and tap it into the stud or bolt. Turn the extractor counter-clockwise to remove the stud or bolt.

Magnaflux and Zyglo are inspection techniques used to locate material flaws, such as stress cracks. Magnafluxing coats the part with fine magnetic particles, and subjects the part to a magnetic field. Cracks cause breaks

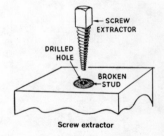

Screw extractor

in the magnetic field, which are outlined by the particles. Since Magnaflux is a magnetic process, it is applicable only to ferrous materials. The Zyglo process coats the material with a fluorescent dye penetrant, and then subjects it to blacklight inspection, under which cracks glow bright-

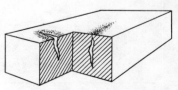

Magnaflux indication of cracks

ly. Parts made of any material may be tested using Zyglo. While Magnaflux and Zyglo are excellent for general inspection, and locating hidden defects, specific checks of suspected cracks may be made at lower cost and more readily using spot check dye. The dye is sprayed onto the suspected area, wiped off, and the area is then sprayed with a developer. Cracks then will show up bright-ly. Spot check dyes will only indicate surface cracks; therefore, structural cracks below the surface may escape detection. When questionable, the part should be tested using Magnaflux or Zyglo.

CYLINDER HEAD RECONDITIONING

Procedure	Method
Identify the valves:  **Valve identification**	Invert the cylinder head, and number the valve faces front to rear, using a permanent felt-tip marker.
Remove the rocker arms:	Remove the rocker arms with shaft(s) or balls and nuts. Wire the sets of rockers, balls and nuts together, and identify according to the corresponding valve.
Remove the valves and springs:	Using an appropriate valve spring compressor (depending on the configuration of the cylinder head), compress the valve springs. Lift out the keepers with needlenose pliers, release the compressor, and remove the valve, spring, and spring retainer.
Check the valve stem-to-guide clearance:  **Checking the valve stem-to-guide clearance**	Clean the valve stem with lacquer thinner or a similar solvent to remove all gum and varnish. Clean the valve guides using solvent and an expanding wire-type valve guide cleaner. Mount a dial indicator so that the stem is at 90° to the valve stem, as close to the valve guide as possible. Move the valve off its seat, and measure the valve guide-to-stem clearance by moving the stem back and forth to actuate the dial indicator. Measure the valve stems using a micrometer, and compare to specifications, to determine whether stem or guide wear is responsible for excessive clearance.
De-carbon the cylinder head and valves: 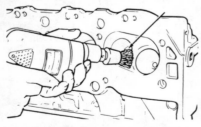 **Removing carbon from the cylinder head**	Chip carbon away from the valve heads, combustion chambers, and ports, using a chisel made of hardwood. Remove the remaining deposits with a stiff wire brush. NOTE: *Ensure that the deposits are actually removed, rather than burnished.*

Procedure	Method
Hot-tank the cylinder head:	Have the cylinder head hot-tanked to remove grease, corrosion, and scale from the water passages. NOTE: *In the case of overhead cam cylinder heads, consult the operator to determine whether the camshaft bearings will be damaged by the caustic solution.*
Degrease the remaining cylinder head parts:	Using solvent (i.e., Gunk), clean the rockers, rocker shaft(s) (where applicable), rocker balls and nuts, springs, spring retainers, and keepers. Do not remove the protective coating from the springs.
Check the cylinder head for warpage: **Checking the cylinder head for warpage** 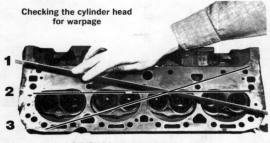 1 & 3 CHECK DIAGONALLY 2 CHECK ACROSS CENTER	Place a straight-edge across the gasket surface of the cylinder head. Using feeler gauges, determine the clearance at the center of the straight-edge. Measure across both diagonals, along the longitudinal centerline, and across the cylinder head at several points. If warpage exceeds .003″ in a 6″ span, or .006″ over the total length, the cylinder head must be resurfaced. NOTE: *If warpage exceeds the manufacturers maximum tolerance for material removal, the cylinder head must be replaced.* When milling the cylinder heads of V-type engines, the intake manifold mounting position is altered, and must be corrected by milling the manifold flange a proportionate amount.
** Porting and gasket matching: 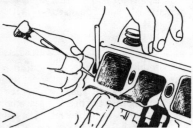 **Marking the cylinder head for gasket matching** 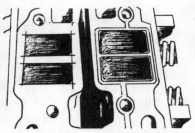 **Port configuration before and after gasket matching**	** Coat the manifold flanges of the cylinder head with Prussian blue dye. Glue intake and exhaust gaskets to the cylinder head in their installed position using rubber cement and scribe the outline of the ports on the manifold flanges. Remove the gaskets. Using a small cutter in a hand-held power tool (i.e., Dremel Moto-Tool), gradually taper the walls of the port out to the scribed outline of the gasket. Further enlargement of the ports should include the removal of sharp edges and radiusing of sharp corners. Do not alter the valve guides. NOTE: *The most efficient port configuration is determined only by extensive testing. Therefore, it is best to consult someone experienced with the head in question to determine the optimum alterations.*

Procedure	Method
** Polish the ports: 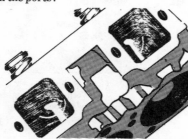 **Relieved and polished ports**	** Using a grinding stone with the above mentioned tool, polish the walls of the intake and exhaust ports, and combustion chamber. Use progressively finer stones until all surface imperfections are removed. NOTE: *Through testing, it has been determined that a smooth surface is more effective than a mirror polished surface in intake ports, and vice-versa in exhaust ports.*
* Knurling the valve guides: 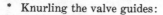 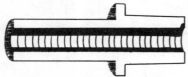 **Cut-away view of a knurled valve guide**	* Valve guides which are not excessively worn or distorted may, in some cases, be knurled rather than replaced. Knurling is a process in which metal is displaced and raised, thereby reducing clearance. Knurling also provides excellent oil control. The possibility of knurling rather than replacing valve guides should be discussed with a machinist.
Replacing the valve guides: NOTE: *Valve guides should only be replaced if damaged or if an oversize valve stem is not available.* 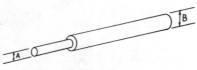 A-VALVE GUIDE I.D. B-SLIGHTLY SMALLER THAN VALVE GUIDE O.D. **Valve guide removal tool**  WASHERS A-VALVE GUIDE I.D. B-LARGER THAN THE VALVE GUIDE O.D.	Depending on the type of cylinder head, valve guides may be pressed, hammered, or shrunk in. In cases where the guides are shrunk into the head, replacement should be left to an equipped machine shop. In other cases, the guides are replaced as follows: Press or tap the valve guides out of the head using a stepped drift (see illustration). Determine the height above the boss that the guide must extend, and obtain a stack of washers, their I.D. similar to the guide's O.D., of that height. Place the stack of washers on the guide, and insert the guide into the boss. NOTE: *Valve guides are often tapered or beveled for installation.* Using the stepped installation tool (see illustration), press or tap the guides into position. Ream the guides according to the size of the valve stem. **Valve guide installation tool (with washers used during installation)**

Procedure	Method
Replacing valve seat inserts:	Replacement of valve seat inserts which are worn beyond resurfacing or broken, if feasible, must be done by a machine shop.

Resurfacing (grinding) the valve face:

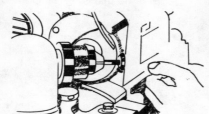

Grinding a valve

Using a valve grinder, resurface the valves according to specifications. CAUTION: *Valve face angle is not always identical to valve seat angle.* A minimum margin of 1/32″ should remain after grinding the valve. The valve stem tip should also be squared and resurfaced, by placing the stem in the V-block of the grinder, and turning it while pressing lightly against the grinding wheel.

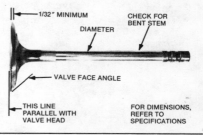

Critical valve dimensions

Resurfacing the valve seats using reamers:

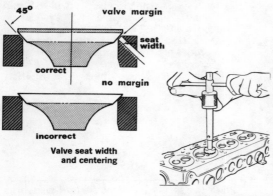

Valve seat width and centering

Reaming the valve seat (© Outboard Marine Corp)

Select a reamer of the correct seat angle, slightly larger than the diameter of the valve seat, and assemble it with a pilot of the correct size. Install the pilot into the valve guide, and using steady pressure, turn the reamer clockwise. CAUTION: *Do not turn the reamer counter-clockwise.* Remove only as much material as necessary to clean the seat. Check the concentricity of the seat (see below). If the dye method is not used, coat the valve face with Prussian blue dye, install and rotate it on the valve seat. Using the dye marked area as a centering guide, center and narrow the valve seat to specifications with correction cutters. NOTE: *When no specifications are available, minimum seat width for exhaust valves should be 5/64″, intake valves 1/16″.* After making correction cuts, check the position of the valve seat on the valve face using Prussian blue dye.

* Resurfacing the valve seats using a grinder:

Grinding a valve seat (© Subaru)

Select a pilot of the correct size, and a coarse stone of the correct seat angle. Lubricate the pilot if necessary, and install the tool in the valve guide. Move the stone on and off the seat at approximately two cycles per second, until all flaws are removed from the seat. Install a fine stone, and finish the seat. Center and narrow the seat using correction stones, as described above.

Procedure	Method
Checking the valve seat concentricity:  **Checking the valve seat concentricity using a dial gauge**	Coat the valve face with Prussian blue dye, install the valve, and rotate it on the valve seat. If the entire seat becomes coated, and the valve is known to be concentric, the seat is concentric.
	* Install the dial gauge pilot into the guide, and rest the arm on the valve seat. Zero the gauge, and rotate the arm around the seat. Run-out should not exceed .002″.
* Lapping the valves: NOTE: *Valve lapping is done to ensure efficient sealing of resurfaced valves and seats. Valve lapping alone is not recommended for use as a resurfacing procedure.* 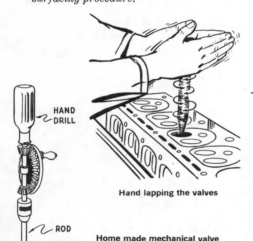 **Hand lapping the valves** **Home made mechanical valve lapping tool**	* Invert the cylinder head, lightly lubricate the valve stems, and install the valves in the head as numbered. Coat valve seats with fine grinding compound, and attach the lapping tool suction cup to a valve head (NOTE: *Moisten the suction cup*). Rotate the tool between the palms, changing position and lifting the tool often to prevent grooving. Lap the valve until a smooth, polished seat is evident. Remove the valve and tool, and rinse away all traces of grinding compound.
	** Fasten a suction cup to a piece of drill rod, and mount the rod in a hand drill. Proceed as above, using the hand drill as a lapping tool. CAUTION: *Due to the higher speeds involved when using the hand drill, care must be exercised to avoid grooving the seat.* Lift the tool and change direction of rotation often.
Check the valve springs: 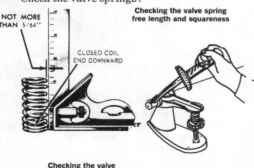 **Checking the valve spring free length and squareness** **Checking the valve spring tension** (© Outboard Marine Corp.)	Place the spring on a flat surface next to a square. Measure the height of the spring, and rotate it against the edge of the square to measure distortion. If spring height varies (by comparison) by more than 1/16″ or if distortion exceeds 1/16″, replace the spring.
	** In addition to evaluating the spring as above, test the spring pressure at the installed and compressed (installed height minus valve lift) height using a valve spring tester. Springs used on small displacement engines (up to 3 liters) should be ± 1 lb. of all other springs in either position. A tolerance of ± 5 lbs. is permissible on larger engines.

Procedure	Method
* Install valve stem seals:  RETAINER SPRING INTAKE VALVE SEAL **Valve stem seal installation**	* Due to the pressure differential that exists at the ends of the intake valve guides (atmospheric pressure above, manifold vacuum below), oil is drawn through the valve guides into the intake port. This has been alleviated somewhat since the addition of positive crankcase ventilation, which lowers the pressure above the guides. Several types of valve stem seals are available to reduce blow-by. Certain seals simply slip over the stem and guide boss, while others require that the boss be machined. Recently, Teflon guide seals have become popular. Consult a parts supplier or machinist concerning availability and suggested usages. NOTE: *When installing seals, ensure that a small amount of oil is able to pass the seal to lubricate the valve guides; otherwise, excessive wear may result.*
Install the valves:	Lubricate the valve stems, and install the valves in the cylinder head as numbered. Lubricate and position the seals (if used, see above) and the valve springs. Install the spring retainers, compress the springs, and insert the keys using needlenose pliers or a tool designed for this purpose. NOTE: *Retain the keys with wheel bearing grease during installation.*
Checking valve spring installed height: 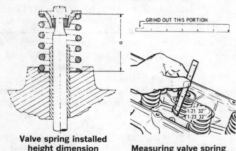 GRIND OUT THIS PORTION **Valve spring installed height dimension** **Measuring valve spring installed height** (© Outboard Marine Corp.)	Measure the distance between the spring pad and the lower edge of the spring retainer, and compare to specifications. If the installed height is incorrect, add shim washers between the spring pad and the spring. CAUTION: *Use only washers designed for this purpose.*
** CC'ing the combustion chambers:	** Invert the cylinder head and place a bead of sealer around a combustion chamber. Install an apparatus designed for this purpose (burette mounted on a clear plate; see illustration) over the combustion chamber, and fill with the specified fluid to an even mark on the burette. Record the burette reading, and fill the combustion chamber with fluid. (NOTE: *A hole drilled in the plate will permit air to escape*). Subtract the burette reading, with the combustion chamber filled, from the previous reading, to determine combustion chamber volume in cc's. Duplicate this procedure in all combustion

Procedure	Method

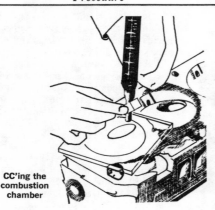

CC'ing the combustion chamber

chambers on the cylinder head, and compare the readings. The volume of all combustion chambers should be made equal to that of the largest. Combustion chamber volume may be increased in two ways. When only a small change is required (usually), a small cutter or coarse stone may be used to remove material from the combustion chamber. NOTE: *Check volume frequently*. Remove material over a wide area, so as not to change the configuration of the combustion chamber. When a larger change is required, the valve seat may be sunk (lowered into the head). NOTE: *When altering valve seat, remember to compensate for the change in spring installed height.*

Inspect the rocker arms, balls, studs, and nuts (where applicable):

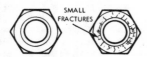

Stress cracks in rocker nuts
(© Ford Motor Co.)

Visually inspect the rocker arms, balls, studs, and nuts for cracks, galling, burning, scoring, or wear. If all parts are intact, liberally lubricate the rocker arms and balls, and install them on the cylinder head. If wear is noted on a rocker arm at the point of valve contact, grind it smooth and square, removing as little material as possible. Replace the rocker arm if excessively worn. If a rocker stud shows signs of wear, it must be replaced (see below). If a rocker nut shows stress cracks, replace it. If an exhaust ball is galled or burned, substitute the intake ball from the same cylinder (if it is intact), and install a new intake ball. NOTE: *Avoid using new rocker balls on exhaust valves.*

Replacing rocker studs:

Reaming the stud bore for oversize rocker studs
(© Buick Div. G.M. Corp.)

Extracting a pressed in rocker stud
(© Buick Div. G.M. Corp.)

FLAT WASHERS

AS STUD BEGINS TO PULL UP, IT WILL BE NECESSARY TO REMOVE THE NUT AND ADD MORE WASHERS.

In order to remove a threaded stud, lock two nuts on the stud, and unscrew the stud using the lower nut. Coat the lower threads of the new stud with Loctite, and install.

Two alternative methods are available for replacing pressed in studs. Remove the damaged stud using a stack of washers and a nut (see illustration). In the first, the boss is reamed .005-.006″ oversize, and an oversize stud pressed in. Control the stud extension over the boss using washers, in the same manner as valve guides. Before installing the stud, coat it with white lead and grease. To retain the stud more positively, drill a hole through the stud and boss, and install a roll pin. In the second method, the boss is tapped, and a threaded stud installed. Retain the stud using Loctite Stud and Bearing Mount.

Procedure	*Method*
Inspect the rocker shaft(s) and rocker arms (where applicable): 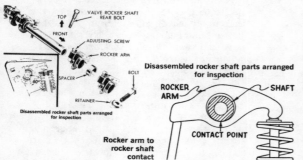 Disassembled rocker shaft parts arranged for inspection **ROCKER ARM** **SHAFT** **CONTACT POINT** **Rocker arm to rocker shaft contact**	Remove rocker arms, springs and washers from rocker shaft. NOTE: *Lay out parts in the order they are removed.* Inspect rocker arms for pitting or wear on the valve contact point, or excessive bushing wear. Bushings need only be replaced if wear is excessive, because the rocker arm normally contacts the shaft at one point only. Grind the valve contact point of rocker arm smooth if necessary, removing as little material as possible. If excessive material must be removed to smooth and square the arm, it should be replaced. Clean out all oil holes and passages in rocker shaft. If shaft is grooved or worn, replace it. Lubricate and assemble the rocker shaft.
Inspect the camshaft bushings and the camshaft (overhead cam engines):	See next section.
Inspect the pushrods:	Remove the pushrods, and, if hollow, clean out the oil passages using fine wire. Roll each pushrod over a piece of clean glass. If a distinct clicking sound is heard as the pushrod rolls, the rod is bent, and must be replaced.
	* The length of all pushrods must be equal. Measure the length of the pushrods, compare to specifications, and replace as necessary.
Inspect the valve lifters:  CHECK FOR CONCAVE WEAR ON FACE OF TAPPET USING TAPPET FOR STRAIGHT EDGE **Checking the lifter face** (© American Motors Corp.)	Remove lifters from their bores, and remove gum and varnish, using solvent. Clean walls of lifter bores. Check lifters for concave wear as illustrated. If face is worn concave, replace lifter, and carefully inspect the camshaft. Lightly lubricate lifter and insert it into its bore. If play is excessive, an oversize lifter must be installed (where possible). Consult a machinist concerning feasibility. If play is satisfactory, remove, lubricate, and reinstall the lifter.
* Testing hydraulic lifter leak down: 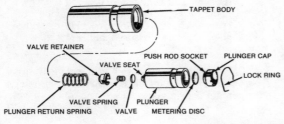 TAPPET BODY VALVE RETAINER PUSH ROD SOCKET PLUNGER CAP VALVE SEAT LOCK RING PLUNGER RETURN SPRING VALVE SPRING PLUNGER VALVE METERING DISC **Exploded view of a typical hydraulic lifter** (© American Motors Corp.)	Submerge lifter in a container of kerosene. Chuck a used pushrod or its equivalent into a drill press. Position container of kerosene so pushrod acts on the lifter plunger. Pump lifter with the drill press, until resistance increases. Pump several more times to bleed any air out of lifter. Apply very firm, constant pressure to the lifter, and observe rate at which fluid bleeds out of lifter. If the fluid bleeds very quickly (less than 15 seconds), lifter is defective. If the time exceeds 60 seconds, lifter is sticking. In either case, recondition or replace lifter. If lifter is operating properly (leak down time 15-60 seconds), lubricate and install it.

CYLINDER BLOCK RECONDITIONING

Procedure	Method

Checking the main bearing clearance:

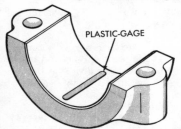

PLASTIC-GAGE

Installing Plastigage on lower bearing shell (© Chrysler Corp.)

Measuring Plastigage to determine bearing clearance (© Chrysler Corp.)

SCRATCHES — SCRATCHED BY DIRT / DIRT IMBEDDED INTO BEARING MATERIAL / OVERLAY WIPED OUT — LACK OF OIL / BRIGHT (POLISHED) SECTIONS — IMPROPER SEATING

OVERLAY GONE FROM ENTIRE SURFACE — TAPERED JOURNAL / RADIUS RIDE — RADIUS RIDE / CRATERS OR POCKETS — FATIGUE FAILURE

Causes of bearing failure
(© Ford Motor Co.)

Invert engine, and remove cap from the bearing to be checked. Using a clean, dry rag, thoroughly clean all oil from crankshaft journal and bearing insert. NOTE: *Plastigage is soluble in oil; therefore, oil on the journal or bearing could result in erroneous readings.* Place a piece of Plastigage along the full length of journal, reinstall cap, and torque to specifications. Remove bearing cap, and determine bearing clearance by comparing width of Plastigage to the scale on Plastigage envelope. Journal taper is determined by comparing width of the Plastigage strip near its ends. Rotate crankshaft 90° and retest, to determine journal eccentricity. NOTE: *Do not rotate crankshaft with Plastigage installed.* If bearing insert and journal appear intact, and are within tolerances, no further main bearing service is required. If bearing or journal appear defective, cause of failure should be determined before replacement.

* Remove crankshaft from block (see below). Measure the main bearing journals at each end twice (90° apart) using a micrometer, to determine diameter, journal taper and eccentricity. If journals are within tolerances, reinstall bearing caps at their specified torque. Using a telescope gauge and micrometer, measure bearing I.D. parallel to piston axis and at 30° on each side of piston axis. Subtract journal O.D. from bearing I.D. to determine oil clearance. If crankshaft journals appear defective, or do not meet tolerances, there is no need to measure bearings; for the crankshaft will require grinding and/or undersize bearings will be required. If bearing appears defective, cause for failure should be determined prior to replacement.

Checking the connecting rod bearing clearance: – –

Connecting rod bearing clearance is checked in the same manner as main bearing clearance, using Plastigage. Before removing the crankshaft, connecting rod side clearance also should be measured and recorded.

* Checking connecting rod bearing clearance, using a micrometer, is identical to checking main bearing clearance. If no other service

Procedure	Method

is required, the piston and rod assemblies need not be removed.

Removing the crankshaft:

Connecting rod matching marks

Using a punch, mark the corresponding main bearing caps and saddles according to position (i.e., one punch on the front main cap and saddle, two on the second, three on the third, etc.). Using number stamps, identify the corresponding connecting rods and caps, according to cylinder (if no numbers are present). Remove the main and connecting rod caps, and place sleeves of plastic tubing over the connecting rod bolts, to protect the journals as the crankshaft is removed. Lift the crankshaft out of the block.

Remove the ridge from the top of the cylinder:

RIDGE CAUSED BY CYLINDER WEAR

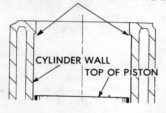

CYLINDER WALL
TOP OF PISTON

Cylinder bore ridge
(© Pontiac Div. G.M. Corp.)

In order to facilitate removal of the piston and connecting rod, the ridge at the top of the cylinder (unworn area; see illustration) must be removed. Place the piston at the bottom of the bore, and cover it with a rag. Cut the ridge away using a ridge reamer, exercising extreme care to avoid cutting too deeply. Remove the rag, and remove cuttings that remain on the piston. CAUTION: *If the ridge is not removed, and new rings are installed, damage to rings will result.*

Removing the piston and connecting rod:

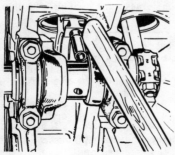

Removing the piston

Invert the engine, and push the pistons and connecting rods out of the cylinders. If necessary, tap the connecting rod boss with a wooden hammer handle, to force the piston out. CAUTION: *Do not attempt to force the piston past the cylinder ridge* (see above).

Procedure	*Method*
Service the crankshaft:	Ensure that all oil holes and passages in the crankshaft are open and free of sludge. If necessary, have the crankshaft ground to the largest possible undersize.
	** Have the crankshaft Magnafluxed, to locate stress cracks. Consult a machinist concerning additional service procedures, such as surface hardening (e.g., nitriding, Tuftriding) to improve wear characteristics, cross drilling and chamfering the oil holes to improve lubrication, and balancing.
Removing freeze plugs:	Drill a hole in the center of the freeze plugs, and pry them out using a screwdriver or drift.
Remove the oil gallery plugs:	Threaded plugs should be removed using an appropriate (usually square) wrench. To remove soft, pressed in plugs, drill a hole in the plug, and thread in a sheet metal screw. Pull the plug out by the screw using pliers.
Hot-tank the block:	Have the block hot-tanked to remove grease, corrosion, and scale from the water jackets. NOTE: *Consult the operator to determine whether the camshaft bearings will be damaged during the hot-tank process.*
Check the block for cracks:	Visually inspect the block for cracks or chips. The most common locations are as follows: Adjacent to freeze plugs. Between the cylinders and water jackets. Adjacent to the main bearing saddles. At the extreme bottom of the cylinders. Check only suspected cracks using spot check dye (see introduction). If a crack is located, consult a machinist concerning possible repairs.
	** Magnaflux the block to locate hidden cracks. If cracks are located, consult a machinist about feasibility of repair.
Install the oil gallery plugs and freeze plugs:	Coat freeze plugs with sealer and tap into position using a piece of pipe, slightly smaller than the plug, as a driver. To ensure retention, stake the edges of the plugs. Coat threaded oil gallery plugs with sealer and install. Drive replacement soft plugs into block using a large drift as a driver.
	* Rather than reinstalling lead plugs, drill and tap the holes, and install threaded plugs.

Procedure	*Method*

Check the bore diameter and surface:

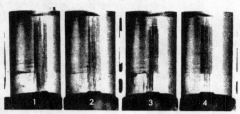

1, 2, 3 Piston skirt seizure resulted in this pattern. Engine must be rebored

4. Piston skirt and oil ring seizure caused this damage Engine must be rebored

Visually inspect the cylinder bores for roughness, scoring, or scuffing. If evident, the cylinder bore must be bored or honed oversize to eliminate imperfections, and the smallest possible oversize piston used. The new pistons should be given to the machinist with the block, so that the cylinders can be bored or honed exactly to the piston size (plus clearance). If no flaws are evident, measure the bore diameter using a telescope gauge and micrometer, or dial gauge, parallel and perpendicular to the engine centerline, at the top (below the ridge) and bottom of the bore. Subtract the bottom measurements from the top to determine taper, and the parallel to the centerline measurements from the perpendicular measurements to determine eccentricity. If the measurements are not within specifications, the cylinder must be bored or honed, and an oversize piston installed. If the measurements are within specifications the cylinder may be used as is, with only finish honing (see below). NOTE: *Prior to submitting the block for boring, perform the following operation(s).*

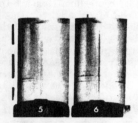

5, 6 Score marks caused by a split piston skirt. Damage is not serious enough to warrant reboring

7. Ring seized longitudinally, causing a score mark 1 3/16" wide, on the land side of the piston groove. The honing pattern is destroyed and the cylinder must be rebored

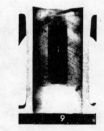

Cylinder wall damage
(© Daimler-Benz A.G.)

8. Result of oil ring seizure. Engine must be rebored

9. Oil ring seizure here was not serious enough to warrant reboring. The honing marks are still visible

Cylinder bore measuring positions
(© Ford Motor Co.)

Measuring the cylinder bore with a telescope gauge
(© Buick Div. G.M. Corp.)

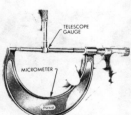

Determining the cylinder bore by measuring the telescope gauge with a micrometer
(© Buick Div. G.M. Corp.)

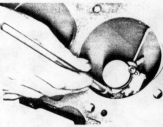

Measuring the cylinder bore with a dial gauge
(© Chevrolet Div. G.M. Corp.)

Procedure	Method
Check the block deck for warpage:	Using a straightedge and feeler gauges, check the block deck for warpage in the same manner that the cylinder head is checked (see Cylinder Head Reconditioning). If warpage exceeds specifications, have the deck resurfaced. NOTE: *In certain cases a specification for total material removal (Cylinder head and block deck) is provided. This specification must not be exceeded.*
* Check the deck height:	The deck height is the distance from the crankshaft centerline to the block deck. To measure, invert the engine, and install the crankshaft, retaining it with the center main cap. Measure the distance from the crankshaft journal to the block deck, parallel to the cylinder centerline. Measure the diameter of the end (front and rear) main journals, parallel to the centerline of the cylinders, divide the diameter in half, and subtract it from the previous measurement. The results of the front and rear measurements should be identical. If the difference exceeds .005″, the deck height should be corrected. NOTE: *Block deck height and warpage should be corrected concurrently.*
Check the cylinder block bearing alignment:  Checking main bearing saddle alignment	Remove the upper bearing inserts. Place a straightedge in the bearing saddles along the centerline of the crankshaft. If clearance exists between the straightedge and the center saddle, the block must be align-bored.
Clean and inspect the pistons and connecting rods:  RING EXPANDER Removing the piston rings	Using a ring expander, remove the rings from the piston. Remove the retaining rings (if so equipped) and remove piston pin. NOTE: *If the piston pin must be pressed out, determine the proper method and use the proper tools; otherwise the piston will distort.* Clean the ring grooves using an appropriate tool, exercising care to avoid cutting too deeply. Thoroughly clean all carbon and varnish from the piston with solvent. CAUTION: *Do not use a wire brush or caustic solvent on pistons.* Inspect the pistons for scuffing, scoring, cracks, pitting, or excessive ring groove wear. If wear is evident, the piston must be replaced. Check the connecting rod length by measuring the rod from the inside of the large end to the inside of the small end using calipers (see

Procedure	Method

Connecting rod length checking dimension

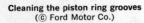

Ring Groove Cleaner

Cleaning the piston ring grooves
(© Ford Motor Co.)

illustration). All connecting rods should be equal length. Replace any rod that differs from the others in the engine.

* Have the connecting rod alignment checked in an alignment fixture by a machinist. Replace any twisted or bent rods.

* Magnaflux the connecting rods to locate stress cracks. If cracks are found, replace the connecting rod.

Fit the pistons to the cylinders:

Measuring the piston for fitting
(© Buick Div. G.M. Corp.)

90°

Using a telescope gauge and micrometer, or a dial gauge, measure the cylinder bore diameter perpendicular to the piston pin, 2½″ below the deck. Measure the piston perpendicular to its pin on the skirt. The difference between the two measurements is the piston clearance. If the clearance is within specifications or slightly below (after boring or honing), finish honing is all that is required. If the clearance is excessive, try to obtain a slightly larger piston to bring clearance within specifications. Where this is not possible, obtain the first oversize piston, and hone (or if necessary, bore) the cylinder to size.

Assemble the pistons and connecting rods:

Installing piston pin lock rings

Inspect piston pin, connecting rod small end bushing, and piston bore for galling, scoring, or excessive wear. If evident, replace defective part(s). Measure the I.D. of the piston boss and connecting rod small end, and the O.D. of the piston pin. If within specifications, assemble piston pin and rod. CAUTION: *If piston pin must be pressed in, determine the proper method and use the proper tools; otherwise the piston will distort.* Install the lock rings; ensure that they seat properly. If the parts are not within specifications, determine the service method for the type of engine. In some cases, piston and pin are serviced as an assembly when either is defective. Others specify reaming the piston and connecting rods for an oversize pin. If the connecting rod bushing is worn, it may in many cases be replaced. Reaming the piston and replacing the rod bushing are machine shop operations.

Procedure	*Method*

Clean and inspect the camshaft:

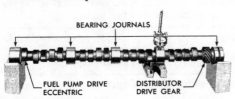

BEARING JOURNALS

FUEL PUMP DRIVE ECCENTRIC   DISTRIBUTOR DRIVE GEAR

Checking the camshaft for straightness
(© Chevrolet Motor Div. G.M. Corp.)

Camshaft lobe measurement
(© Ford Motor Co.)

Degrease the camshaft, using solvent, and clean out all oil holes. Visually inspect cam lobes and bearing journals for excessive wear. If a lobe is questionable, check all lobes as indicated below. If a journal or lobe is worn, the camshaft must be reground or replaced. NOTE: *If a journal is worn, there is a good chance that the bushings are worn.* If lobes and journals appear intact, place the front and rear journals in V-blocks, and rest a dial indicator on the center journal. Rotate the camshaft to check straightness. If deviation exceeds .001″, replace the camshaft.

* Check the camshaft lobes with a micrometer, by measuring the lobes from the nose to base and again at 90° (see illustration). The lift is determined by subtracting the second measurement from the first. If all exhaust lobes and all intake lobes are not identical, the camshaft must be reground or replaced.

Replace the camshaft bearings:

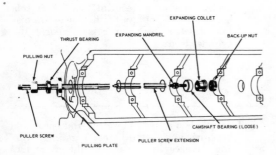

EXPANDING COLLET

THRUST BEARING   EXPANDING MANDREL   BACK-UP NUT

PULLING NUT

PULLER SCREW   PULLING PLATE   PULLER SCREW EXTENSION   CAMSHAFT BEARING (LOOSE)

Camshaft removal and installation tool (typical)
(© Ford Motor Co.)

If excessive wear is indicated, or if the engine is being completely rebuilt, camshaft bearings should be replaced as follows: Drive the camshaft rear plug from the block. Assemble the removal puller with its shoulder on the bearing to be removed. Gradually tighten the puller nut until bearing is removed. Remove remaining bearings, leaving the front and rear for last. To remove front and rear bearings, reverse position of the tool, so as to pull the bearings in toward the center of the block. Leave the tool in this position, pilot the new front and rear bearings on the installer, and pull them into position. Return the tool to its original position and pull remaining bearings into position. NOTE: *Ensure that oil holes align when installing bearings.* Replace camshaft rear plug, and stake it into position to aid retention.

Finish hone the cylinders:

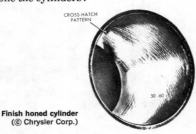

CROSS-HATCH PATTERN

50-60

Finish honed cylinder
(© Chrysler Corp.)

Chuck a flexible drive hone into a power drill, and insert it into the cylinder. Start the hone, and move it up and down in the cylinder at a rate which will produce approximately a 60° cross-hatch pattern (see illustration). NOTE: *Do not extend the hone below the cylinder bore.* After developing the pattern, remove the hone and recheck piston fit. Wash the cylinders with a detergent and water solution to remove abrasive dust, dry, and wipe several times with a rag soaked in engine oil.

Procedure	*Method*
Check piston ring end-gap:  **Checking ring end-gap** (© Outboard Marine Corp.)	Compress the piston rings to be used in a cylinder, one at a time, into that cylinder, and press them approximately 1″ below the deck with an inverted piston. Using feeler gauges, measure the ring end-gap, and compare to specifications. Pull the ring out of the cylinder and file the ends with a fine file to obtain proper clearance. CAUTION: *If inadequate ring end-gap is utilized, ring breakage will result.*
Install the piston rings: 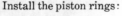  **Checking ring side clearance** (© Chrysler Corp.) 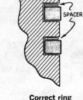 CORRECT INCORRECT **Correct ring spacer installation** **Piston groove depth**	Inspect the ring grooves in the piston for excessive wear or taper. If necessary, recut the groove(s) for use with an overwidth ring or a standard ring and spacer. If the groove is worn uniformly, overwidth rings, or standard rings and spacers may be installed without recutting. Roll the outside of the ring around the groove to check for burrs or deposits. If any are found, remove with a fine file. Hold the ring in the groove, and measure side clearance. If necessary, correct as indicated above. NOTE: *Always install any additional spacers above the piston ring.* The ring groove must be deep enough to allow the ring to seat below the lands (see illustration). In many cases, a "go-no-go" depth gauge will be provided with the piston rings. Shallow grooves may be corrected by recutting, while deep grooves require some type of filler or expander behind the piston. Consult the piston ring supplier concerning the suggested method. Install the rings on the piston, lowest ring first, using a ring expander. NOTE: *Position the ring markings as specified by the manufacturer (see car section).*
Install the camshaft:	Liberally lubricate the camshaft lobes and journals, and slide the camshaft into the block. CAUTION: *Exercise extreme care to avoid damaging the bearings when inserting the camshaft.* Install and tighten the camshaft thrust plate retaining bolts.
Check camshaft end-play: **Checking camshaft end-play with a feeler gauge** (© Outboard Marine Corp.)  0.0025″-0.0075″	Using feeler gauges, determine whether the clearance between the camshaft boss (or gear) and backing plate is within specifications. Install shims behind the thrust plate, or reposition the camshaft gear and retest end-play.

Procedure	Method

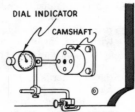

DIAL INDICATOR
CAMSHAFT

Checking camshaft end-play with a dial indicator

* Mount a dial indicator stand so that the stem of the dial indicator rests on the nose of the camshaft, parallel to the camshaft axis. Push the camshaft as far in as possible and zero the gauge. Move the camshaft outward to determine the amount of camshaft end-play. If the end-play is not within tolerance, install shims behind the thrust plate, or reposition the camshaft gear and retest.

Install the rear main seal (where applicable):

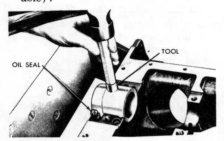

OIL SEAL

TOOL

Seating the rear main seal

Position the block with the bearing saddles facing upward. Lay the rear main seal in its groove and press it lightly into its seat. Place a piece of pipe the same diameter as the crankshaft journal into the saddle, and firmly seat the seal. Hold the pipe in position, and trim the ends of the seal flush if required.

Install the crankshaft:

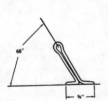

60°

⅝″

Home made bearing roll-out pin
(© Pontiac Div. G.M. Corp.)

INSTALLING BEARING SHELL

REMOVING BEARING SHELL

Removal and installation of upper bearing insert using a roll-out pin
(© Buick Div. G.M. Corp.)

Thoroughly clean the main bearing saddles and caps. Place the upper halves of the bearing inserts on the saddles and press into position. NOTE: *Ensure that the oil holes align.* Press the corresponding bearing inserts into the main bearing caps. Lubricate the upper main bearings, and lay the crankshaft in position. Place a strip of Plastigage on each of the crankshaft journals, install the main caps, and torque to specifications. Remove the main caps, and compare the Plastigage to the scale on the Plastigage envelope. If clearances are within tolerances, remove the Plastigage, turn the crankshaft 90°, wipe off all oil and retest. If all clearances are correct, remove all Plastigage, thoroughly

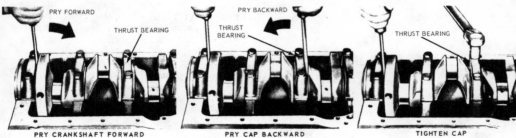

PRY FORWARD

THRUST BEARING

PRY CRANKSHAFT FORWARD

PRY BACKWARD

THRUST BEARING

PRY CAP BACKWARD

THRUST BEARING

TIGHTEN CAP

Aligning the thrust bearing
(© Ford Motor Co.)

Procedure	Method
	lubricate the main caps and bearing journals, and install the main caps. If clearances are not within tolerance, the upper bearing inserts may be removed, without removing the crankshaft, using a bearing roll out pin (see illustration). Roll in a bearing that will provide proper clearance, and retest. Torque all main caps, excluding the thrust bearing cap, to specifications. Tighten the thrust bearing cap finger tight. To properly align the thrust bearing, pry the crankshaft the extent of its axial travel several times, the last movement held toward the front of the engine, and torque the thrust bearing cap to specifications. Determine the crankshaft end-play (see below), and bring within tolerance with thrust washers.
Measure crankshaft end-play:	Mount a dial indicator stand on the front of the block, with the dial indicator stem resting on the nose of the crankshaft, parallel to the crankshaft axis. Pry the crankshaft the extent of its travel rearward, and zero the indicator. Pry the crankshaft forward and record crankshaft end-play. NOTE: *Crankshaft end-play also may be measured at the thrust bearing, using feeler gauges* (see illustration).

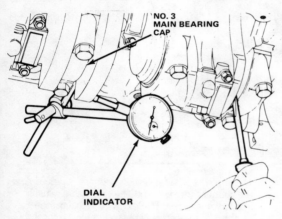

NO. 3
MAIN BEARING
CAP

DIAL
INDICATOR

**Checking crankshaft
end-play with a
dial indicator**

**Checking crankshaft
end-play with a
feeler gauge**

Install the pistons:	Press the upper connecting rod bearing halves into the connecting rods, and the lower halves into the connecting rod caps. Position the piston ring gaps according to specifications (see car section), and lubricate the pistons. Install a ring compresser on a piston, and press two long (8″) pieces of plastic tubing over the rod bolts. Using the plastic tubes as a guide, press the pistons into the bores and onto the crankshaft with a wooden hammer handle. After seating the rod on the crankshaft journal, remove the tubes and install the cap finger tight. Install the remaining pistons in the same man-

Procedure	*Method*

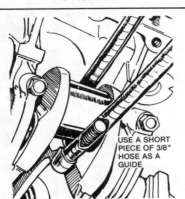

USE A SHORT
PIECE OF 3/8"
HOSE AS A
GUIDE

Tubing used as guide when installing a piston

ner. Invert the engine and check the bearing clearance at two points (90° apart) on each journal with Plastigage. NOTE: *Do not turn the crankshaft with Plastigage installed.* If clearance is within tolerances, remove *all* Plastigage, thoroughly lubricate the journals, and torque the rod caps to specifications. If clearance is not within specifications, install different thickness bearing inserts and recheck. CAUTION: *Never shim or file the connecting rods or caps.* Always install plastic tube sleeves over the rod bolts when the caps are not installed, to protect the crankshaft journals.

Installing a piston

Check connecting rod side clearance:

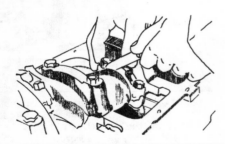

Checking connecting rod side clearance

Determine the clearance between the sides of the connecting rods and the crankshaft, using feeler gauges. If clearance is below the minimum tolerance, the rod may be machined to provide adequate clearance. If clearance is excessive, substitute an unworn rod, and recheck. If clearance is still outside specifications, the crankshaft must be welded and reground, or replaced.

Inspect the timing chain:

Visually inspect the timing chain for broken or loose links, and replace the chain if any are found. If the chain will flex sideways, it must be replaced. Install the timing chain as specified. NOTE: *If the original timing chain is to be reused, install it in its original position.*

Procedure	Method
Check timing gear backlash and runout:	Mount a dial indicator with its stem resting on a tooth of the camshaft gear (as illustrated). Rotate the gear until all slack is removed, and zero the indicator. Rotate the gear in the opposite direction until slack is removed, and record gear backlash. Mount the indicator with its stem resting on the edge of the camshaft gear, parallel to the axis of the camshaft. Zero the indicator, and turn the camshaft gear one full turn, recording the runout. If either backlash or runout exceed specifications, replace the worn gear(s).

Checking camshaft gear backlash

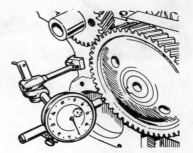

Checking camshaft gear runout

Completing the Rebuilding Process

Following the above procedures, complete the rebuilding process as follows:

Fill the oil pump with oil, to prevent cavitating (sucking air) on initial engine start up. Install the oil pump and the pickup tube on the engine. Coat the oil pan gasket as necessary, and install the gasket and the oil pan. Mount the flywheel and the crankshaft vibrational damper or pulley on the crankshaft. NOTE: *Always use new bolts when installing the flywheel.* Inspect the clutch shaft pilot bushing in the crankshaft. If the bushing is excessively worn, remove it with an expanding puller and a slide hammer, and tap a new bushing into place.

Position the engine, cylinder head side up. Lubricate the lifters, and install them into their bores. Install the cylinder head, and torque it as specified in the car section. Insert the pushrods (where applicable), and install the rocker shaft(s) (if so equipped) or position the rocker arms on the pushrods. If solid lifters are utilized, adjust the valves to the "cold" specifications.

Mount the intake and exhaust manifolds, the carburetor(s), the distributor and spark plugs. Adjust the point gap and the static ignition timing. Mount all accessories and install the engine in the car. Fill the radiator with coolant, and the crankcase with high quality engine oil.

Break-in Procedure

Start the engine, and allow it to run at low speed for a few minutes, while checking for leaks. Stop the engine, check the oil level, and fill as necessary. Restart the engine, and fill the cooling system to capacity. Check the point dwell angle and adjust the ignition timing and the valves. Run the engine at low to medium speed (800-2500 rpm) for approximately ½ hour, and retorque the cylinder head bolts. Road test the car, and check again for leaks.

Follow the manufacturer's recommended engine break-in procedure and maintenance schedule for new engines.

Chapter 4

Emission Controls and Fuel System

Emission Controls

DESCRIPTION

Positive Crankcase Ventilation (PCV)

All models are equipped with a positive crankcase ventilation system which draws air into the engine through the oil filler cap or the air cleaner and circulates it through the engine. The air combines with vapors in the crankcase and exits the engine through a metering valve mounted in the rocker arm cover. The air-vapor mixture then re-enters the engine through the carburetor or intake manifold and passes into the combustion chamber where it is burned.

Orifice Spark Advance Control (OSAC) Valve

This valve is located on the air cleaner. Most models are equipped with OSAC. The valve controls No_x and HC emissions by delaying the vacuum advance for 17 or 27 seconds (depending on engine) during acceleration. Some OSAC valves contain a temperature control device to improve driveability during engine warm-up.

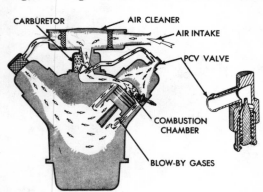

PCV system schematic

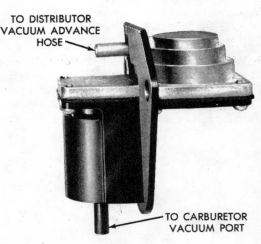

OSAC valve

Air Injection System (Air Pump)

This system is used on most 1976 models and all 1977–78 California models. A belt-driven air pump, mounted on the front of the engine, is used to inject air into the exhaust ports. This causes oxidation of these gases and a considerable reduction in carbon monoxide and hydrocarbons. The system consists of the pump, a check valve to protect the hoses and pump from hot gases, and a diverter/pressure relief valve assembly.

Service to the air injection system is limited to belt tension adjustment every 12,000 miles. In addition, if any part fails in service, repair is effected by removal and replacement only. Pumps are not rebuildable.

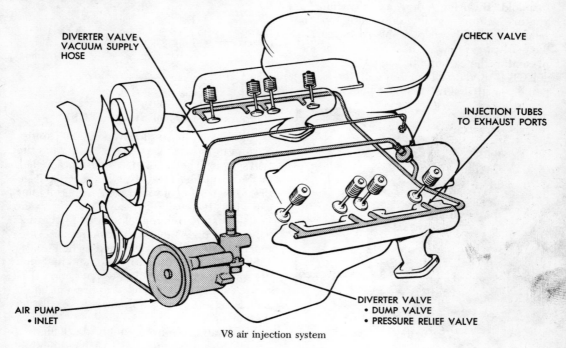

V8 air injection system

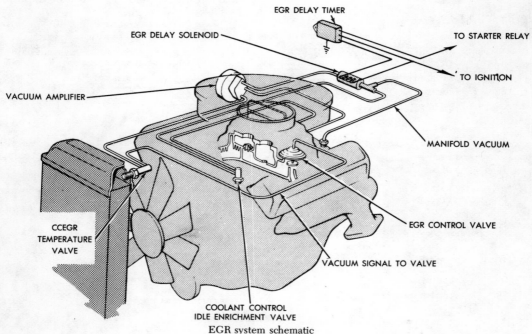

EGR system schematic

Exhaust Gas Recirculation (EGR)

In order to reduce the emission of oxides of nitrogen (NO_x), exhaust gases are ducted from the intake manifold crossover passage to contaminate the fuel/air mixture. These gases are introduced to the intake manifold floor by an EGR control valve. This valve directs exhaust gas from the crossover passage into the intake manifold. By using either ported-vacuum or venturi-vacuum signals, depending on the model, the EGR valve is able to proportion the exhaust gas flow to the amount of vacuum present in the carburetor.

EGR is used on all engines with the exception of the 1978 49 state 360 4 bbl engine.

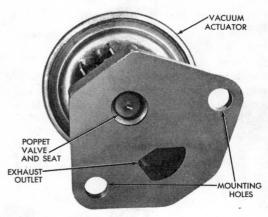

EGR valve—bottom view

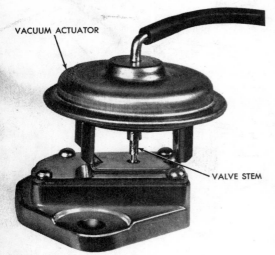

EGR valve

Evaporation Control System (ECS)

All vehicles have an Evaporation Control System to reduce evaporation losses from the fuel system. The system has an expansion tank in the main fuel tank. This prevents spillage due to expansion of warm fuel. A special filler cap with a two-way relief valve is used. An internal pressure differential, caused by thermal expansion, opens the valve, as does an external pressure differential, caused by fuel usage. Fuel vapors from the carburetor and fuel tank are routed to the crankcase ventilation system. A separator is installed to prevent liquid fuel from entering the crankcase ventilation system.

Evaporation control systems also include a charcoal canister and an overflow limiting valve.

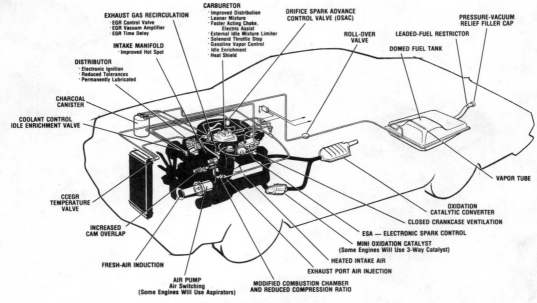

An overall view of the emission controls system

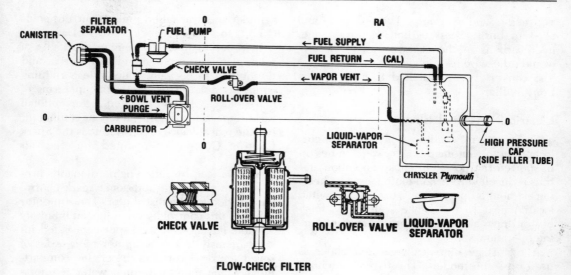

Fuel and evaporative control system

The limiting valve prevents the fuel tank from being overfilled by trapping fuel in the filler when the tank is full. When pressure in the tank becomes greater than the valve operating pressure, the valve opens and allows the gasoline vapors to flow into the charcoal canister.

The charcoal canister is mounted in the engine compartment. It absorbs vapors and retains them until clean air is drawn through a line from it which tuns to the PCV valve. Absorption occurs while the car is parked and cleaning occurs when the car engine is running.

Catalytic Converter

All models are equipped with catalytic converters except some 1976 318 engines with

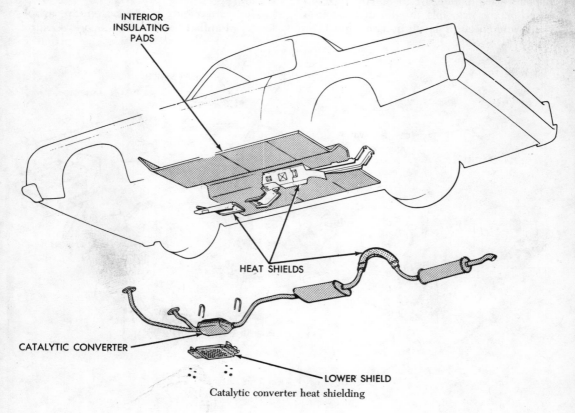

Catalytic converter heat shielding

Torqueflite and air pump. These devices are used to burn excess carbon monoxide and hydrocarbons in the exhaust system, which would otherwise escape out the exhaust pipe. The converters are installed in front of the front mufflers.

Electrically Assisted Choke

During warm weather, a heating element, located in the automatic choke well, comes on to shorten the period of choke operation and thus reduce hydrocarbon emissions. The heating element is operated by a time-delay switch located next to the choke well. The choke heater draws about three amps of current during operation.

A two stage electrically-assisted choke is used on some models. The two stage choke may be identified by its external resistor. Below 58° F., the heating element gets full, low amperage current from the choke control. Above 58° F, the control opens the circuit so that the heating element gets no current at all.

Lean Burn System

The Chrysler Corporation Lean Burn System, introduced in 1976 on the Cordoba, has been made available on a number of Aspen/Volare models for 1978. This system is based on the principle that lower NO_x emissions would occur if the air/fuel ratio inside the

cylinder area was raised from its current point (15.5:1) to a much leaner point (18:1).

In order to make the engine workable, a solution to the problems of carburetion and timing had to be found since a lean running engine is not the most efficient in terms of driveability. Chrysler adapted a conventional carburetor to handle the added air coming in, but the real advance of the system is the Spark Control Computer mounted on the air cleaner.

Since a lean burning engine demands precise ignition timing, additional spark control was needed for the distributor. The computer supplies this control by providing an infinitely variable advance curve. Input data is fed instantaneously to the computer by a series of seven sensors located in the engine compartment which monitor timing, water temperature, air temperature, throttle position, idle/off-idle operation, and intake manifold vacuum. The program schedule module of the spark control computer receives the information from the sensors, processes it, and then directs the ignition control module to advance or retard the timing as necessary. This whole process is going on continuously as the engine is running, taking only a thousandth of a second to complete a circuit from sensor to distributor.

The components of the system are as follows: Modified carburetor; Spark Control

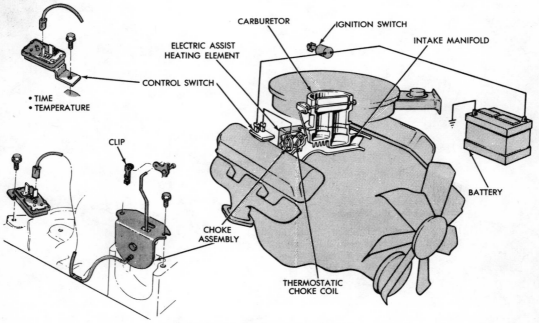

Electric assist choke system schematic

Computer, consisting of two interacting modules: the Program Schedule Module which is responsible for translating input data, and the Ignition Control Module which transmits data to the distributor to advance or retard the timing; and the following sensors.

Start Pick-up Sensor, located inside the distributor, supplies a signal to the computer providing a fixed timing point which is only used for starting the car. It also has a back-up function of taking over engine timing in case the run pick-up fails. Since the timing in this pick-up is fixed at one point, the engine will be able to run, but not very well.

The Run Pick-up Sensor, also located in the distributor, provides timing data to the computer once the engine is running. It also monitors engine speed and helps the computer decide when the piston is reaching the top of its compression stroke.

Coolant Temperature Sensor, located on the water pump housing, informs the computer when the coolant temperature is below 150°.

Air Temperature Sensor, inside the computer itself, monitors the temperature of the air coming into the air cleaner.

Throttle Position Transducer, located on the carburetor, monitors the position and rate of change of the throttle plates. When the throttle plates start to open and as they continue to open toward full throttle, more and more spark advance is called for by the computer. If the throttle plates are opened quickly even more spark advance is given for about one second. The amount of maximum advance is determined by the temperature of the air coming into the air cleaner. Less advance under acceleration will be given if the air entering the air cleaner is hot, while more advance will be given if the air is cold.

Carburetor Switch Sensor, located on the end of the idle stop solenoid, tells the computer if the engine is at idle or off-idle.

Vacuum Transducer, located on the computer, monitors the amount of intake manifold vacuum present; the more vacuum, the more spark advance to the distributor. In order to obtain this spark advance in the distributor, the carburetor switch sensor has to remain open for a specified amount of time during which the advance will slowly build up to the amount indicated as necessary by the vacuum transducer. If the carburetor switch should close during that time, the advance to the distributor will be cancelled. From here the computer will start with an advance count-

down. If the carburetor switch is reopened within a certain amount of time, the advance will continue from a point where the computer decides it should. If the switch is reopened after the computer has counted down to "no advance," the vacuum advance process must start over again.

OPERATION

When you turn the ignition key on, the start pick-up sends its signal to the computer which relays back information for more spark advance during cranking. As soon as the engine starts, the run pick-up takes over and receives more advance for about one minute. This advance is slowly eliminated during the one minute warm-up period. While the engine is cold (coolant temperature below 150° as monitored by the coolant temperature sensor), no more advance will be given to the distributor until the engine reaches normal operating temperature, at which time normal operation of the system will begin.

In normal operation, the basic timing information is relayed by the run pick-up to the computer along with input signals from all the other sensors. From this data the computer determines the maximum allowable advance or retard to be sent to the distributor for any situation.

If either the run pick-up or the computer should fail, the back-up system of the start pick-up takes over. This supplies a fixed timing signal to the distributor which allows the car to be driven until it can be repaired. In this mode, very poor fuel economy and performance will be experienced. If the start pick-up or the ignition control module section of the computer should fail, the engine will not start or run.

EMISSION CONTROL TROUBLESHOOTING

Positive Crankcase Ventilation (PCV) System

VALVE TEST

1. See if there are any deposits in the carburetor passages, the oil filler cap, or the hoses. Clean these as required.

2. Connect a tachometer to the engine.

3. With the engine idling, remove the PCV valve .

NOTE: *If the valve and the hoses are not clogged-up, there should be a hissing sound.*

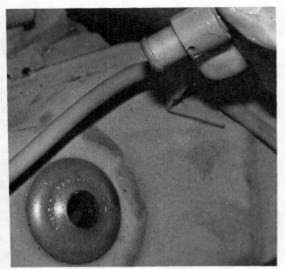

Pull the PCV valve out of the valve cover to test it

4. Check the tachometer reading. Place a finger over the valve or hose opening (a suction should be felt).

5. Check the tachometer again. The engine speed should have dropped at least 50 rpm. It should return to normal when the finger is removed from the opening.

6. If the engine does not change speed or if the change is less than 50 rpm, the hose is clogged or the valve is defective. Check the hose first. If the hose is not clogged replace, do not attempt to repair, the PCV valve.

7. Test the new valve to make sure that it is operating properly.

NOTE: *There are several commercial PCV valve testers available. Be sure that the one used is suitable for the valve to be tested, as the testers are not universal.*

Air Injection System

CAUTION: *Do not hammer on, pry, or bend the pump housing while tightening the drive belt or testing the pump.*

BELT TENSION AND AIR LEAKS

1. Check the pump drive belt tension. There should be about ½ in. play in the longest span of belt between pulleys.

2. Turn the pump by hand. If it has seized, the belt will slip, producing noise. Disregard any chirping, squealing, or rolling sounds from inside the pump; these are normal when it is turned by hand.

3. Check the hoses and connections for leaks. Hissing or a blast of air is indicative of a leak. Soapy water, applied lightly around the

area in question, is a good method for detecting leaks.

AIR OUTPUT TEST

1. Disconnect the air supply hose at the antibackfire valve.

2. Connect a pressure gauge to the air supply hose.

NOTE: *If there are two hoses plug the second one.*

3. With the engine at normal operating temperature, increase the idle speed and watch the vacuum gauge.

4. The airflow from the pump should be steady and between 2–6 psi. If it is unsteady or falls below this, the pump is defective and must be replaced.

PUMP NOISE DIAGNOSIS

The air pump is normally noisy; as engine speed increases, the noise of the pump will rise in pitch. The rolling sound the pump bearings make is normal.

CHECK VALVE TEST

1. Before starting the test, check all of the hoses and connections for leaks.

2. Detach the air supply hose(s) from the check valve(s).

3. Insert a probe into the check valve and depress the plate. Release it; the plate should return to its original position against the valve seat. If binding is evident, replace the valve.

4. Repeat Step 3 if two valves are used.

5. With the engine running at normal operating temperature, gradually increase its speed to 1,500 rpm. Check for exhaust gas leakage. If there is any, replace the valve assembly.

NOTE: *Vibration and flutter of the check valve at idle speed is a normal condition and does not mean that the valve should be replaced.*

Thermostatically Controlled Air Cleaner

AIR DOOR TEST

1. Remove the air cleaner from the carburetor and allow it to cool to 90° F. Connect a vacuum source with a vacuum gauge to the sensor.

2. Apply 20 in. Hg to the sensor. The door should be in the "heat on" (up) position. If it remains in the "off" position, test the vacuum motor.

3. Connect the motor to a vacuum source.

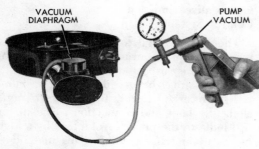

VACUUM
DIAPHRAGM

PUMP
VACUUM

Air door testing

In addition to the vacuum gauge, a hose clamp and a bleed valve are necessary. Connect them in the following order:

    a. Vacuum source;
    b. Hose clamp (or shut-off valve);
    c. Bleed valve;
    d. Vacuum gauge;
    e. Vacuum motor.

4. Apply 20 in. Hg vacuum to the motor. Use the hose clamp to block the line, so that the motor will retain the vacuum. The door operating motor should retain this amount of vacuum for five minutes. Release the hose clamp.

NOTE: *If the vacuum cannot be built up to the specified amount, the diaphragm has a leak and the valve will require replacement.*

5. By slowly closing the bleed valve, check the operation of the door. The door should open at no less than 5 in. Hg.

Orifice Spark Advance

CONTROL VALVE TEST

The OSAC valve is located on the air cleaner. Warm the engine to normal operating temperature for this test.

1. Check the vacuum hoses and connections for leaks or plugging.

2. Detach the vacuum line which runs from the distributor to the OSAC valve at the distributor end. Connect a vacuum gauge to this line.

3. Connect a tachometer to the engine. Rapidly open the throttle and then stabilize the engine speed at 2,000 rpm in neutral. When the throttle is rapidly opened the vacuum gauge reading should drop to zero. With the engine speed at a steady 2,000 rpm, it should take about 20 seconds for the vacuum level to rise and then stabilize.

NOTE: *The length of time may vary slightly with different engines; 20 seconds is an approximate figure.*

5. If the vacuum level rises immediately, the valve is defective and must be replaced.

Carburetor Controls

ANTIDIESELING
SOLENOID TEST

NOTE: *Antidieseling solenoids are also referred to as "throttle stop" or "idle stop" solenoids.*

CAUTION: *Cars with catalytic converters have an additional solenoid; this is NOT an antidieseling solenoid, and no attempt to adjust the idle speed with it should be made. See "Catalytic Converter" for details.*

1. Turn the ignition key on and open the throttle. The solenoid plunger should extend (solenoid energized).

2. Turn the ignition off. The plunger should retract, allowing the throttle to close.

NOTE: *With the antidieseling solenoid de-energized, the carburetor idle speed adjusting screw must make contact with the throttle shaft to prevent the throttle plates from jamming in the throttle bore when the engine is turned off.*

3. If the solenoid is functioning properly and the engine is still dieseling, check for one of the following:

    a. High idle or engine shut off speed;
    b. Engine timing not set to specification;
    c. Binding throttle linkage;
    d. Too low an octane fuel being used.

Correct any of these problems, as necessary.

4. If the solenoid fails to function as outlined in Steps 1–2, disconnect the solenoid leads; the solenoid should be de-energized. If it does not, it is jammed and must be replaced.

5. Connect the solenoid to a 12 V power source and to ground. Open the throttle so that the plunger can extend. If it does not, the solenoid is defective.

6. If the solenoid is functioning correctly and no other source of trouble can be found, the fault probably lies in the wiring between the solenoid and the ignition switch or in the ignition switch itself. Reconnect the solenoid when finished testing.

ELECTRICALLY ASSISTED
CHOKE TEST

CAUTION: *Do not immerse the choke heating element in any type of liquid, especially solvent, for any reason.*

NOTE: *A short circuit in the choke wiring or in the heater will show up as a short in the ignition system.*

Choke control unit identification

1. Disconnect the electrical leads from the choke control switch before starting the engine.

2. Connect a test light between the smaller of the two terminals on the choke control switch and a ground.

3. Start the engine and run it until it reaches normal operating temperature.

4. Apply power from a 12V source to the terminal marked "BAT" on the choke control switch.

5. The test light should light for at least a few seconds or for as long as five minutes. If the light does not come on at all or if it stays on longer than five minutes, replace the switch.

6. Disconnect the test light and reconnect the electrical leads to the choke switch, if it is functioning properly.

7. Detach the lead from the choke switch which runs to the choke heating element.

8. Connect the lead from an ohm-meter to the crimped section at the choke end of the wire, which was removed in Step 7.

CAUTION: *Do not connect the metallic heater housing.*

9. Ground the other ohmmeter test lead to the engine manifold.

10. The meter should indicate a resistance of 4–6 ohms.

11. If the reading is not within specifications, or if it indicates an opened (zero resistance) or a shorted (infinite resistance) heater coil, replace the heater assembly.

NOTE: *The electrically assisted choke does not change any carburetor service procedures. If any parts of the electrically assisted choke are defective, they must be replaced. Adjustment is not possible.*

Evaporative Emission Control System

There are several things to check for if a malfunction of the evaporative emission control system is suspected.

1. Leaks may be traced by using an infrared hydrocarbon tester. Run the test probe along the lines and connections. The meter will indicate the presence of a leak by a high hydrocarbon (HC) reading. This method is much more accurate than a visual inspection which would indicate only the presence of a leak large enough to pass liquid.

2. Leaks may be caused by any of the following, so always check these areas when looking for them:
    a. Defective or worn lines;
    b. Disconnected or pinched lines;
    c. Improperly routed lines;
    d. A defective filler cap.

NOTE: *If it becomes necessary to replace any of the lines used in the evaporative emission control system, use only those hoses which are fuel resistant or are marked "EVAP."*

3. If the fuel tank has collapsed, it may be the fault of clogged or pinched vent lines, a defective vapor separator, or a plugged or incorrect fuel filler cap.

4. To test the filler cap, clean it and place it against the mouth. Blow into the relief valve housing if the cap passes pressure with light blowing or if it fails to release with hard blowing, it is defective and must be replaced.

NOTE: *Replace the cap with one marked "pressure/vacuum" only. An incorrect cap will render the system inoperative or damage its components.*

Exhaust Gas Recirculation (EGR) System

EGR SYSTEM TEST

NOTE: *Air temperature should be above 68° F for this test.*

1. Check all of the vacuum hoses which run between the carburetor, intake manifold, EGR valve, and the vacuum amplifier (if so equipped). Replace the hoses and tighten the connections, as required.

2. Allow the engine to warm up. Connect a tachometer to it. Start with the engine idling in neutral and rapidly increase the engine speed to 2,000 rpm.

3. If the EGR valve stem moves (watch

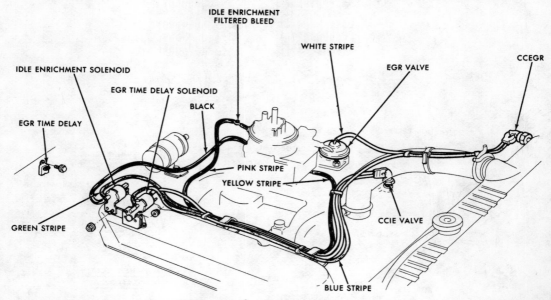

EGR vacuum hose routing—318 automatic

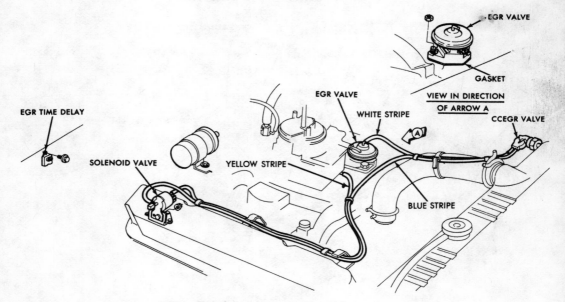

EGR vacuum hose routing—318 manual transmission

the groove on the stem), the valve and the rest of the system are functioning properly. If the stem does not move, proceed with the rest of the EGR system tests.

4. Disconnect the vacuum supply hose from the EGR valve. Apply a vacuum of at least 10 in. Hg to the valve with the engine warmed-up and idling and the transmission in Neutral.

NOTE: *A source of more than adequate vacuum is the intake manifold vacuum connection. Run a hose from the EGR valve directly to the connection.*

5. When vacuum is applied to the EGR valve, the engine speed should drop at least 150 rpm. In some cases the engine may even stall. If the engine does not slow down the EGR valve does not operate, the valve is defective or dirty. Replace it or remove the deposits from it.

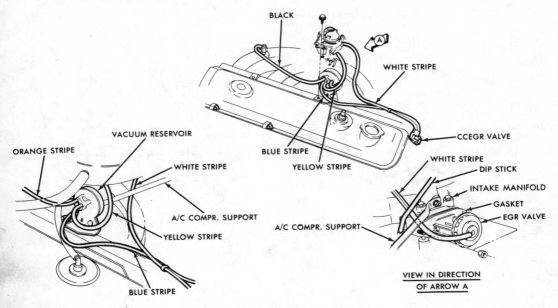

EGR vacuum hose routing—six cylinder engine

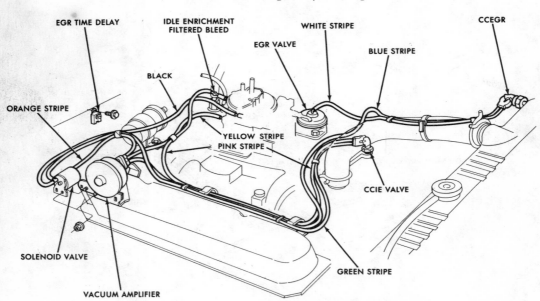

EGR vacuum hose routing—318 California engine

NOTE: *Always replace the EGR valve gasket when the valve is removed for service, even if the valve itself is not replaced.*

6. If the EGR valve is functioning properly, reconnect its vacuum line and test the temperature control valve.

7. Test the EGR system coolant temperature operated control valve for leaks. The valve is located on either the right or left-side of the radiator top tank.

8. Disconnect the vacuum hose from the EGR coolant temperature operated control valve, then connect a vacuum source and gauge to the valve fitting, in place of the hose.

9. Apply 10 in. Hg of vacuum to the valve. If the valve loses more than 1 in. Hg in one minute, the valve is defective and must be replaced.

10. If everything else is functioning properly, the EGR system does not work and the

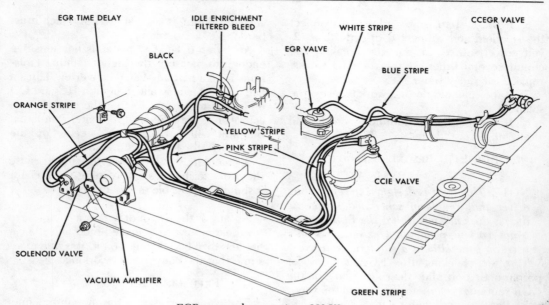

EGR vacuum hose routine—360 V8 engine

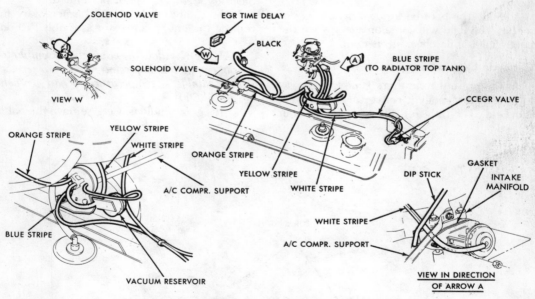

EGR vacuum hose routing—California six cylinder

engine is equipped with a vacuum amplifier, the amplifier is at fault. Replace it and repeat the system test.

NOTE: *Before replacing the amplifier, check the vacuum port in the carburetor. If it is clogged, clean it with solvent; do not use a drill.*

EGR DELAY SYSTEM TEST

1. Unfasten the distributor-to-coil lead.
2. Disconnect the vacuum line which runs from the delay solenoid to the vacuum amplier at the amplifier end.

3. Turn the car's ignition switch to "START" and then release it, so that it returns to "RUN."

4. Suck on the end of the disconnected hose; the hose should be blocked.

5. After about 35 seconds from the time that the ignition switch was turned to "START," the solenoid should open, allowing air to flow through the line.

6. If the system isn't working, disconnect the solenoid and connect it directly to a 12-volt power source, making and breaking the circuit several times. If the solenoid works, replace the delay timer.

7. If the solenoid doesn't work, replace the solenoid.

8. Reconnect the vacuum lines and the coil after completing the test.

1976 EGR REMINDER LIGHT

NOTE: *This light is designed to remind the driver that regularly scheduled service is due; it does not mean that the EGR system is not working properly. This system is only used on cars without a catalytic converter.*

1. After checking the EGR system for proper operation, slide the rubber boot on the EGR reminder odometer up, out of the way.

2. Reset the odometer with a small screwdriver.

3. Slide the boot back down over the odometer. The light will come on again when the next 15,000 mile check-up is due.

Catalytic Converter

At the present time there is no known way to reliably test catalytic converter operation in the field. The only reliable test is a 12 hour and 40 minute "soak test" (CVS) which must be done in a laboratory.

An infrared HC/CO tester is not sensitive enough to measure the higher tailpipe emissions from a partially-failed converter. Thus, a bad converter may allow enough HC and CO emissions to escape, so that the car is not in compliance with Federal (or state) standards, but still will not cause the needle on the HC/CO tester to move off zero.

A completely failed converter should cause the tester to show a slight reading. As a result, it should be possible to spot one of these in the shop.

As long as the driver of the car avoids severe overheating or use of leaded fuels and the car has less than 50,000 miles on it, it is safe to assume that the converter is working.

REPLACING THE CONVERTER

The converter used is the monolithic (one-piece) type which cannot be refilled.

If the catalyst fails, it will be necessary to replace the entire converter assembly. To do so:

CAUTION: *Allow the converter assembly to cool completely before attempting to service it; catalyst temperatures can reach 1500°–1600° F.*

1. If a grass shield is used, remove the bolts

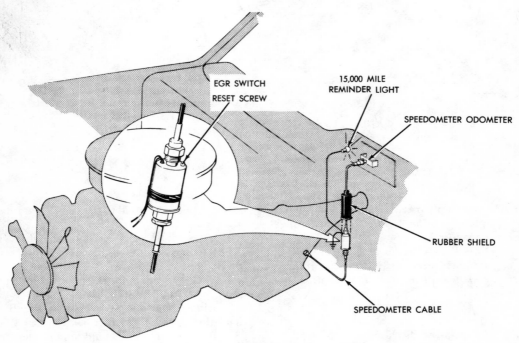

EGR reminder light

which secure it and lower the shield from underneath the vehicle.

2. Unbolt the converter assembly at the mounting flanges, just as you would a normal exhaust pipe from the manifold.

NOTE: *Support the exhaust pipe while the converter is removed.*

3. Replace the old converter with the new unit.

4. Remove the plastic plugs from the ends of the new converter (if used) and install it in the reverse order of removal, being sure to use all required gaskets to ensure a leak-free fit.

5. Install the grass shields.

Lean Burn System Testing and Service

Some of the procedures in this section refer to an adjustable timing light. This is also known as a spark advance tester, i.e., a device which will measure how much spark advance is present going from one point, a base figure, to another. Since precise timing is very important to the Lean Burn System, do not attempt to perform any engine tests calling for an adjustable timing light without the one. In places where a regular timing light can be used, it will be noted in the text.

TROUBLESHOOTING

1. Remove the coil wire and hold it about ¼ in. away from an engine ground, then have someone crank the engine while you check for spark.

2. If you have a good spark, slowly move the coil wire away from the engine and check for arcing at the coil while cranking.

3. If you have good spark and it is not arcing at the coil, check the rest of the parts of the ignition system, if they are alright, the problem is not in the ignition system. Check the "Troubleshooting" section following Chapter 2.

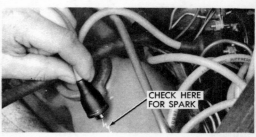

Checking for spark during cranking

Checking for arcing at coil tower

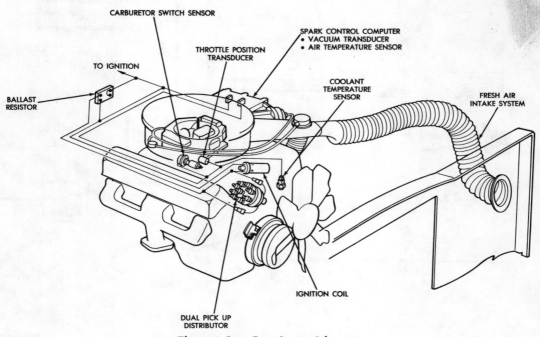

Electronic Lean Burn System Schematic

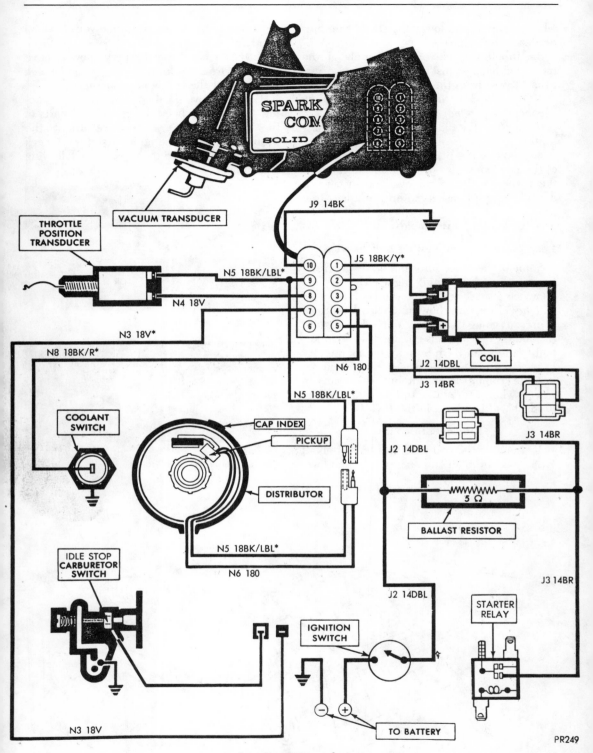

Lean Burn wiring schematic

Engine Not Running—Will Not Start

1. Check the battery specific gravity; it must be at least 1.220 to deliver the necessary voltage to fire the plugs.

2. Remove the terminal connector from the coolant switch and put a piece of paper or plastic between the curb idle adjusting screw and the carburetor switch. This is unnecessary if the screw and switch are not touching.

3. Connect the negative lead of a voltmeter to a good engine ground, turn the ignition switch to the "Run" position and measure the voltage at the carburetor switch terminal. If you receive a reading of more than five volts, go on to Step 7; if not, proceed to the next step.

4. Turn the ignition switch "Off" and disconnect the double terminal connector from the bottom of the Spark Control Computer. Turn the ignition switch back to the "Run" position and measure the voltage at terminal No. 2; if the voltage is not within 1 volt of the voltage you received in Step 3, check the wiring between terminal No. 2 and the ignition switch. If the voltage is correct, go on to the next step.

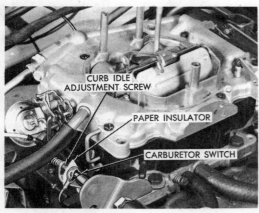

Preparing for power check

5. Turn the ignition switch "off" and disconnect the single connector from the bottom of the Spark Control Computer. Using an ohmmeter, check for continuity between terminal No. 7 and the carburetor switch terminal. There should be continuity present, if not, check the wiring.

6. Check for continuity between terminal No. 10 (double connector) and ground. If there is continuity, replace the Spark Control Computer; if not, check the wiring. If the engine still will not start, proceed to the next step.

7. Turn the ignition switch to the "Run" position and check for voltage at terminal No. 1 and ground of the double connector. If you received voltage within 1 volt of that recorded in Step 3, proceed to the next step. If you do not get the correct voltage, check the wiring between the connector and the ignition switch.

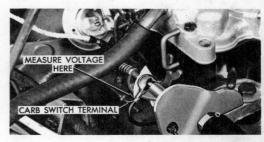

Power check

8. Turn the ignition switch "Off" and with an ohmmeter, measure resistance between terminals Nos. 5 and 9 of the dual connector. If you do not receive a reading of 150–900 ohms, disconnect the start pick-up leads at the distributor and measure the resistance going into the distributor. If you get a reading of 150–900 ohms here, the wiring between terminals Nos. 5 and 9 and the distributor is faulty. If you still do not get a reading between 150–900 ohms, replace the start pick-up. If you received the proper reading when you initially checked terminals Nos. 5 and 9, proceed to the next step.

9. Connect one lead of an ohmmeter to a good engine ground and with the other lead, check the continuity of both start pick-up leads going into the distributor. If there is not continuity, go on to the next step. If you do get a reading, replace the start pick-up.

10. Remove the distributor cap and check the air gap of the start pick-up coil. Adjust, if necessary, and proceed to the next step.

11. Replace the distributor cap, and start the engine; if it still will not start, replace the Spark Control Computer. If the engine still does not work, put the old one back and retrace your steps, paying close attention to any wiring which may be shorted.

Engine Running Badly (Run Pick-Up Tests)

1. Start the engine and let it run for a couple of minutes. Disconnect the start pick-

up lead. If the engine still runs, leave this test and go on to the "Start Timer Advance Test." If the engine died, proceed to Step 2.

Checking Run Pickup at distributor leads

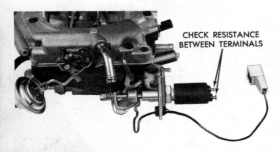

Checking for resistance at throttle transducer terminals

2. Disconnect the run pick-up coil from the distributor. Use an ohmmeter to check for continuity at each of the leads going into the distributor. If there is continuity shown, replace the pick-up coil and repeat Step 1. If you do not get a reading of continuity, proceed to the next step.

3. Remove the distributor cap, check the gap of the run pick-up and adjust it if necessary.

4. Reinstall the distributor cap, check the wiring, and try to start the engine. If it does not start, replace the computer and try again. If it still does not start, repeat the test paying close attention to all wiring connections.

START TIMER ADVANCE TEST

1. Hook up an *adjustable* timing light to the engine.

2. Have an assistant start the engine, place his foot firmly on the brake, then open and close the throttle, then place the transmission in Drive.

3. Locate the timing signal immediately after the transmission is put in Drive. The meter on the timing light should show about 5–9° advance. This advance should slowly decrease to the basic timing signal after about one minute. If it did not increase the 5–9° or return after one minute, replace the spark control computer. If it did operate properly, proceed to the next test.

THROTTLE ADVANCE TEST

Before performing this test, the throttle position transducer must be adjusted. The adjustments are as follows:

1. The air temperature sensor inside the spark control computer must be cool (below 135°). If the engine is at operating temperature, either turn it off and let it cool down or remove the top of the air cleaner and inject a spray coolant into the computer over the air temperature sensor for about 15 seconds. If Steps 2–5 take longer than 3–4 minutes, recool the sensor.

2. Start the engine and wait about 90 seconds, then connect a jumper wire between the carburetor switch terminal and ground.

3. Disconnect the electrical connector from the transducer and check the timing, adjusting if necessary. Reconnect the electrical connector to the transducer and recheck the timing.

4. If the timing is more than specified on the tune-up decal, loosen the transducer locknut and turn the transducer clockwise until it comes within limits, then turn it an additional ½ turn clockwise and tighten the locknut.

5. If the timing is at the specified limits, loosen the locknut and turn the transducer counterclockwise until the timing just begins to advance. At that point, turn the transducer ½ turn clockwise and tighten the locknut. After this step you are ready to begin the throttle advance test.

6. Turn the ignition switch "Off" and disconnect the single connector from the bottom of the spark control computer.

7. With an ohmmeter, measure the resistance between terminals Nos. 8 and 9 of the single connector. The measured resistance should be between 60–90 ohms. If it is, go on to the next step, if not, remove the connector from the throttle position transducer and measure the resistance at the transducer terminals. If you now get a reading of 60–90 ohms, check the wiring between the computer terminals and the transducer terminal. If you do

not get the 60–90 reading, replace the transducer and proceed to the next step.

8. Reconnect the wiring and turn the switch to the "Run" position without starting the engine. Hook up a voltmeter, negative lead to an engine ground, and touch the positive lead to one terminal of the transducer while opening and closing the throttle all the way. Do the same thing to the other terminal of the transducer. Both terminals should show a 2 volt change when opening and closing the throttle. If not proceed to the next step.

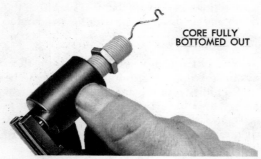

CORE FULLY
BOTTOMED OUT

Checking with test transducer

9. Position the throttle linkage on the fast idle cam and ground the carb switch with a jumper wire. Disconnect the wiring connector from the transducer and connect it to a transducer that you know is good.

10. Move the core of the transducer all the way in, start the engine, wait about 90 seconds, and then move the core out about an inch.

11. Adjust the timing light so that it registers the basic timing signal. The timing light should show the additional amount of advance as given in the "Transducer Advance Specifications" chart in this section. If it is within the specifications, move the core back into the transducer, and the timing should go back to the original position. If the timing did advance and return, go on to the next step. If it did not advance and/or return, replace the spark control computer and try this test over again. If it still fails, replace the transducer.

12. Reset the timing light meter, and have an assistant move the transducer core in and out 5–6 times quickly. The timing should advance 7–12° for about a second and then return to the base figure. If it did not, replace the spark control computer. If you did not get the 2 volt change in reading in Step 8, you should now replace the transducer since you

have proved that the spark control computer is not causing it to check out faulty.

13. Remove the test transducer (from Step 9), and reconnect all wiring.

VACUUM ADVANCE TEST (VACUUM TRANSDUCER)

1. Hook up an adjustable timing light.

2. Turn the ignition switch to the "Run" position, but do not start the engine. Disconnect the idle stop solenoid wire and the wiring connector from the coolant switch. Push the solenoid plunger in all the way, and while holding the throttle linkage open, reconnect the solenoid wire. The solenoid plunger should pop out and when the throttle linkage is released, it should also hold the linkage in place. If it does not, replace the idle stop solenoid.

3. Start the engine and let it warm up; make sure that the transmission is in Neutral and the parking brake is on.

4. Place a small piece of plastic or paper between the carburetor switch and the curb idle adjusting screw; if the screw is not touching the switch, make sure that the fast idle cam is not on or binding; the linkage is not binding, or the throttle stop screw is not overadjusted. Adjust the timing light for the basic timing figure. The meter of the timing light should show 2–5° advance with a minimum of 16 in. of vacuum at the vacuum transducer (checked with a vacuum gauge). If this advance is not present, replace the spark control computer and try the test again. If the advance is present, let the engine run for about 6–9 minutes, then go on to the next step.

5. After the 6–9 minute waiting period, adjust the timing light so that it registers the basic timing figure. The timing light meter should now register 32–35° of advance. If the advance is not shown, replace the spark control computer and repeat the test; if it is shown, proceed to Step 6.

6. Remove the insulator (paper or plastic) which was installed in Step 4; the timing should return to its base setting. If it does not, make sure that the curb idle adjusting screw is not touching the carburetor switch. If that is alright, turn the engine off and check the wire between terminal No. 7 of the single connector (from the bottom of the spark control computer), and the carburetor switch terminal for a bad connection. If it turns out alright, and the timing still will not return to its base setting, replace the spark control computer.

COOLANT SWITCH TEST

1. Connect one lead of the ohmmeter to a good engine ground, the other to the black wire with a tracer in it. Disregard the orange wire if there is one on the switch.

2. If the engine is cold (below 150°), there should be continuity present in the switch. With the thermostat open, and the engine warmed up, there should be no continuity. If either of the conditions in this step are not met, replace the switch.

LEAN BURN TIMING

This procedure is to set the basic timing signal as shown on the engine tune-up decal in the engine compartment.

1. Connect a jumper wire between the carburetor switch terminal and the ground. Connect a standard timing light to the No. 1 cylinder.

2. Block the wheels and set the parking brake. If the car has an automatic release type parking brake, remove and plug the vacuum line which controls it from the fitting on the rear of the engine.

3. Start and warm the engine up; raise engine speed above 1,500 rpm for a second, then drop the speed and let it idle for a minute or two.

4. With the engine idling at the point specified on the tune-up decal with the transmission in Drive, adjust the timing to the figure given on the tune-up decal.

IDLE SPEED AND MIXTURE

1. Follow the first three steps under "Lean Burn Timing," then insert an exhaust gas analyzer into the tailpipe.

2. Place the transmission in Drive, the air conditioning and headlights off. Adjust the idle speed to the specification shown on the tune-up decal by turning the idle solenoid speed screw.

3. Adjust the carbon monoxide level to 0.1% with the mixture screws while trying to keep hydrocarbons to a minimum and the idle speed to specification. Turn the screws alternately over their range to coordinate all three factors.

4. Place the transmission in Neutral; disconnect the wire at the idle stop solenoid and adjust the curb idle speed screw to obtain 650 rpm. Reconnect the wire.

5. Remove the air cleaner cover and lift and support the air cleaner assembly high enough to gain access to the fast idle adjustment screw.

6. Place the fast idle speed screw on the highest step of the cam and adjust the idle speed to the specification shown on the tune-up decal.

7. Drop the idle back down to the curb idle position and turn the ignition switch off. Reconnect any hoses or electrical connections taken off in the procedure.

8. If the procedure has to be performed a second time, make sure that you start from the beginning or the readings will be inaccurate.

REMOVAL AND OVERHAUL

None of the components of the Lean Burn System (except the carburetor), are able to be disassembled and repaired. When one part is known to be defective, it is replaced.

The Spark Control Computer is secured by mounting screws inside the air cleaner. To remove the Throttle Position Transducer, loosen the locknut and unscrew it from the mounting bracket, then unsnap the core from the carburetor linkage.

Transducer Advance Specifications

Core Moved Out 1 in.	7–12° @ 75° F
	4–7° @ 104° F
Moved 5–6 Times	7–12°
	(One second duration each time)

Pick-Up Gaps

Start Pick-up	(set to)	0.008 in.
	(check at)	0.010 in.
Run Pick-Up	(set to)	0.012 in.
	(check at)	0.014 in.

Idle Enrichment System Test

The purpose of the idle enrichment system is to reduce cold engine stalling by use of a metering system related to the basic carburetor instead of the choke. The system enriches carburetor mixtures in the curb idle and fast idle area.

A small vacuum-controlled diaphragm mounted near the top of the carburetor controls idle system air. When control vacuum is applied to the diaphragm, idle system air is reduced. Air losses strengthen the small vacuum signal within the idle system and fuel flow increases. As a result of more fuel and less air, the engine will idle better when cold.

To test the system, proceed as follows:

1. Run the engine to normal operating temperatures.

2. Remove the air cleaner, but *do not* cap any of the vacuum fittings opened by hose removal. The vacuum leakage is needed for the test.

3. Disconnect the hose to the idle enrichment diaphragm at the plastic connector. Remove the plastic connector from the carburetor hose.

4. With the engine running, place the fast idle screw on the lowest step of the fast idle cam.

5. Connect three or four feet of hose to the enrichment diaphragm hose with a suitable connector.

6. Use a hand vacuum pump and apply vacuum to the hose. Listen for a change in engine speed. If the engine speed can be controlled by vacuum, then the system is OK. If the speed cannot be controlled, replace the valve assembly (Holley carburetors) or proceed to the next step (Carter carburetors).

7. Place a finger over the air inlet passage and listen for an engine speed change. If you can control engine speed this way, the diaphragm is leaking or the air valve is stuck open. If speed cannot be controlled this way, the air valve is stuck closed. In either case, clean the air valve, and repeat step six. If speed control is still absent, replace the diaphragm.

Coolant Controlled Engine Vacuum Switch Test

The Cooland Controlled Engine Vacuum Switch (CCEVS) is used to improve hot drive ability by preventing the operation of the idle enrichment system (if equipped), power valve heat system (if equipped), and air injection switching system (if equipped) after the coolant temperature reaches a predetermined level. The CCEVS valve is mounted in the cylinder head on six-cylinder engines and in the intake manifold on V8 engines.

To test the system, proceed as follows:

1. First make sure the vacuum hoses are routed correctly and the engine coolant level is correct.

2. Disconnect the molded connector from

Coolant control engine vacuum switch (CCEVS)

the valve. Attach a ⅛ in. hose to the bottom port on the valve.

3. Run the engine to normal operating temperature.

4. With the top tank warm to the touch (but no warmer than 75 F.), blow through the hose. If it is not possible to blow through the valve, then it is defective and must be replaced.

5. Attach a vacuum pump to the bottom port of the valve. Apply 10 in. of vacuum. If the vacuum level drops more than one inch in 15 seconds, replace the valve.

Fuel System

FUEL PUMP

Removal and Installation

1. Disconnect the fuel inlet and outlet lines. Plug the fuel inlet line to prevent emptying the fuel tank.

2. Remove the two fuel pump securing bolts.

3. Remove the fuel pump from the car.

4. Reverse the above steps to install.

Testing

Fuel pump output can be tested by rigging the pump to discharge into a container. It should pump one quart of fuel in a minute or less, with the engine running at idle speed.

CAUTION: *Use a big container so that it doesn't overflow. Have an assistant ready to stop the engine. Be extremely careful not to spill fuel on hot engine parts.*

CARBURETORS

The Holley 1945 one barrel carburetor is used on six-cylinder engines. The Carter BBD

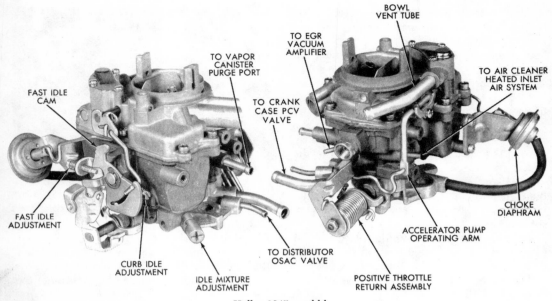

Holley 1945 one-bbl

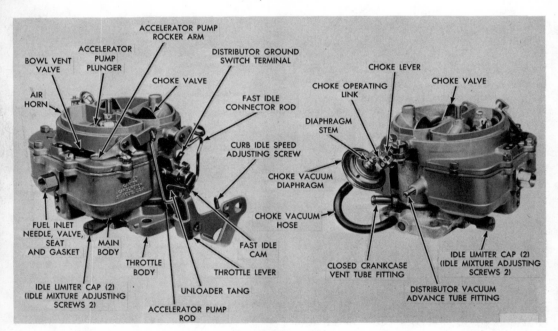

Carter BBD two bbl

two barrel is used on the "Super" six cylinder engine and on the 318 cu. in. V8. The Holley 2245 two barrel carburetor is used on the 360 V8. Both the 318 and 360 four barrel engines use the Carter Thermo-Quad carburetor.

Removal and Installation

1. Remove the air cleaner.
2. Disconnect the fuel and vacuum lines.

It might be a good idea to tag them to avoid confusion when the time comes to put them back.

3. Disconnect the choke rod.
4. Disconnect the accelerator linkage.
5. Disconnect the automatic transmission linkage.
6. Unbolt and remove the carburetor.
7. Remove the base gasket.

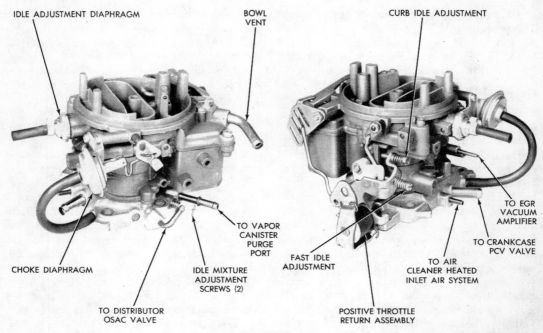

Holley 2245 two-bbl

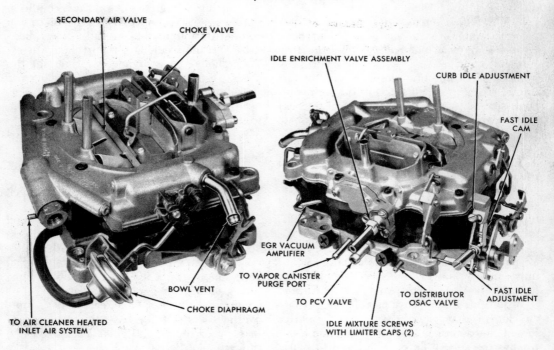

Carter Thermo-Quad Carburetor

8. Before installation, make sure that the carburetor and manifold sealing surfaces are clean.

9. Install a new carburetor base gasket, making sure that the "top front" marking is correctly located on six-cylinder engines.

10. Install the carburetor and start the fuel and vacuum lines.

11. Bolt down the carburetor evenly.

12. Tighten the fuel and vacuum lines.

13. Connect the accelerator and automatic transmission linkage. If the transmission link-

age was disturbed, it will have to be adjusted. The procedure is in this Chapter.

14. Connect the choke rod.

15. Install the air cleaner. Adjust the idle speed and mixture as described in Chapter 2.

Overhaul

Whenever wear or dirt causes a carburetor to perform poorly, there are two possible solutions to the problem. The simplest is to trade in the old unit for a rebuilt one. The other, cheaper alternative is to buy an overhaul kit and rebuild the original unit. Some of the better overhaul kits contain complete step-by-step instructions along with exploded views and gauges. Other kits, intended for the professional, have only a few general overhaul hints. The second type can be confusing to the novice, especially since a kit may have extra parts so that one kit can cover several variations of the same carburetor. In any event, it is not a good idea to dismantle any carburetor without at least replacing all the gaskets. The carburetor adjustments should all be checked during or after overhaul.

NOTE: *Before you tear off to the parts store for a rebuilding kit, make sure that you know what make and model your carburetor is.*

Efficient carburetion depends greatly on careful cleaning and inspection during overhaul, since dirt, gum, water, or varnish in or on the carburetor parts are often responsible for poor performance.

Overhual a carburetor in a clean, dust-free area. Carefully disassemble the carburetor, referring often to illustrations. Keep all similar and look-alike parts segregated during disassembly and cleaning to avoid accidental interchange during assembly. Make a note of all jet sizes.

When the carburetor is disassembled, wash all parts (except diaphragms, electric choke units, pump plunger, and any other plastic, leather, fiber, or rubber parts) in clean carburetor solvent. Do not leave parts in the solvent any longer than is necessary to sufficiently loosen the deposits. Excessive cleaning may remove the special finish from the float bowl and choke valve bodies, leaving these parts unfit for service. Rinse all parts in clean solvent and blow them dry with compressed air or allow them to air dry. Wipe clean all cork, plastic, leather, and fiber parts with a clean, lint-free cloth.

Blow out all passages and jets with compressed air and be sure that there are no re-

strictions or blockages. Never use wire or similar tools to clean jets, fuel passages, or air bleeds. Clean all jets and valves separately to avoid accidental interchange.

Check all parts for wear or damage. If wear or damage is found, replace the defective parts. Especially check the following:

1. Check the float needle and seat for wear. If wear is found, replace the complete assembly.

2. Check the float hinge pin for wear and the float(s) for dents or distortion. Replace the float if fuel has leaked into it.

3. Check the throttle and choke shaft bores for wear or an out-of-round condition. Damage or wear to the throttle arm, shaft, or shaft bore will often require replacement of the throttle body. These parts require a close tolerance of fit; wear may allow air leakage, which could affect starting and idling.

NOTE: *Throttle shafts and bushings are not included in overhaul kits. They can be purchased separately.*

4. Inspect the idle mixture adjusting needles for burrs or grooves. Any such condition requires replacement of the needle, since you will not be able to obtain a satisfactory idle.

5. Test the accelerator pump check valves. They should pass air one way but not the other. Test for proper seating by blowing and sucking on the valve. Replace the valve as necessary. If the valve is satisfactory, wash the valve again to remove breath moisture.

6. Check the bowl cover for warped surfaces with a straightedge.

7. Closely inspect the valves and seats for wear and damage, replacing as necessary.

8. After the carburetor is assembled, check the choke valve for freedom of operation.

Carburetor overhaul kits are recommended for each overhaul. These kits contain all gaskets and new parts to replace those that deteriorate most rapidly. Failure to replace all parts supplied with the kit (especially gaskets) can result in poor performance later.

Some carburetor manufacturers supply overhaul kits of three basic types: minor repair; major repair; and gasket kits. Basically, they contain the following:

Minor Repair Kits:
    All gaskets
    Float needle valve
    All diaphragms
    Spring for the pump diaphragm
Major repair kits:
    All jets and gaskets
    All diaphragms

Float needle valve
Volume control screw
Pump ball valve
Float
Some cover hold-down screws and washers
Gasket Kits:
All gaskets

After cleaning and checking all components, reassemble the carburetor, using new parts and referring to illustrations. When reassembling, make sure that all screws and jets are tight in their seats, but do not overtighten as the tips will be distorted. Tighten all screws gradually, in rotation. Do not tighten needle valves into their seats; uneven jetting will result. Always use new gaskets. Be sure to adjust the float level when reassembling.

Throttle and Automatic Transmission Linkage Adjustments

Throttle linkage adjustments are rarely required unless the transmission linkage has been disturbed. However, it is a good idea to check that the throttle valve(s) open all the way when the accelerator pedal is held all the way down. This is occasionally the source of poor performance on new cars.

ALL AUTOMATIC TRANSMISSION

1. Lubricate the friction points of the linkage.

2. Disconnect the choke at the carburetor or otherwise make sure that the throttle is off the fast idle cam.

3. Loosen the adjustment swivel lockscrew at the transmission.

4. The swivel must be free to slide along the flat end of the throttle rod.

5. Hold the transmission lever firmly forward against its internal stop and tighten the swivel lockscrew. The adjustment is completed and linkage slack removed by the preload spring.

6. Pull the transmission throttle rod slowly back and release it. It should go back forward slowly.

7. Loosen the cable clamp nut. Adjust the position of the outer cable in the clamp so that all slack is removed. Move the outer cable away from the carburetor to do this. Move the outer cable back ¼ in. to allow slack at idle.

ALL MANUAL TRANSMISSION

1. Lubricate the friction points of the throttle linkage.

2. Disconnect the choke at the carburetor and make sure that the throttle is off the fast idle cam.

3. Loosen the cable clamp nut. Adjust the cable by moving the cable housing so that there is about ¼ in. of slack in the cable at idle.

4. Tighten the cable clamp nut.

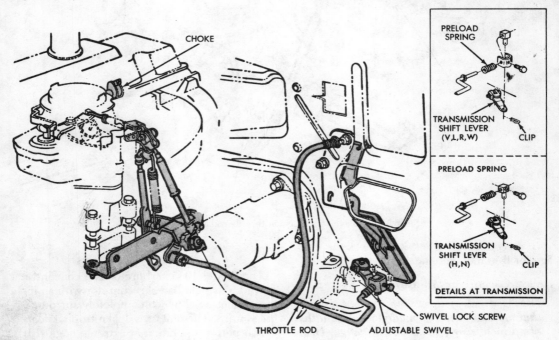

Six cylinder automatic transmission throttle rod adjustment

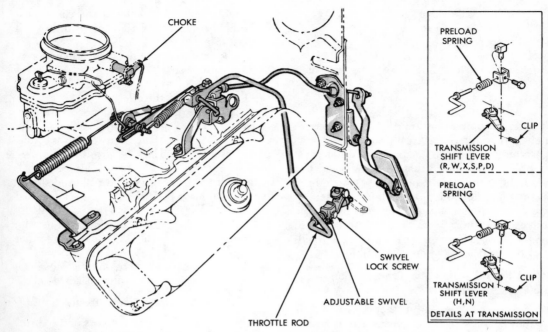

V8 automatic transmission throttle rod adjustment

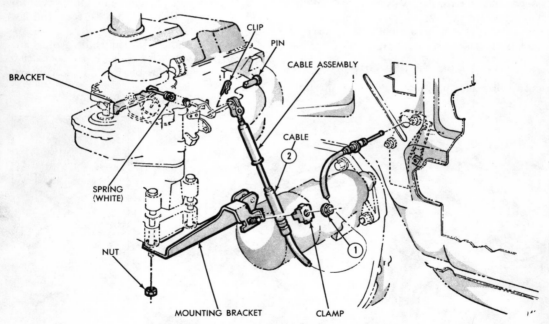

Six cylinder manual transmission throttle rod adjustment

5. Reconnect the choke and check the linkage for free movement.

Holley Carburetor Adjustments

NOTE: *Most of these adjustments require that measurements be made in thousandths of an inch, using some sort of gauge. Drill bits are ideal for this purpose.*

MODEL 1945

The model 1945 carburetor is a concentric downdraft single-barrel carburetor with an internal float bowl which completely surrounds the venturi. The unit uses dual nitrophyl floats which permit operation at extreme angles. It is used on six-cylinder engines.

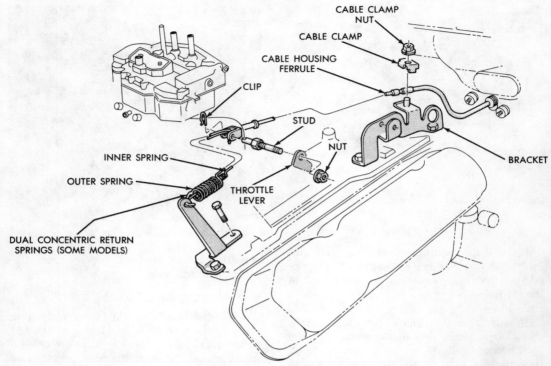

V8 manual transmission throttle rod adjustment

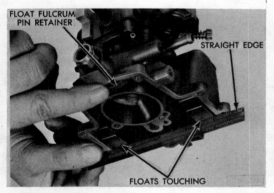

Holley 1945—float level check

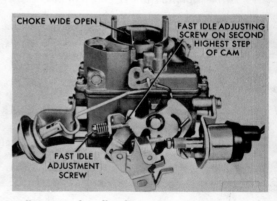

Holley 1945—fast idle adjustment

FLOAT LEVEL

1. Remove the float bowl cover and invert the bowl. Hold the retaining spring in place.

2. Place a straightedge across the surface of the bowl. It should just clear the toes of the floats by the specified measurement.

3. If adjustment is necessary, bend the float tang to obtain the correct adjustment.

FAST IDLE

1. Remove the air cleaner and disconnect the vacuum lines to the heated air control and the OSAC (Orifice Spark Advance Control)

valve. If there is no OSAC valve, disconnect the hose to the distributor and the EGR hose. Cap all carburetor vacuum fittings.

2. With the engine off, transmission in Neutral and the parking brake set, open the throttle and close the choke.

3. Close the throttle. This will place the fast idle speed screw on the highest step.

4. Move the fast idle cam until the screw drops to the second highest speed step.

5. Start the engine and stabilize the engine speed. Rotate the idle speed screw to obtain the specified setting. See "Specifications" chart.

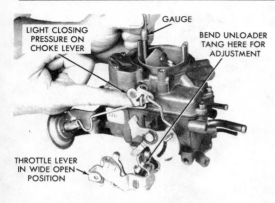

Holley 1945—choke unloader adjustment

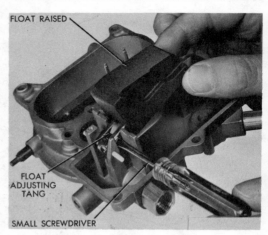

Holley 2245—float level adjustment

CHOKE UNLOADER

1. Hold the throttle valves wide-open and insert the specified gauge between the upper edge of the choke valve and the inner wall of the air horn.

2. Place slight pressure against the control lever and attempt to remove the gauge. There should be a slight drag as the gauge is being withdrawn. If adjustment is necessary, bend the unloader tang on the throttle lever until the correct opening has been obtained.

Model 2245

The model 2245 carburetor is a two-barrel unit used on 360 cubic inch engines. The carburetor uses four fuel metering systems. The Idle and Idle Enrichment System provides the correct mixture for idle and low-speed performance; the Accelerator Pump System furnishes additional fuel during acceleration; the Main Metering System gives an economical mixture for normal cruising conditions; and the Power Enrichment System enriches the mixture when high power output is desired.

FLOAT LEVEL

1. Invert the air horn so that the weight of the float is forcing the metering needle against its seat.

2. Measure the distance from the top of the float and the float stop. The clearance should be the same as given in the "Specifications" chart. Make certain that the gauge is level when making the measurement.

3. If adjustment is necessary, bend the float adjusting tab toward or away from the needle. A narrow-bladed screwdriver may be used to bend the tab.

4. Check the float drop by holding the air horn upright. The bottom edge of the float should be parallel to the underside of the air horn. If an adjustment is necessary, bend the tang on the float arm.

FAST IDLE CAM POSITION

1. Position the fast idle speed adjusting screw on the second highest notch on the fast idle cam. Move the choke valve toward the closed position by applying light pressure on the choke shaft lever.

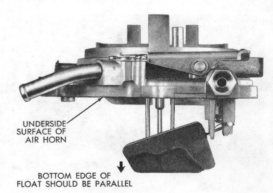

Holley 2245—checking float drop

2. Insert the correct gauge (see "Specifications" chart) between the top of the choke valve and the wall of the air horn. An adjustment will be necessary if there is not a slight drag when the gauge is removed.

3. If an adjustment is necessary, bend the fast idle connector rod at the angle.

VACUUM KICK

1. The adjustment must be made with some type of vacuum source. If the adjustment is made with the engine running, disconnect the fast idle linkage to allow the choke to close to the kick position with the engine at

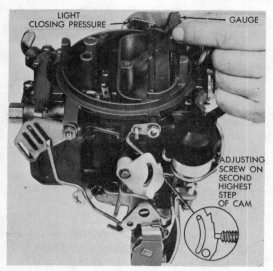

Holley 2245—fast idle cam position adjustment

curb idle. If an auxiliary vacuum source is to be used, open the throttle valves and move the choke to the closed position. Release the throttle first and then the choke.

2. If an auxiliary vacuum source is used, disconnect the vacuum hose from the carburetor and connect it to the hose from the vacuum supply with a small length of extra hose. Apply a vacuum of 15 in. or more of mercury.

3. Insert the correct gauge (see "Specifications" chart) between the top of the choke valve and the wall of the air horn. Apply pressure to the choke rod without distorting the diaphragm link. The cylindrical stem of the diaphragm will extend as the internal spring is compressed. This spring must be fully compressed for proper measurement of the vacuum kick adjustment.

4. If a slight drag is not felt when the gauge is removed, adjustment is necessary. Adjust the diaphragm link to obtain the correct choke

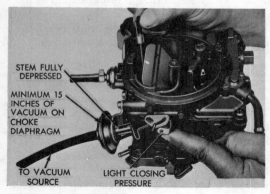

Holley 2245—Vacuum kick adjustment

valve opening. Adjustments can be made by carefully opening or closing the U-bend in the link.

CAUTION: *Do not twist or bend the diaphragm.*

5. Connect the vacuum hose to the correct carburetor fitting. Replace the linkage.

6. Make the following check. With no vacuum source attached to the diaphragm, the choke valve should move freely between open and closed positions. If the movement is not free, examine the linkage for misalignment or interferences caused by the bending operation.

CHOKE UNLOADER (WIDE OPEN KICK)

1. Place the throttle valves in the wide-open position and insert the proper gauge (see "Specifications" chart) between the upper edge of the choke valve and the inner wall of the air horn.

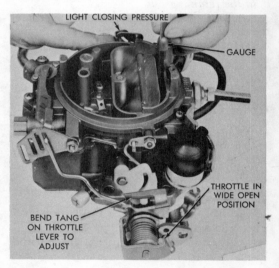

Holley 2245—Choke unloader adjustment

2. While holding pressure on the shaft lever, a slight drag should be felt as the gauge is removed.

3. If an adjustment is necessary, bend the unloader tang on the throttle lever.

ACCELERATOR PUMP

1. Back off the curb idle adjusting screw and open the choke valve so that the fast idle cam allows the throttle valves to be completely seated in their bores.

NOTE: *Make certain that the pump connector rod is placed in the correct slot of the accelerator pump rocker arm. On manual*

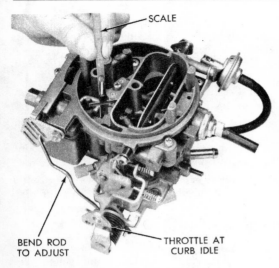

Holley 2245—accelerator pump adjustment

transmission models, it is the first slot next to the retaining nut.

2. Close the throttle valves and measure the distance from the top of the air horn to the end of the plunger shaft. See "Specifications" chart.

3. If adjustment is needed, bend the pump operating rod at its loop.

Carter Carburetor Adjustments

NOTE: *Most of these adjustments require that measurements be made in thousandths of an inch, using some sort of gauge. Drill bits are ideal for this purpose.*

MODEL BBD

The BBD carburetor is a two-barrel unit. This is sometimes called a Ball & Ball carburetor. It is used on 318 cu. in. V8s and the "Super" six cylinder.

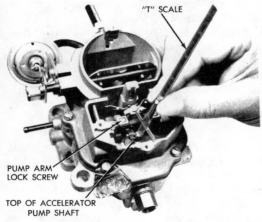

Carter BBD—accelerator pump stroke adjustment

ACCELERATOR PUMP

1. Back off the idle adjusting screw. Open the choke valve so that the fast idle cam allows the throttle valves to close. Be sure that the acclerator pump "S" link is in the outer hole of the pump arm.

2. With the throttle valves closed tightly, measure the distance between the top of the air horn and the top of the pump plunger shaft. If the dimension is not as specified, loosen the pump arm adjusting lockscrew (near the plunger shaft) and rotate the sleeve to obtain the correct dimension.

FAST IDLE CAM POSITION

1. With the fast idle speed adjusting screw contacting the second highest speed step on the fast idle cam, move the choke valve toward the closed position with light pressure on the choke shaft lever.

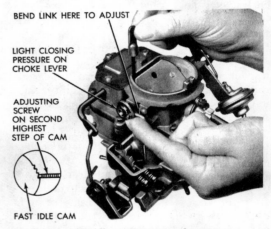

Carter BBD—fast idle cam position adjustment

2. Insert the specified drill (refer to "Specifications"), between the choke valve and the wall of the air horn. An adjustment will be necessary if a slight drag is not obtained as the drill is being removed.

3. If an adjustment is required, bend the fast idle connector rod at the lower angle.

CHOKE UNLOADER (WIDE OPEN KICK)

1. Hold the throttle valves in the wide open position. Insert the specified drill (see "Specifications") between the upper edge of the choke valve and the inner wall of the air horn.

2. With a finger lightly pressing against the choke lever, a slight drag should be felt as the drill is being withdrawn. If an adjustment is necessary, bend the unloader tang on the

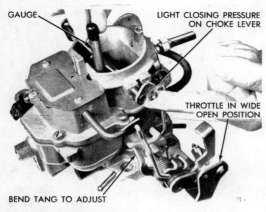

Carter BBD—choke unloader adjustment

throttle lever until the correct opening has been obtained.

FAST IDLE SPEED

1. Disconnect and plug the connections for the heated air control and OSAC valve or distributor. With the engine off and the transmission in Park or Neutral position, open the throttle slightly.

2. Close the choke valve until the fast idle screw can be positioned on the highest speed step of the fast idle cam.

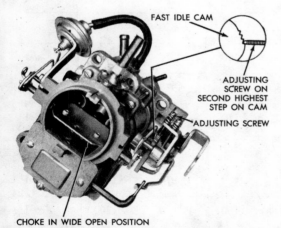

Carter BBD—fast idle speed adjustment

3. Start the engine and let the idle stabilize. Turn the fast idle speed screw in or out to obtain the specified speed.

4. Stopping the engine between adjustments is not necessary. However, reposition the fast idle speed screw on the cam after each speed adjustment to provide the correct throttle closing torque.

VACUUM KICK

1. If the adjustment is to be made with the engine running, disconnect the fast idle linkage to allow the choke to close to the kick position with engine at curb idle. If an auxiliary vacuum source is to be used, open the throttle valves (engine not running) and move the choke to the closed position. Release the throttle first, then release the choke.

2. When using an auxiliary vacuum source, disconnect the vacuum hose from the carburetor and connect it to the hose from the vacuum supply with a small length of tube to act as a fitting. Removal of the hose from the diaphragm may require sufficient force to damage the diaphragm. Apply a vacuum of 15 or more in. of mercury.

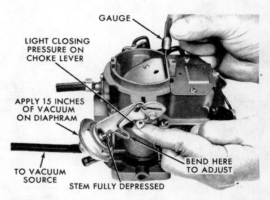

Carter BBD—vacuum kick adjustment

3. Insert the specified drill (refer to "Specifications") between the choke valve and the upper wall of the air horn. Apply sufficient closing pressure on the lever to which the choke rod attaches to provide a minimum choke valve opening without distortion of the diaphragm link. Note that the cylindrical stem of the diaphragm will extend as the internal spring is compressed. This spring must be fully compressed for proper measurement of the vacuum kick of adjustment.

4. An adjustment will be necessary if a slight drag is not obtained as the drill is being removed. Shorten or lengthen the diaphragm link to obtain the correct choke opening. Length changes should be made carefully by bending the U-bend provided in the diaphragm link.

CAUTION: *Do not apply twisting or bending force to the diaphragm.*

5. Reinstall the vacuum hose on the correct carburetor fitting. Return the fast idle linkage

to its original condition if it was disturbed, as suggested in Step 1.

6. Make the following check: With no vacuum applied to the diaphragm, the choke valve should move freely between the open and closed positions. If its movement is not free, examine the linkage for misalignment or interference caused by the bending operation. Repeat the adjustment if necessary to provide proper link operation.

FLOAT LEVEL

1. Invert the carburetor so that the weight of the floats is the only force on the needle and seat.

2. Use a T-scale to check the float level. Measure the area from the surface of the fuel bowl to the crown of each float at center.

3. To adjust, hold the floats on the bottom

of the bowl and bend the float lip to give the specified dimension.

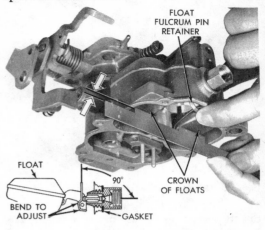

Carter BBD—checking float setting

Carter BBD Specifications

Year	Carburetor Number	Float Level (in.)	Accelerator Pump Travel (in.)	Choke Unloader (in.)	Choke Vacuum Kick (in.)	Fast Idle Cam Position (in.)	Fast Idle Speed (rpm)	Choke Setting
1976	8069S	¼	0.500	.310	.070	.070	1200	Fixed
	8070S	¼	0.500	.310	.110	.070	1500	Fixed
	8071S	¼	0.500	.280	.130	.070	1500	Fixed
	8072S	¼	0.500	.310	.070	.070	1500	Fixed
	8077S	¼	0.500	.280	.110	.070	1250	Fixed
1977	8087S	¼	$\frac{15}{32}$	.280	.100	.070	1600	Fixed
	8089S	¼	$\frac{15}{32}$	.280	.130	.070	1600	Fixed
	8090S	¼	$\frac{15}{32}$	.280	.130	.070	1700	Fixed
	8093S	¼	$\frac{15}{32}$	.310	.130	.070	1400	Fixed
	8094S	¼	$\frac{15}{32}$	.310	.070	.070	1400	Fixed
	8096S	¼	$\frac{15}{32}$	.310	.110	.070	1500	Fixed
	8126S	¼	$\frac{15}{32}$	.310	.110	.070	1500	Fixed
	8127S	¼	$\frac{15}{32}$	.280	.110	.070	1500	Fixed

Carter BBD Specifications (cont.)

Year	Carburetor Number	Float Level (in.)	Accelerator Pump Travel (in.)	Choke Unloader (in.)	Choke Vacuum Kick (in.)	Fast Idle Cam Position (in.)	Fast Idle Speed (rpm)	Choke Setting
1978	8137S	¼	½	.280	.100	.070	1600	Fixed
	8177S	¼	½	.280	.100	.070	1600	Fixed
	8136S	¼	½	.280	.110	.070	1500	Fixed
	8175S	¼	½	.280	.160	.070	1400	Fixed
	8143S	¼	½	.280	.150	.070	1500	Fixed

Holley 1945 Specifications

Year	Carburetor Number	Float Level (in.) Dry Setting	Bowl Vent (in.)	Accelerator Pump Travel (in.)	Choke Unloader (in.)	Vacuum Kick (in.)	Fast Idle Cam (in.)	Fast Idle Speed (rpm)	Choke Setting
1976	R-7356A	Flush with top of bowl cover gasket (all models)	1/16	2 7/32	.250	.110	.080	1600	Fixed
	R-7357A		1/16	2 21/32	.250	.100	.080	1700	Fixed
	R-7360A		——	2 7/32	.250	.110	.080	1600	Fixed
	R-7361A		——	2 21/32	.250	.100	.080	1700	Fixed
	R-7362A		——	2 7/32	.250	.110	.080	1600	Fixed
	R-7363A		——	2 21/32	.250	.100	.080	1700	Fixed
1977	R-7632A	Flush with top of bowl cover gasket (all models)	1/16	2 7/32	.250	.110	.080	1400	Fixed
	R-7633A		1/16	2 21/64	.250	.110	.080	1700	Fixed
	R-7635A		——	2 21/64	.250	.110	.080	1700	Fixed
	R-7744A		1/16	2 21/64	.250	.130	.080	1700	Fixed
	R-7745A		1/16	2 7/32	.250	.150	.080	1600	Fixed
	R-7746A		1/16	2 21/64	.250	.110	.080	1700	Fixed

Holley 1945 Specifications (cont.)

Year	Carbu- retor Number	Float Level (in.) Dry Setting	Bowl Vent (in.)	Accelerator Pump Travel (in.)	Choke Unloader (in.)	Vacuum Kick (in.)	Fast Idle Cam (in.)	Fast Idle Speed (rpm)	Choke Setting
1977	R-7764A		$\frac{1}{16}$	$2\frac{7}{32}$	.250	.110	.080	1700	Fixed
	R-7765A		$\frac{1}{16}$	$2\frac{21}{64}$	.250	.110	.080	1700	Fixed
1978	R-7988A	Flush with top of bowl cover gasket (all models)	$\frac{1}{16}$	$2\frac{7}{32}$	.250	.110	.080	1400	Fixed
	R-7989A		$\frac{1}{16}$	$2\frac{21}{64}$	.250	.110	.080	1600	Fixed
	R-8394A		$\frac{1}{16}$	$2\frac{21}{64}$	.250	.110	.080	1700	Fixed
	R-8010A		$\frac{1}{16}$	$2\frac{21}{64}$	.250	.130	.080	1500	Fixed
	R-8008A		$\frac{1}{16}$	$2\frac{21}{64}$	.250	.110	.080	1700	Fixed

Holley 2245 Specifications

Year	Carbu- retor Number	Float Level (in.)	Bowl Vent (in.)	Accelerator Pump Travel (in.)	Choke Unloader (in.)	Vacuum Kick (in.)	Fast Idle Cam (in.)	Fast Idle Speed (rpm)	Choke Setting
1976	R-7364A	$\frac{3}{16}$	.025	$\frac{5}{16}$	.170	.150	.110	1600	Fixed
	R-7366A	$\frac{3}{16}$	.025	$\frac{5}{16}$	.170	.150	.110	1600	Fixed
1977	R-7671A	$\frac{3}{16}$	.250	$\frac{5}{16}$	.170	.110	.110	1700	Fixed
1978	R-7991A	$\frac{3}{16}$	.025	$\frac{17}{64}$	.170	.110	.110	1600	Fixed
	R-8326A	$\frac{3}{16}$	.025	$\frac{17}{64}$	.170	.110	.110	1600	Fixed

Carter Thermo-Quad Specifications

Year	Carburetor Number	Float Level (in.)	Bowl Vent (in.)	Accelerator Pump Travel (in.)	Choke Unloader (in.)	Vacuum Kick (in.)	Fast Idle Cam (in.)	Fast Idle Speed (rmp)	Choke Setting
1978	TQ-9147S	$\frac{29}{32}$	——	$\frac{31}{64}$	.310	.100	.100	1600	Fixed
	TQ-9137S	$\frac{29}{32}$	$1\frac{3}{16}$	$\frac{31}{64}$	.310	.100	.100	1600	Fixed
	TQ-9134S	$\frac{29}{32}$	——	$\frac{31}{64}$	.310	.100	.100	1500	Fixed
	TQ-9104S	$\frac{29}{32}$	——	$\frac{31}{64}$	.310	.150	.100	1500	Fixed

Chapter 5

Chassis Electrical

Heater

On non-air conditioned cars, it is necessary to remove the heater assembly to remove either the blower motor or the heater core. Use the following procedure.

Removal and Installation

CAUTION: *This is a major disassembly ope, ation.*

1. Disconnect the battery ground cable and drain the coolant.

2. Disconnect the heater hoses at the firewall. Plug the core tubes to prevent spillage.

3. Slide the front seat all the way back.

4. Remove the core tube firewall seals and retainer.

5. Remove the instrument cluster bezel by removing the four screws along the lower edge, placing the automatic transmission selector in 1, and pulling out to detach the upper edge clips.

6. Remove the instrument panel upper cover by removing the mounting screws at the top inner surface of the glove box, at the brow above the instrument cluster, at the left end cap mounting, at the right side of the pad brow, and in the defroster outlets.

7. Remove the steering column cover (the instrument panel piece under the column).

8. Remove the right intermediate side

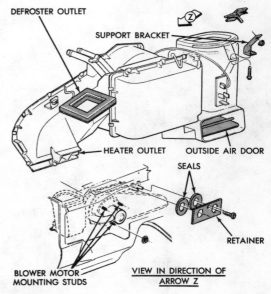

Heater assembly

cowl trim panel. Remove the lower instrument panel (the part with the glove box). Remove the instrument panel center to lower reinforcement.

9. Remove the right vent control cable, the temperature, and heating mode door control cables from the unit.

10. Disconnect the blower motor resistor block wiring.

11. Remove the mounting nuts on the engine side of the firewall.

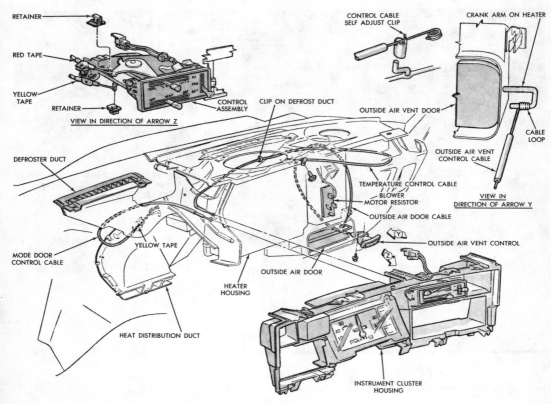

Heater control cable assembly

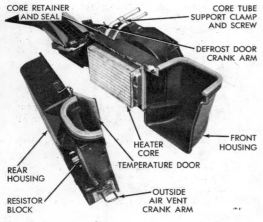

Heater core removal

12. Remove the heater support-to-plenum bracket.

13. Remove the heater unit.

Use the following procedure to remove the core or blower motor.

1. Remove the heater assembly from the car.

2. Remove the retainer clips and separate the housing halves.

3. Remove the screw attaching the seal re-

tainer and seal around the core tubes. Remove the core tube support clamp.

4. Slide the core out.

5. Remove the blower vent tube and the blower mounting nuts. Remove the blower motor.

HEATER BLOWER

Removal and Installation

AIR CONDITIONED CARS

The blower motor is removed from inside the car.

1. Disconnect the motor wiring.

2. Remove the motor mounting nuts from the bottom of the recirculation housing.

3. Separate the lower blower motor housing from the upper housing.

4. Remove the mounting plate screws and remove the mounting plate and blower motor.

HEATER CORE

Removal and Installation

AIR CONDITIONED CARS

CAUTION: *This job requires that the air conditioning system be evacuated. Have*

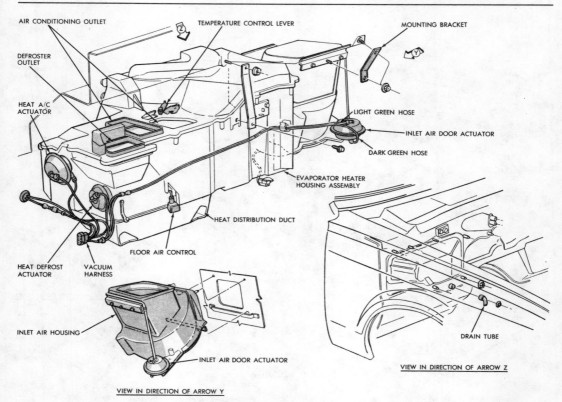

AIR CONDITIONING OUTLET

DEFROSTER OUTLET

HEAT A/C ACTUATOR

TEMPERATURE CONTROL LEVER

MOUNTING BRACKET

LIGHT GREEN HOSE

INLET AIR DOOR ACTUATOR

DARK GREEN HOSE

EVAPORATOR HEATER HOUSING ASSEMBLY

HEAT DISTRIBUTION DUCT

FLOOR AIR CONTROL

HEAT DEFROST ACTUATOR

VACUUM HARNESS

INLET AIR HOUSING

INLET AIR DOOR ACTUATOR

VIEW IN DIRECTION OF ARROW Y

DRAIN TUBE

VIEW IN DIRECTION OF ARROW Z

Air conditioning and heater assembly

this done by a professional if you are not familiar with air conditioning service, and then remove the heater core.

1. Discharge the air conditioning system.
2. Disconnect the battery ground cable, drain the coolant, remove the air cleaner, and disconnect the heater hoses. Plug the core tubes to prevent spillage.
3. Remove the H-type expansion valve.
4. Slide the front seat all the way back.

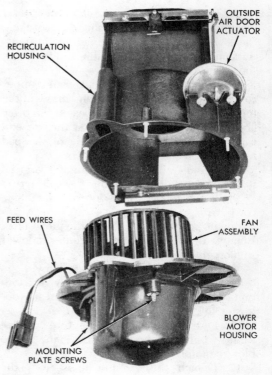

OUTSIDE AIR DOOR ACTUATOR

RECIRCULATION HOUSING

FEED WIRES

FAN ASSEMBLY

BLOWER MOTOR HOUSING

MOUNTING PLATE SCREWS

Blower motor assembly

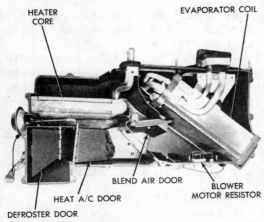

HEATER CORE

EVAPORATOR COIL

BLEND AIR DOOR

BLOWER MOTOR RESISTOR

HEAT A/C DOOR

DEFROSTER DOOR

Evaporator and heater housing assembly

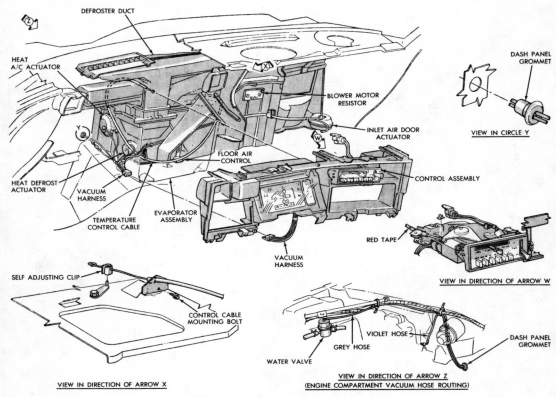

Evaporative assembly and controls

5. Remove the instrument cluster bezel assembly by removing the four screws along the lower edge, placing the automatic transmission selector in 1, and pulling out to detach the upper edge clips.

6. Remove the instrument panel upper cover by removing the mounting screws at the top inner surface of the glove box, at the brow above the instrument cluster, at the left end cap mounting, at the right side of the pad brow, and in the defroster outlets.

7. Remove the steering column cover (the instrument panel piece under the column).

8. Remove the right intermediate side cowl trim panel. Remove the lower instrument panel (the part with the glove box). Remove the instrument panel center to lower reinforcement.

9. Remove the floor console, if any.

10. Remove the right center air distribution duct. Detach the locking tab on the defroster duct.

11. Disconnect the temperature control cable from the housing. Disconnect the blower motor resistor block wiring.

12. Detach the vacuum lines from the water valve and tee in the engine compart-

ment. Detach the wiring from the evaporator housing. Remove the vacuum lines from the inlet air housing and disconnect the vacuum harness coupling.

13. Remove the drain tube in the engine compartment. Remove the mounting nuts from the firewall.

14. Remove the hanger strap from the rear of the evaporator and plenum stud.

15. Roll the unit back so that the pipes clear and remove it.

16. Remove the blend air door lever from the shaft. Remove the screws and lift off the top cover. Lift the heater core out.

17. Reverse the procedure for installation. Have the air conditioning system recharged and checked for leaks. Refill the cooling system.

Radio

Removal and Installation

1. Disconnect the battery ground cable.
2. Remove the instrument cluster bezel by

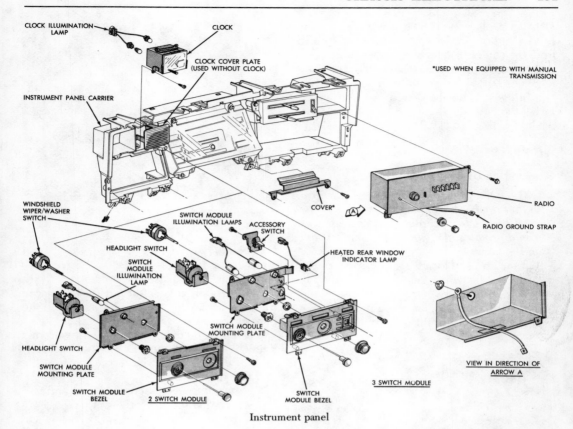

CLOCK ILLUMINATION LAMP

CLOCK

CLOCK COVER PLATE (USED WITHOUT CLOCK)

*USED WHEN EQUIPPED WITH MANUAL TRANSMISSION

INSTRUMENT PANEL CARRIER

RADIO

COVER*

RADIO GROUND STRAP

WINDSHIELD WIPER/WASHER SWITCH

SWITCH MODULE ILLUMINATION LAMPS

ACCESSORY SWITCH

HEADLIGHT SWITCH

SWITCH MODULE ILLUMINATION LAMP

HEATED REAR WINDOW INDICATOR LAMP

SWITCH MODULE MOUNTING PLATE

HEADLIGHT SWITCH

SWITCH MODULE MOUNTING PLATE

SWITCH MODULE BEZEL

2 SWITCH MODULE

SWITCH MODULE BEZEL

VIEW IN DIRECTION OF ARROW A

3 SWITCH MODULE

Instrument panel

removing the four screws along the lower edge, placing the automatic transmission selector in the 1 position, and pulling the bezel out to detach the clips along the top edge.

3. Remove the radio mounting screws.

4. Pull the radio out of the panel and disconnect the wiring and the antenna cable.

5. Remove the radio.

6. Installation is the reverse of removal.

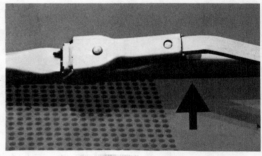

The release lever is under the arm (arrow)

Windshield Wipers

When your wiper blades wear out, you can either replace the entire wiper blade assembly or just the rubber inserts. The wiper arms can also be replaced if necessary.

WIPER BLADES

Removal and Installation

1. Non-concealed wipers usually have a release lever under the arm. Push the lever, wiggle the blade, and pull it off. Just push the blade back onto the arm to replace.

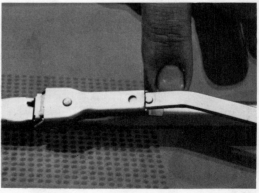

Press down on the lever to release the blade assembly

2. To replace the blade inserts, push the release button on the end bridge to release it from the center bridge. Sometimes there is an end clip on replacement inserts; if so, remove it. Slide the old insert out of the claws of the two bridges. Slide the new insert into place, install the end clip, if any, and reassemble the blade.

WIPER ARMS

Removal and Installation

CAUTION: *Make sure to position the arm so that the blade doesn't hit the edge of the windshield when running at top speed. This would produce annoying noise and a strain on the motor.*

Lift the arm and look for a spring retainer at the bottom. If there is one, hold it out of the way with a screwdriver. Wiggle the arm and pull it off. To replace, just push it on, making sure that the latch is out of the way.

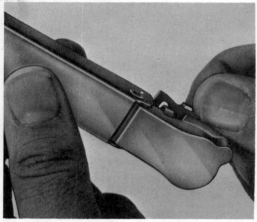

Wiper arm removal

MOTOR

Removal and Installation

1. Disconnect the battery ground cable.
2. Remove the wiper arms.
3. Remove the cowl screen.
4. Hold the motor crank with a wrench while removing the crank arm nut.
5. Remove the three mounting nuts and the motor.
6. Position the motor on the three studs on the dash panel. Be sure that the rubber gasket and spacers between the motor and dash panel are correctly positioned.
7. Install the 3 nuts that retain the motor to the dash panel and connect the wiring to

Wiper motor (arrow)

the motor. Don't forget to install the ground strap under 1 nut.
8. Match the flats on the crank arm with those on the motor shaft. Start the crank arm nut carefully so that the crank arm stays in the correct position.
9. While holding the crank arm with one wrench, tighten the nut to 8 ft lbs.
10. Reconnect the battery ground cable and test the wipers.
11. Install the cowl screen. Be careful that the screen doesn't pinch the washer hoses.
12. Install the windshield wiper arms and blades.

Instrument Cluster

Removal and Installation

1. Make sure the gearshift lever is in Park.
2. Remove the four screws which are located in the lower edge of the instrument cluster bezel.
3. The bezel is retained by clips along the upper edge. Pull the bezel toward while disengaging the clips to remove the bezel.
4. Installation is in the reverse order of removal.

Headlights

Removal and Installation

1. Remove the headlight cover (surrounding trim panel).

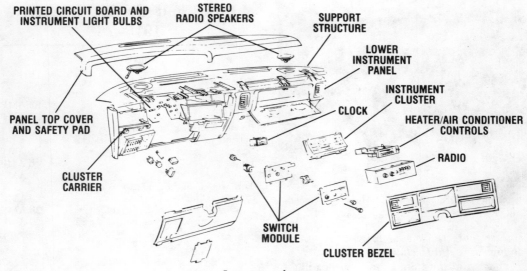

PRINTED CIRCUIT BOARD AND
INSTRUMENT LIGHT BULBS

STEREO
RADIO SPEAKERS

SUPPORT
STRUCTURE

LOWER
INSTRUMENT
PANEL

INSTRUMENT
CLUSTER

CLOCK

HEATER/AIR CONDITIONER
CONTROLS

RADIO

PANEL TOP COVER
AND SAFETY PAD

CLUSTER
CARRIER

SWITCH
MODULE

CLUSTER BEZEL

Instrument cluster

Trim cover removal

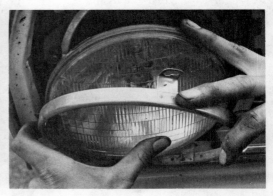

Rotate the ring to remove it

Retainer ring removal

2. Loosen the screws holding the headlight retainer ring in place.

NOTE: *The screws directly above and to one side of the headlight are for adjusting the vertical and horizontal headlight aim.*

Don't confuse these with the retaining ring screws.

3. Rotate the retainer ring to disengage the ring from the screws. Remove the ring.

4. Pull the headlight out and pull the wire plug off the back.

There are currently only 3 types of round headlights commonly in use on U.S. cars:

    a. Four-lamp system high beam.

    b. Four-lamp system combined high and low beam;

    c. Two-lamp system combined high and low beam.

Knowing this, you can check your required headlight number against the "Light Bulb Specifications" chart and charge off to the discount or auto parts store.

NOTE: *If your two-lamp system takes a 6014 headlight, don't buy the 6012 headlight. This is an older headlight that is being*

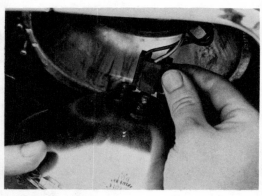

Pull on the plug, not the wires, when removing the headlight

phased out. It isn't as bright as a 6014, though it will interchange.

5. Push the plug onto the new headlight. Position the headlight. There are lugs on the headlight to make it impossible to put it in wrong.

6. Replace the retainer ring and tighten the screws.

7. Replace the headlight cover.

Fuses

The fuses are behind this panel

Fuses and Circuit Breakers 1976–78

FUSES

Switch lamps, instrument cluster lights, tailgate lock	5 AMP
Clock, cigar lighter, tail lights, side marker lights, turn signal, parking lights, license lights	20 AMP

Fuses and Circuit Breakers 1976–78

FUSES

Trunk hazard, brake lights, seatbelt buzzer, dome, map, courtesy, glove box, seat belt lamps	20 AMP
Horn, horn relay	20 AMP
Power windows, warning lamps, trunk release, seat belt interlock, ignition feed	20 AMP
Radio	5 AMP
Accessories	20 AMP
Turn signal flasher, back-up lights voltage limiter, gauges	20 AMP
Heater/AC blower motor/relay	20 AMP
AC high speed blower	30 AMP

INLINE FUSES

Automatic temperature control	1 AMP
Spot lights	10 AMP

CIRCUIT BREAKERS

Power door lights	15 AMP
Power windows, tailgate windows, tailgate latch	30 AMP
Trailer lights, trailer (spare battery)	40 AMP

Light Bulbs

Headlights	6014
Side marker	168
Park and turn signal	1159NA
Tail/stop/turn signal	1157
Fender turn signal	168
License	
Sedan	168
Wagon	67
Back-up lights	1156
Speedometer	158
Clock	158
Heater/AC	363
Switches	
Headlight	1815
Wipe/Wash	1815
Rear defrost	1892
Rear unlock	1892
Cigarette lighter	158
Radio	168
Radio w/8-track	1893
Warning lights	158
Key light	1455
Glove box	1891
Dome lamp	211-2
Courtesy lamp	90
Trunk light	1003
Underhood light	1003
Seat belt warning	158
Door ajar	158
Hot temp indication	158
Washer fluid level	158

Chapter 6

Clutch and Transmission

Manual Transmission

Two manual transmissions are available on the Aspen and Volaré, a 3-speed and 4-speed. The 4-speed transmission features an overdrive high gear for better fuel economy.

Linkage Adjustment

COLUMN SHIFT

1. Loosen both shift rod swivels at the ends of the two long rods from the column.
2. Make sure the transmission levers are in the neutral or middle positions.
3. Move the column shift lever into neutral to line up the locating slots in the bottom of the steering column shift housing and the bearing housing. Install a tool into the slot to hold the lever in place.
4. Place a screwdriver between the cross-over blade (between the two column levers) and the second-third (the upper one) lever so that both lever pins are engaged by the cross-over blade.
5. Tighten both swivel bolts to 125 in. lbs.
6. Remove the gearshift housing locating tool.
7. Remove the screwdriver.
8. Shift through all gears to check the adjustment and cross-over (through neutral) smoothness.

CROSS-OVER BLADE IN NEUTRAL

Holding crossover blade in neutral position

9. Check that the ignition switch will lock with the shift lever in reverse only, without applying any pressure to the shift lever.

THREE-SPEED FLOORSHIFT

1. Make an alignment tool out of $1/16$ in. thick metal. It should be $5/8$ in. wide and $2\frac{3}{8}$ in. long.

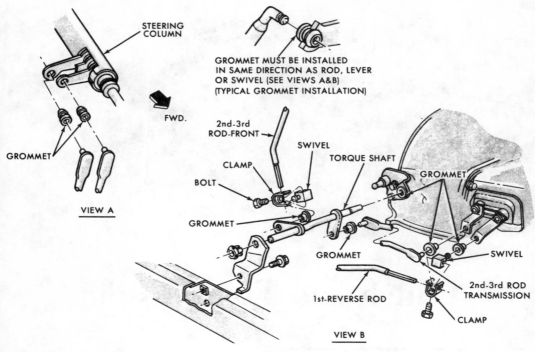

Column shift linkage

2. Detach the shift rod swivels.

3. From under the car, insert the alignment tool through the shifter levers and the shifter to hold the levers in the neutral positions.

4. Place both shift levers on the transmis-sion side cover in the neutral or middle position.

5. Adjust the swivels so that they can be installed freely in the shifter lever holes.

6. Remove the alignment tool and check the shifting action.

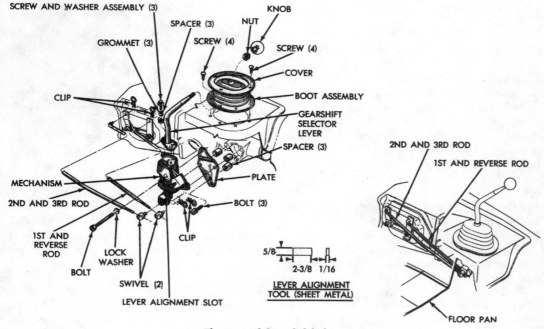

Three speed floor shift linkage

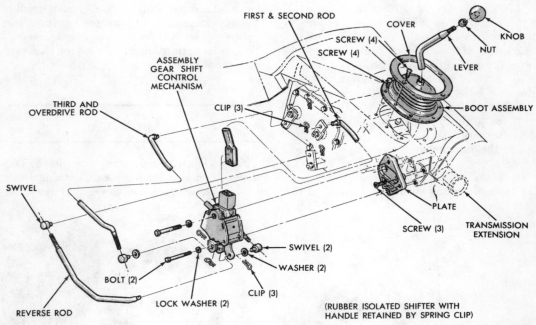

Four speed floor shift linkage

FOUR-SPEED FLOORSHIFT

1. Remove all the shift rods from the transmission shift levers.

2. Place all the transmission shift levers in their neutral positions.

3. From under the car, insert a ¼ in. rod or drill bit about 2¼ in. long through the shifter levers and the shifter to hold the levers in the neutral positions.

4. Adjust the shift rods so that they can be installed freely in the shifter lever holes.

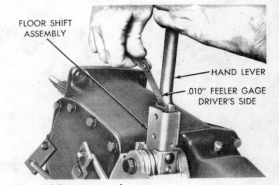

Floor shift lever removal

have a drain plug, you can get most of the lubricant out by using a suction gun at the fill hole. Remove the shift rods from the transmission levers.

3. After marking both parts for reassembly, detach the driveshaft and the rear universal joint.

CAUTION: *Don't nick or scratch the ground surface on the sliding spline yoke.*

4. Disconnect the speedometer cable and back-up light switch. Remove the console, if necessary, and unbolt the shifter from the extension housing on floor-shift models. The shift lever unbolts from the shifter.

5. Unfasten the transmission extension housing from the center crossmember and jack up the engine and transmission about 1 in.

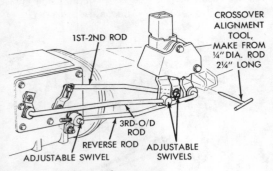

Four speed linkage adjustment

5. Remove the aligning tool and check the shifting action.

Removal and Installation

1. Raise and support the car safely.

2. Drain the transmission. If it doesn't

6. Remove the center crossmember.

7. On some models it may be necessary to disconnect or loosen the exhaust system and position it to one side to gain clearance in order to remove the transmission.

8. Support the transmission on a jack. Remove the bolts which secure the transmission to the clutch housing.

9. Slide the transmission toward the rear until the input shaft clears the clutch disc. Lower the transmission and remove it from the car.

10. Installation is the reverse of removal. Lubricate the input shaft pilot bearing in the flywheel and the bearing retainer pilot (for the clutch release sleeve). Do not lubricate the clutch splines or the clutch release levers. Torque the transmission to clutch housing bolts to 50 ft lbs.

Clutch

All models use a coil spring type clutch. The larger diameter clutches have centrifugal rollers which exert a force between the pressure

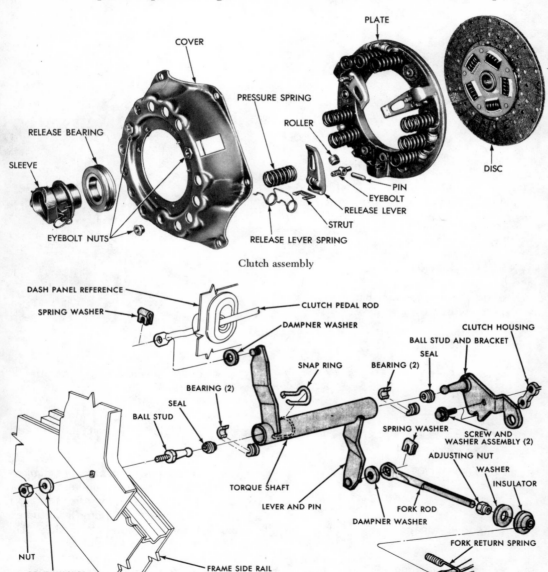

Clutch assembly

Clutch linkage

plate and cover to increase the load on the disc at high engine speeds.

NOTE: *It is normal for the centrifugal rollers to rattle before the cover is installed.*

Free-Play Adjustment

1. Check that the rubber pedal stop is in good shape.
2. Under the car, turn the self-locking adjustment nut on the release fork operating rod to get about 5/32 in. free movement at the end of the fork. If the nut won't turn readily, the swivel is probably binding in the release fork. Tap it to free it.
3. Check the adjustment by making sure that you have 1 in. of free-play at the pedal. The easiest way to measure this is to hold a yardstick alongside the clutch pedal and press the pedal down until you can feel resistance.

Removal and Installation

1. Remove the transmission.
2. Remove the clutch housing pan.
3. Remove the spring washer which secures the clutch fork rod to the torque shaft lever and remove the fork rod.
4. Disconnect the fork return spring at the fork. Disconnect the torque shaft return spring. If so equipped, at the torque shaft assembly.
5. Remove the clutch release (throwout) bearing from the clutch release fork. Remove the release fork and boot from the clutch housing.
6. Using a metal punch, mark the clutch cover (pressure plate) and the flywheel to indicate their correct positions for reassembly.
7. Loosen the clutch cover (pressure plate) securing bolts one or two turns at a time in succession to prevent warping the clutch cover.

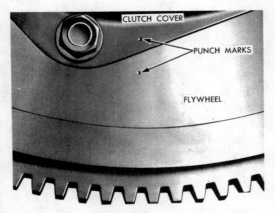

Marking clutch and flywheel

8. Remove the bolts and take out the clutch disc and pressure plate. Do not get any grease or oil on the pressure plate or the clutch disc.
9. Lubricate the pilot bearing in the end of the crankshaft with about half a teaspoon of high temperature grease. Place the grease deep in the cavity. If the bearing is damaged, it will have to be removed with a puller and a new one driven in.
10. Clean the surfaces of the flywheel and pressure plate with fine sandpaper. Check the pressure plate carefully for possible replacement.
11. Place the clutch disc and pressure plate in position and insert a clutch disc aligning tool (dummy shaft) through the clutch disc hub and into the pilot bearing.

NOTE: *The springs on the clutch disc should be facing away from the flywheel when the disc is properly installed.*

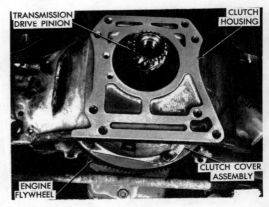

Clutch disc alignment

12. Align the punch marks that were made before the removal on the flywheel and the pressure plate.
13. Install the pressure plate securing bolts and tighten them one to two turns at a time in an alternating sequence. Tighten 5/16 in. bolts to 17 ft lbs and ⅜ in. bolts to 30 ft lbs. Remove the clutch alignment tool.
14. Pack the throwout bearing sleeve and the release fork pads with grease. If the bearing is noisy or worn, it must be pressed off the sleeve and a new one pressed on.
15. Insert the throwout bearing into the bellhousing and place the fork fingers under the throwout bearing retaining springs.
16. Reverse steps 1–6 to finish installation. Do not lubricate the transmission splines.
17. Adjust clutch pedal free-play.

Automatic Transmission

All models use the Torqueflite automatic transmission. There are two versions: A-904 and A-904LA. The A-904 is used only on six-cylinder engines. The A-904LA is used on all V8s.

This section covers in-car automatic transmission service that can readily be handled by the owner. The most common automatic transmission difficulties are those caused by need for band or linkage adjustments or dirty fluid. Though the factory doesn't recommend any periodic fluid changes except for heavy service, it is a good idea to change the fluid and filter whenever periodic transmission adjustments are done. Refer to Chapter 1 for the fluid and filter changing procedure, transmission identification, and the required intervals for adjustments. Throttle linkage adjustments are covered in Chapter 4.

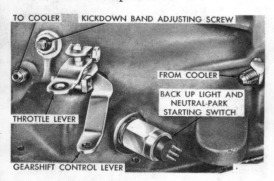

Kickdown band adjustment screw location

Kick-Down Band Adjustment

The kick-down band adjusting screw is located on the left-hand side of the transmission case near the throttle lever shaft.

1. Loosen the locknut and back it off about 5 turns. Be sure that the adjusting screw is free in the case.
2. Torque the adjusting screw to exactly 72 in. lbs.
3. Back off the adjusting screw 2 turns. Hold the adjusting screw and tighten the lock nut to 35 ft lbs.

Low-Reverse Band Adjustment

The pan must be removed from the transmission to gain access to the Low-Reverse band adjusting screw. An in. lb torque wrench is also necessary for accurate adjustment.

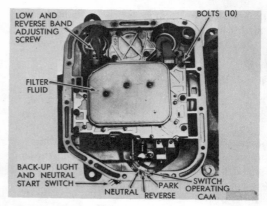

Automatic transmission—pan removed

1. Drain the transmission and remove the pan. See Chapter 1 for the procedure.
2. Loosen the band adjusting screw locknut and back it off about 5 turns. Be sure that the adjusting screw turns freely in the lever.

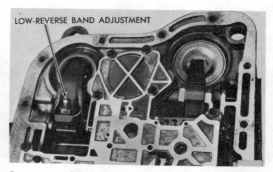

Low-reverse band adjusting screw

3. Torque the adjusting screw to exactly 72 in. lbs. On A-904 transmissions with a six-cylinder engine, torque the adjusting screw to exactly 41 in. lbs.
4. Back off the adjusting screw 4 turns on V8 models or 7 turns on six-cylinder models. Keep the screw from turning and tighten the locknut.
5. Install the pan using a new gasket. Refill the transmission with the correct type of transmission fluid.

Neutral Safety/Backup Light Switch Replacement

The neutral safety switch is mounted in the transmission case. When the gearshift lever is placed in either the Park or Neutral position, a cam, which is attached to the transmission throttle lever inside the transmission, contacts the neutral safety switch and provides a ground to complete the starter solenoid circuit.

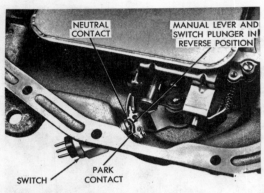

Neutral start switch

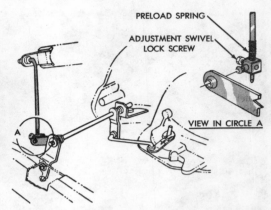

Column gearshift linkage

The back-up lamp switch is incorporated into the neutral safety switch. The center terminal is for the neutral safety switch and the two outer terminals are for the back-up lamps.

There is no adjustment for the switch. If a malfunction occurs, first check to make sure that the transmission gear shift linkage is properly adjusted. If the malfunction continues, the switch must be removed and replaced.

To remove the switch, disconnect the electrical leads and unscrew the switch from the transmission. Use a drain pan to catch the transmission fluid that drains out of the mounting hole. Install a new switch using a new seal and refill the transmission to the proper level.

Shift Linkage Adjustment

1. Under the car, loosen the adjustable rod swivel lock bolt.
2. Put the floorshift or column shift lever into Park.
3. Move the transmission shift lever all the way to the rear.

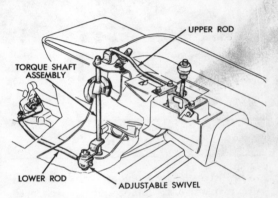

Console gearshift linkage

4. Tighten the swivel lock bolt (torque is 90 in. lbs) without putting any pressure on the linkage.
5. The shift effort must be free and the detents should feel crisp. All gate stops must be positive. It should be possible to start the engine in Park and Neutral only.

Chapter 7

Drive Train

Driveline

The driveshaft is a one-piece tubular shaft with two universal joints, one at each end. The front joint yoke serves as a slip yoke on the transmission output shaft. The rear universal joint is the type that must be disassembled to be removed. The rear axle is a live, or solid, type. Numerous rear axle ratios and several rear axles have been used, depending on the application. See Chapter 1 for rear axle identification. In addition, a limited-

slip feature has been available. Chrysler calls this Sure-Grip.

DRIVESHAFT AND U-JOINTS

Removal and Installation

You can avoid loss of lubricant from the rear of the transmission by raising the rear of the car before removing the driveshaft.

1. Match mark the driveshaft, U-joint and pinion flange before disassembly. These marks must be realigned during reassembly to maintain the balance of the driveline. Failure

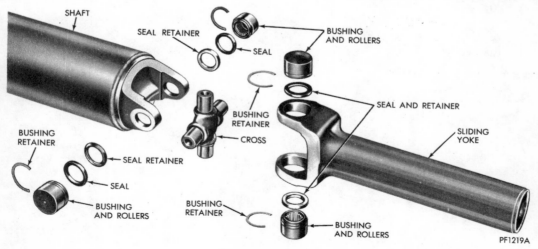

Front universal joint

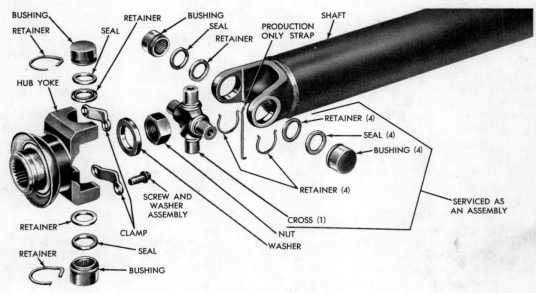

Rear universal joint

to align them may result in excessive vibration.

2. Remove both of the clamps from the differential pinion yoke and slide the driveshaft forward slightly to disengage the U-joint from the pinion yoke. Tape the two loose U-joint bearings together to prevent them from falling off.

CAUTION: *Do not disturb the bearing assembly retaining strap. Never allow the driveshaft to hang from either of the U-joints. Always support the unattached end of the shaft to prevent damage to the joints.*

3. Lower the rear end of the driveshaft and gently slide the front yoke/driveshaft assembly rearward disengaging the assembly from the transmission output shaft. Be careful not to damage the splines or the surface which the output shaft seal rides on.

4. Check the transmission output shaft seal for signs of leakage.

5. Installation is the reverse of removal. Be sure to align the match marks. The torque for the clamp bolts is 170 in. lbs.

U-Joint Overhaul

1. Remove the driveshaft.

2. To remove the bearings from the yoke, first remove the bearing retainer snap rings located at the base or open end of each bearing cap.

3. Pressing on one of the bearings, drive the bearing in toward the center of the joint. This will force the cross to push the opposite

U-joint disassembly

U-joint assembly

bearing out of the universal joint. This step may be performed using a hammer and suitable drift or a vise and sockets of pieces of pipe. However installation of bearings must be done using the vise or a press.

4. After the bearing has been pushed all the way out of the yoke, pull up the cross slightly and pack some washers under it. Then

press on the end of the cross from which the bearing was just removed to force the first bearing out of the yoke. Repeat steps 3 and 4 to remove the remaining two bearings.

5. If a grease fitting is supplied with the new U-joint assembly, install it. If no fitting is supplied, make sure that the joint is amply greased. Pack grease in the recesses in the end of the cross.

6. To reassemble start both bearing cups into the yoke at the same time and hold the cross carefully in the fingers in its installed position. Be careful not to knock any rollers out of position.

7. Squeeze both bearings in a vise or press, moving the bearings into place. Continually check for free movement of the cross in the bearings as they are pressed into the yoke. If there is a sudden increase in the force needed to press the bearings into place, or the cross starts to bind, the bearings are cocked in the yoke. They must be removed and restarted in the yoke. Failure to do so will greatly reduce the life of the bearing. Repeat steps 6 and 7 to reinstall the remaining two bearings.

Rear Axle

The 7¼ in. (ring gear) and 8¼ in. axles are used on all years. Refer to Chapter 1 for identification of the axle in your car.

AXLE SHAFT

Removal and Installation

NOTE: *This procedure also covers axle bearing replacement.*

7¼ IN. AXLE

NOTE: *Whenever this axle assembly is serviced, both the brake support plate gaskets and the inner axle shaft oil seal must be renewed. There is no provision for adjusting the axle shaft end-play.*

Removal

1. Raise the rear of the car and remove the wheels.

2. Detach the clips which secure the brake drum to the axle shaft studs and remove the brake drum.

3. Disconnect the brake lines at the wheel cylinders and block off the lines.

4. Through the access hole in the axle shaft flange, remove the axle shaft retaining nuts.

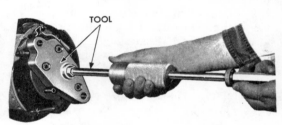

7¼ in. axle shaft removal

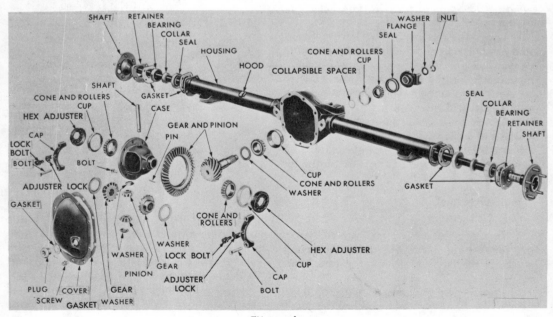

7¼ in. axle

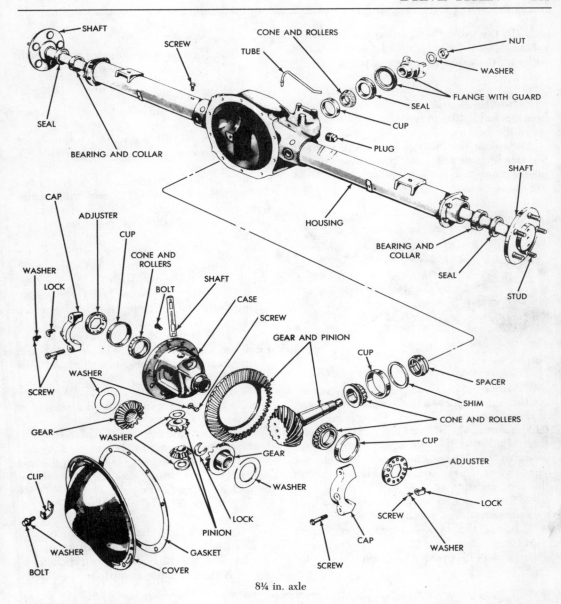

SHAFT

SCREW

CONE AND ROLLERS

TUBE

NUT

WASHER

FLANGE WITH GUARD

SEAL

CUP

SEAL

PLUG

BEARING AND COLLAR

HOUSING

SHAFT

CAP

ADJUSTER

CUP

CONE AND ROLLERS

SHAFT

BEARING AND COLLAR

BOLT

CASE

SEAL

WASHER

SCREW

STUD

LOCK

GEAR AND PINION

CUP

SPACER

SCREW

WASHER

SHIM

CONE AND ROLLERS

GEAR

CONE AND ROLLERS

WASHER

CUP

GEAR

ADJUSTER

CLIP

WASHER

LOCK

LOCK

SCREW

PINION

CAP

WASHER

WASHER

GASKET

BOLT

COVER

SCREW

8¼ in. axle

5. Attach a puller or slide hammer to the axle shaft flange and remove the axle shaft.

6. Remove the brake assembly from the axle housing.

7. Remove the axle shaft oil seal from the axle housing.

CAUTION: *Never use a torch or other heat source as an aid in removing any axle shaft components; this will result in serious damage to the axle assembly.*

Overhaul

1. Place the axle shaft housing retaining collar in a vise. With a chisel, cut deeply into the retaining collar at 90° intervals. Remove the bearing with a puller.

NOTCH COLLAR

Removing axle shaft collar

2. To assemble the axle shaft, replace the retainer plate, bearing, and bearing retainer collar on the axle shaft, using a press.

Installation

1. Insert new axle shaft oil seals in the axle housing and lightly grease the outside diameter of the bearing.

2. Replace the foam gasket on the studs of the axle housing and install the brake support plate assembly on the axle housing studs. Refit the outer gasket.

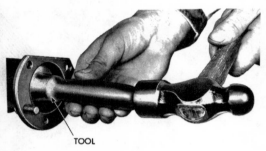

Installing oil seal—7¼ in. axle

3. Very carefully slide the axle shaft assembly through the oil seal and engage the splines of the differential side gear. Using a non-metallic hammer, lightly tap the end of the axle shaft to position the axle shaft bearing in the recess of the axle housing. Install the retainer plate over the axle housing studs and torque the securing nuts to 35 ft lbs.

4. Reconnect the brake lines to the wheel cylinders and bleed the hydraulic system.

5. Install the brake drum and retaining clips.

6. Replace the rear wheels and lower the car.

8¼ IN. AXLE

NOTE: *There is no provision for axle shaft end-play adjustment on this axle.*

Removal

1. Raise the vehicle and remove the rear wheels.

2. Clean all dirt from the housing cover and remove the housing cover to drain the lubricant.

3. Remove the brake drum.

4. Rotate the differential case until the differential pinion shaft lockscrew can be removed. Remove the lockscrew and pinion shaft.

5. Push the axle shafts toward the center of the vehicle and remove the C-locks from the grooves on the axle shafts.

6. Pull the axle shafts from the housing, being careful not to damage the bearing which remains in the housing.

7. Inspect the axle shaft bearings and replace any doubtful parts. Whenever the axle shaft is replaced, the bearings should also be replaced.

8. Remove the axle shaft seal from the bore in the housing, using the button end of the axle shaft.

9. Remove the axle shaft bearing from the housing. Do not reuse the bearing or the seal.

10. Check the bearing shoulder in the axle housing for imperfections. These should be corrected with a file or polish.

Installation

1. Clean the axle shaft bearing cavity.

2. Install the axle shaft bearing in the cavity. Be sure that the bearing is not cocked and that it is seated firmly against the shoulder.

Removing axle shaft bearing—8¼ in. axle

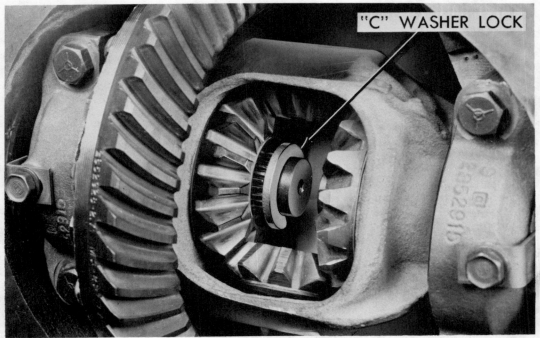

"C" WASHER LOCK

C-lock—8¼ in. axle

3. Install the axle shaft bearing seal. It should be seated beyond the end of the flange face.

4. Insert the axle shaft, making sure that the splines do not damage the seal. Be sure that the splines are properly engaged with the differential side gear splines.

5. Install the C-locks in the grooves on the axle shafts. Pull the shafts outward so that the C-locks seat in the counterbore of the differential side gears.

6. Install the differential pinion shaft

through the case and pinions. Install the lockscrew and secure it in position.

7. Clean the housing and gasket surfaces. Install the cover and a new gasket.

NOTE: *Replacement gaskets may not be available for differential covers. In this case, the use of gel type nonsticking sealant is recommended. See Chapter 1.*

Be sure that the rear axle ratio identification tag is replaced under one of the cover bolts. Refill the axle with the specified lubricant.

8. Install the brake drum and wheel.

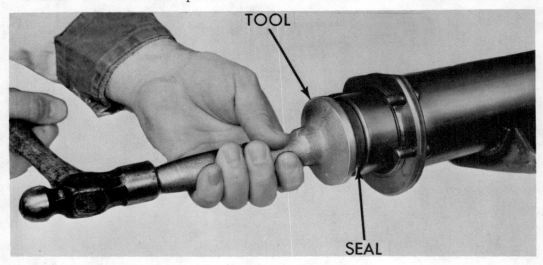

TOOL

SEAL

Axle seal installation—8¼ in. axle

9. Lower the vehicle to the ground and test the operation of the brakes.

REAR AXLE NOISE DIAGNOSIS

Your hearing can be the best guide to rear end problems. Rear end noise usually appears as gear noise from the ring and pinion gears or bearing noise coming from the pinion bearing, wheel bearings, or side bearings. No rear axle is silent. A slight noise peaking in volume at varying speeds is to be considered normal. If the noise is loud, unusual, or occurs at all speeds, the car should be carefully inspected to find the source. Noise from the tires, transmission, driveshaft, or universal joints may seem to be coming from the rear axle so each of these possibilities should be considered. Abnormal gear noise can occur as a high-pitched whine that gets higher and lower, and louder and softer, but is most pronounced at certain speeds. Gear noise usually occurs when the ring and pinion become scored due to insufficient lubrication. Gear noise varies in pitch while faulty bearings produce a whine that is constant in pitch. Bearing whine is lower pitched than gear whine and usually grows louder when accelerating under load rather than when coasting. When faulty, each bearing has its own characteristic sound. A faulty pinion bearing emits a constant rough sound. Pinion bearings rotate at a higher speed than the other bearings, so the noise it makes would be faster and high-pitched, but steady. The noise gets louder during acceleration but, unlike wheel bearings, does not change when the car is turned right or left or made to swerve.

It is advisable that noise tests be performed on a smooth road to avoid confusing road sounds with possible axle noises. Tires may produce a whining sound when contacting a smooth, black top road. Do not confuse this whine with the whine of a faulty axle component. Bad wheel bearings are a frequent cause of bearing noise. To determine if wheel bearings are bad, drive down a smooth road and, when safe to do so, swerve from right to left. If the noise is coming from the wheel bearings, it will get louder due to the increased side load imposed upon them. Worn side bearings will produce a rough sound similar to a pinion bearing but at a lower frequency. Swerving the car from side-to-side will not affect side bearing noise. Other signs of axle trouble are not so difficult to spot. A car with a broken axle shaft will not move if equipped with a conventional differential and will move only slightly if equipped with limited-slip. A ruptured grease seal is made obvious by the presence of great amounts of oil covering the exterior of the assembly. Wheel bearing seals usually give out before the other seals since they undergo a greater amount of stress. Broken gear teeth are somewht rare but are made apparent by clunking sounds.

Chapter 8

Suspension and Steering

Front Suspension

The Aspen/Volaré front suspension is of a unique design. Transverse torsion bars are used on these cars in place of the traditional Chrysler longitudinal torsion bars. The torsion bars react on the outboard ends of the lower control arms. The torsion bars are anchored in the front crossmember opposite the wheel on which they react. Upper and lower control arms locate the wheel spindle. A stabilizer bar is used to resist front roll and to act as the lower control arm strut.

TORSION BARS

Removal and Installation

The torsion bars are not interchangeable from right to left. They are marked with an R or an L, according to their location.

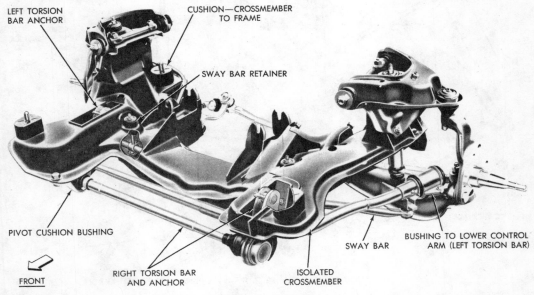

LEFT TORSION BAR ANCHOR

CUSHION—CROSSMEMBER TO FRAME

SWAY BAR RETAINER

PIVOT CUSHION BUSHING

FRONT

RIGHT TORSION BAR AND ANCHOR

ISOLATED CROSSMEMBER

SWAY BAR

BUSHING TO LOWER CONTROL ARM (LEFT TORSION BAR)

Front suspension

1. Raise the car so that the front suspension hangs free.

2. Release the load on the torsion bar by turning the anchor adjusting bolts counterclockwise.

3. Remove the adjusting bolt on the bar to be removed.

4. Raise the lower control arms until there is 2⅞ in. clearance between the crossmember ledge at the jounce bumper and the torsion bar bushing on the lower control arm.

5. Unbolt the sway bar from the control arm.

6. Unbolt the torsion bar pivot bushing from the crossmember. Remove the bar and anchor assembly from the crossmember.

7. Check the seals on the bar for damage. If corrosion is evident, replace the bar assembly. Touch up any paint nicks or scratches. Check the adjusting bolt and swivel for corrosion or damage. Replace them if necessary.

8. Slide the balloon seal over the end of the bar with the cupped end toward the hex.

9. Coat the hex end of the bar with high-temperature waterproof grease.

10. Install the hex end of the bar into the anchor bracket. The ears of the bracket should be nearly straight up.

11. Install the bar anchor bracket assembly into the crossmember anchor retainer. Install the adjusting bolt and bearing. Attach the pivot bushing to the crossmember, finger tight.

12. Support the lower control arms at the height specified in Step 4 and install the torsion bar bushing to lower control arm bolts. Tighten them to 50 ft lbs.

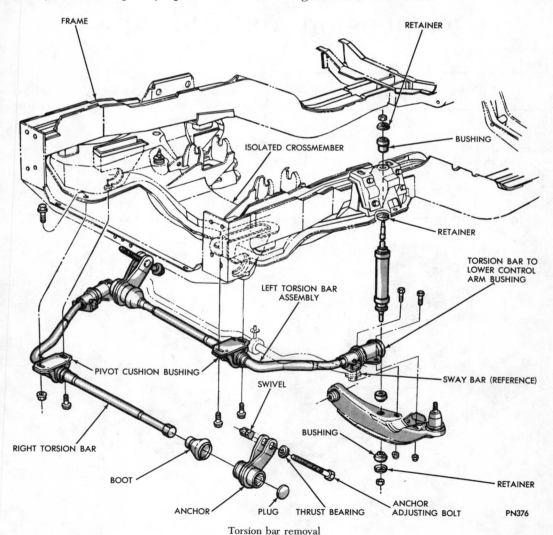

Torsion bar removal

Anchor adjusting bolt (arrow)

13. Check that the anchor bracket is fully seated in the crossmember. Tighten the pivot bushing bolts to 75 ft lbs.

14. Put the balloon seal over the anchor bracket.

15. Install a new sway bar end bolt and tighten to 50 ft lbs.

16. Load the bar by turning the adjusting bolt clockwise. Lower the car and adjust the front end height.

SHOCK ABSORBERS

Testing

To test the shock absorbers, bounce the front of the car up and down a few times. When released, the car should return to its normal ride height and stop bouncing immediately. If the shocks are worn, they should be replaced in pairs to provide equal damping. Heavy-duty replacements are available to provide a more stable and slightly firmer ride.

Removal and Installation

Sometimes this job is easier with the wheel and tire removed. If you remove one shock at a time, you won't have any problem installing all the parts.

1. Remove the nut and retainer from the top of the shock.

2. Remove the lower nut and retainer from the shock.

NOTE: *Steps 1 and 2 sound easy, but very often the retaining nuts are rusted in place. Penetrating oil helps, and very often you have to find a way to stop the shock absorber shaft from turning while you remove the top nut.*

3. Fully compress the shock and remove it downward.

4. If the upper bushing needs to be re-

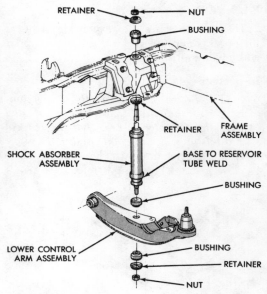

Front shock assembly

placed, it can be cut or pried out. To install the new one, wet it and start it into the bracket hole with a twisting motion. Tap it into position with a hammer.

5. Purge the new shock of air by extending it in its normal position and compressing it while inverted. Do this several times. It is normal for there to be more resistance to extension than to compression.

6. Compress the new shock and insert the upper end through the lower retainer, the bushing, and the upper retainer. Tighten the nut to 25 ft lbs.

NOTE: *All retainers must be installed with the concave side in contact with the rubber bushing.*

7. Align the lower mount and install the nut and bolt finger tight. Tighten the nut to 35 ft lbs with the weight of the car on the wheels.

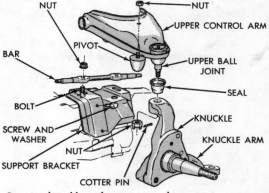

Steering knuckle and upper control arm

BALL JOINTS

The ball joints are the suspension pivots at the outer (steering knuckle) ends of the upper and lower control arms.

Inspection

NOTE: *Before performing the inspection, make sure the wheel bearings are adjusted ocrrectly (Chapter 9) and that the control arm bushings are in good condition.*

1. Place a jack under the lower control arm as close to the wheel as possible.

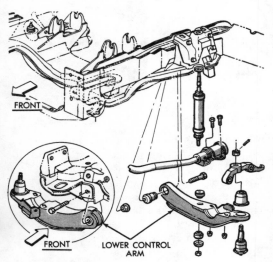

FRONT

FRONT   LOWER CONTROL ARM

Lower control arm

2. Raise the car until there is 1–2 ın. of clearance under the wheel.

3. Insert a bar under the wheel and pry upward. If the wheel raises noticeably the ball joints are worn. Determine if the upper or lower ball joint is worn by visual inspection while prying on the wheel.

NOTE: *Due to the distribution of forces in the suspension, the lower ball joint is usually the defective joint. The manufacturer's limit for lower ball joint play, measured at the joint, is 0.030 in. This limit may not agree with your state's inspection regulations.*

Removal and Installation

UPPER BALL JOINT

1. Raise the car by placing a jack stand under the lower control arm as close to the wheel as possible.

2. Remove the nut that attaches the upper ball joint to the steering knuckle. Loosen the

Ball joint removal

ball joint stud from the steering knuckle. Ball joint removal tools are available at auto parts stores and large mail order houses to press the ball joint out. Follow the manufacturer's directions for operating the tool. Never strike the ball joint stud.

3. Unscrew the upper ball joint from the upper control arm and remove it from the vehicle.

4. Position a new ball joint on the upper control arm and screw the joint into the arm. Be careful not to cross thread the joint in the arm.

5. Position a new seal on the ball joint stud and install the seal in the ball joint making sure the seal is fully seated on the ball joint housing.

6. Position the ball joint stud in the steering knuckle and install the retaining nut. Torque the nut to 100 ft lbs.

7. Lubricate the ball joint.

8. Lower the car.

LOWER BALL JOINT

1. Remove the lower control arm rebound bumper.

2. Raise the vehicle so that the front suspension drops to the downward limit of its travel. Position jackstands beneath the front frame for extra support.

3. Remove the wheel and tire assembly.

4. Remove the brake caliper from its mounts and tie it up out of the way so that there is no strain on the flexible brake hose.

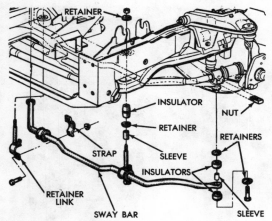

Front sway bar

3. Remove the upper ball joint stud nut and cotter pin.

4. To remove the stud from the steering knuckle, use a ball joint removal tool to press it out. Do not attempt to force the stud out by striking the stud.

5. Remove the rubber splash shield and remove the control arm pivot shaft bolts and nuts. Remove the control arm from the car.

6. Installation is the reverse of removal. It will be necessary to realign the front end and check front suspension height. Tighten the upper ball joint stud nut to 100 ft lbs and the pivot shaft nuts to 150 ft lbs.

LOWER CONTROL ARM

Removal and Installation

1. Raise the car and remove the wheel.

2. Remove the brake caliper and wire it up.

3. Remove the lower shock absorber attachment.

4. Remove the hub, rotor and splash shield.

5. Unload both torsion bars by turning the adjusting bolts counterclockwise.

CAUTION: *Unload both bars even if you are removing only one control arm.*

6. Raise the lower control arm until there is 2⅞ in. clearance between the crossmember ledge at the jounce bumper and the torsion bar bushing on the lower control arm. Unbolt the torsion bar bushing from the control arm.

7. Separate the lower ball joint from the steering knuckle arm.

8. Remove the lower control arm pivot bolt and the control arm.

9. Position the control arm, install the pivot bolt, and make the flange nut finger tight.

10. Install the ball joint stud in the steering knuckle arm, tighten the nut to 100 ft lbs, and install a new cotter pin.

11. Hold the control arm at the height used in Step 6. Tighten the torsion bar bushing bolts to 50 ft lbs. Tighten the control arm pivot bolt to 100 ft lbs.

12. Replace the shock absorber and tighten the lower nut to 35 ft lbs.

13. Replace the brake assembly. Tighten the caliper bolts to 15 lbs.

14. Turn the adjusting screws clockwise to load the torsion bars.

15. Lower the car and adjust suspension height and wheel alignment.

5. Remove the hub and rotor assembly, splash shield, and lower shock absorber mounting nut and bolt.

6. Unload the torsion bar by rotating the adjusting bolt counterclockwise.

7. Remove the upper ball joint stud cotter pin and nut. Use a ball joint removal tool to press the ball joint out. Never strike the ball joint stud.

8. Press the ball joint out of the lower control arm.

9. Press the new ball joint into the lower control arm.

10. Place a new seal over the ball joint. Press the retainer portion of the seal down over the ball joint housing until it locks into position.

11. Insert the ball joint stud through the opening in the knuckle arm and install the stud retaining nut. Tighten to 100 ft lbs. Install the cotter pin and lubricate the ball joint.

12. Load the torsion bar by rotating the adjusting bolt clockwise.

13. Install the shock absorber nut and bolt, the splash shield, hub and rotor assembly, and brake caliper. Install the wheel and tire assembly.

14. Adjust the front wheel bearings. Remove the jackstands and lower the car. Install the rebound bumper. Adjust the front suspension height and alignment.

UPPER CONTROL ARM

Removal and Installation

1. Jack up the car and support it under the lower control arm as near to the wheel as possible.

2. Remove the wheel and tire.

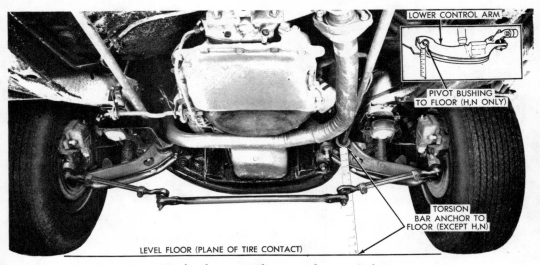

Height adjustment. The inset is for Aspen/Volare

FRONT END HEIGHT ADJUSTMENT

The front end height should be checked whenever suspension components are replaced and before front end alignment.

1. Bounce the front of the car several times, releasing it on a downward bounce.

2. Measure from the lowest point of the lower control arm inner pivot bushing to the floor. This should be between 10⅛–10¼ in.

3. Adjust by turning the long bolts at the ends of the torsion bars. The left side bolt adjusts the right side height and vice-versa.

4. Maximum side-to-side variation is ⅛ in.

FRONT END ALIGNMENT

Only caster, camber, and toe-in settings are adjustable. Specifications for steering axis inclination and wheel pivot ratio are useful only in detecting damaged components. Caster and camber cannot be set accurately without professional equipment. Toe-in can be adjusted with some degree of success without any special equipment. Front end height should be checked before adjusting front end alignment.

Caster Adjustment

Caster is the backward or forward tilt from the vertical of the steering knuckle centerline at the top, measured in degrees. A steering knuckle centerline tilted backward at the top has positive (+) caster, while one tilted forward has negative (−) caster. Most American cars have negative or zero caster to reduce steering effort. Positive caster produces greater directional stability and requires greater steering effort, since it also increases the self-centering effect at the steering wheel.

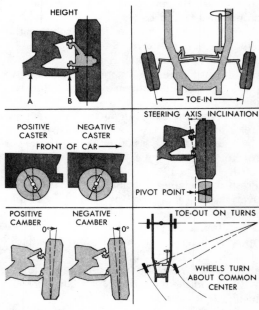

Alignment factors

Caster is adjusted by loosening either one of the upper control arm pivot bar adjusting bolts and moving the pivot bar. The bolts should be tightened to 150 ft lbs after adjustment.

Camber Adjustment

Camber is the inward or outward tilt, measured in degrees, of the wheel at the top. A wheel tilted out at the top has positive (+) camber. A wheel tilted in has negative (−) camber. Camber has a great effect on tire wear.

Camber is adjusted by loosening both the

upper control arm pivot bar adjusting bolts and moving both ends of the pivot bar equal amounts. The bolts should be tightened to 150 ft lbs after adjustment. Caster should always be rechecked after setting camber.

Toe-In Adjustment

Toe-in is the amount, measured in inches, that the centerlines of the wheels are closer together at the front than at the rear. Virtually all cars, except some with front wheel drive, are set with toe-in. Front wheel drive cars usually require toe-out to prevent excessive toe-in under power.

Toe-in must be checked after caster and camber have been adjusted, but it can be adjusted without checking the other two settings.

Toe-in is adjusted at the tie-rod sleeves. The wheels must be straight-ahead when adjusting toe-in.

1. Loosen the clamp bolts on the tie-rod sleeves.

2. Rotate the sleeves equally (in opposite directions) to obtain the correct measurement. If the sleeves are not adjusted equally, the steering wheel will be crooked.

NOTE: *If your steering wheel is already crooked, it can be straightened by turning the sleeves equally in the same direction.*

3. Toe-in can be determined by measuring the distance between the centers of the tire treads, front and rear.

4. When the adjustment is complete, turn the U of the clamps down and tighten the bolts to 11 ft lbs. A torque wrench isn't essential here, but don't overtighten the clamps.

Rear Suspension

SPRINGS

Removal and Installation

1. Raise and support the car and remove the wheels. Position jack stands under the axle

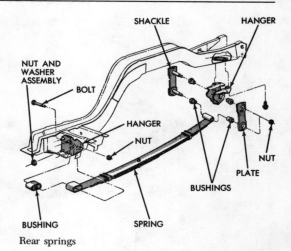

Rear springs

to remove the weight of the rear axle from the springs.

2. Disconnect the rear shock absorbers at the bottom attaching bolts. Lower the axle assembly to allow the rear springs to hang free.

3. Remove the U-bolt nuts and remove the U-bolts and plate. Remove the nuts which secure the front spring hanger to the body mounting bracket.

4. Remove the rear spring hanger bolts and let the spring drop far enough to allow the front spring hanger bolts to be removed.

5. Remove the front pivot bolt from the front spring hanger.

6. Remove the shackle nuts and remove the shackle from the rear of the spring.

7. To start installation, assemble the shackle and bushings in the rear of the spring and hanger. Start the shackle bolt nut. Do not lubricate the rubber bushings and do not tighten the bolt nut.

8. Install the front spring hanger to the front spring eye and insert the pivot bolt and nut but do not tighten them.

9. Install the rear spring hanger to the body bracket and tighten the bolts to 30 ft lbs.

10. Raise the spring and insert the bolts in the spring hanger mounting bracket holes. Tighten the bracket nuts to 30 ft lbs.

Wheel Alignment Specifications

Year	Model	CASTER		CAMBER		Toe-in (in.)	Steering Axis Inclin (deg)	Wheel Pivot Ratio (deg)	
		Range (deg)	Pref Setting (deg)	Range (deg)	Pref Setting (deg)			Inner Wheel	Outer Wheel
'76–'78	Aspen, Volare	1½P to 3¾P	2½P	①	②	⅟₁₆ to ¼	8	20	18

① Left wheel— 0 to 1P; Right wheel—¼N to ¾P
② Left wheel—½P; Right wheel—¼P

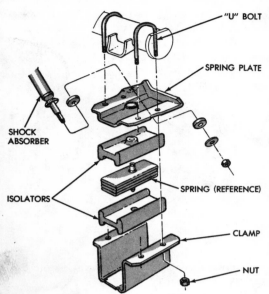

Rear spring isolator

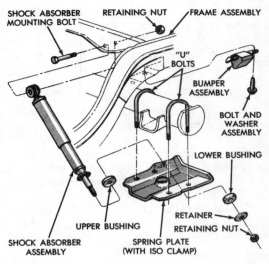

Rear shock assembly

11. Position the axle assembly so it is correctly aligned with the spring center bolt.

12. Position the center bolt over the lower spring plate. Insert the U-bolt and nut and tighten the nuts to 45 ft lbs.

13. Install the shock absorbers. Tighten to lower mount to 35 ft lbs.

14. Lower the car. Tighten the pivot bolts to 125 ft lbs and shackle nuts to 40 ft lbs.

15. If springs were replaced, check the front suspension height and adjust if necessary.

SHOCK ABSORBERS

Testing

To test the shock absorbers, bounce the rear of the car up and down a few times. When released, the car should return to its normal ride height and stop bouncing immediately. If the shocks are worn, they should both be replaced to provide equal damping.

Heavy-duty replacements are available to provide a more stable and slightly firmer ride. Air adjustable shock absorbers can be used to maintain a level ride with heavy loads.

CAUTION: *Air adjustable shock absorbers should not be used to raise the car to provide clearance for outsize rear tires. The results of a sudden pressure loss underway could be disastrous.*

Removal and Installation

1. Raise the car and support it under the rear axle to relieve the load from the shock absorber.

2. Remove the nut which attaches the shock to the spring mounting plate stud and then pull the shock from the stud.

3. At the upper mount, remove the shock attaching bolt and nut and remove the shock from the car.

4. Purge the new shock of air by extending it in its normal position and compressing it while inverted. Do this several times. It is normal for there to be more resistance to extension than to compression.

5. To install the shock, position it so the upper bolt may be inserted. Hand tighten the nut and bolt.

6. Align the shock with the spring mounting plate stud, install the retainer, nut, and washer, and hand tighten the nut.

7. Lower the car and tighten the upper nut to 70 ft lbs and the lower to 35 ft lbs.

Steering

A worm and recirculating ball type steering gear is used with the manual steering system.

Power steering is an option on all models. Hydraulic power is provided by a constant displacement type, belt driven pump. A collapsible, energy-absorbing steering column is used. No service operations involving removal or disassembly of the steering column are given here. Such critical and delicate operations should be entrusted to qualified service personnel.

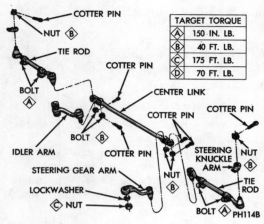

TARGET TORQUE	
Ⓐ	150 IN. LB.
Ⓑ	40 FT. LB.
Ⓒ	175 FT. LB.
Ⓓ	70 FT. LB.

Steering linkage

STEERING WHEEL

Removal and Installation

NOTE: *All models are equipped with collapsible steering columns. A sharp blow or excessive pressure on the column will cause it to collapse. Do not hammer on the steering wheel.*

1. Disconnect the ground cable from the battery.

2. Remove the padded center assembly. This center assembly is often held on only by spring clips. There are usually holes in the back of the wheel so the pad can be pushed off. However, on some deluxe interiors it is held on by screws behind the arms of the wheel.

3. Remove the large center nut. Mark the steering wheel and steering shaft so that the wheel may be replaced in its original position. In most cases, the wheel can only go on one way.

4. Using a puller, pull the steering wheel from the steering shaft. It is possible to make a puller by drilling two holes in a piece of steel exactly the same distance apart as the two threaded holes on either side of the large nut. Drill another hole in the center of the piece the same diameter as the steering shaft. Find a bolt of a slightly smaller diameter than the steering shaft. Place the puller over the steering shaft and thread the two bolts into the holes in the wheel. Tighten the two bolts, and then tighten the center bolt to draw the wheel off the shaft.

5. Reverse the above procedure to install the wheel. When placing the wheel on the shaft, make sure the tires are straight ahead and the match marks are aligned. Tighten the nut to 60 ft lbs.

TURN SIGNAL SWITCH

Removal and Installation

1. Disconnect the battery ground cable.
2. Remove the steering wheel.

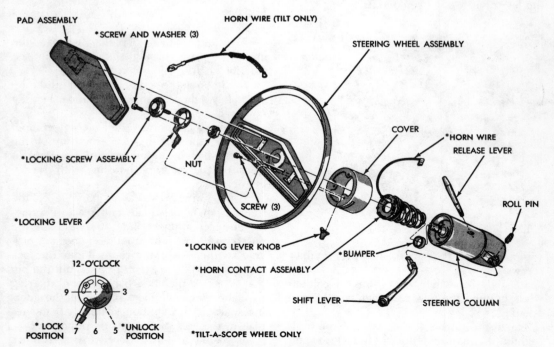

Steering wheel disassembled

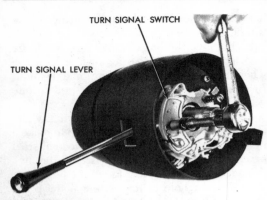

Turn signal switch removal

3. Remove the steering column cover.

4. With tilting steering wheel, remove the shift position indicator, unbolt the steering column from the lower instrument panel reinforcement and the mounting bracket from the column wiring trough.

CAUTION: *Support the steering column to prevent damage.*

5. With standard column, unsnap the wiring trough from the column.

6. Position the automatic transmission column shift lever fully clockwise. Set the tilting steering wheel at its midpoint.

7. Disconnect the harness wire connector.

8. Remove the turn signal lever screw and the lever. If the car has speed control, just let the lever hang; don't remove it.

Turn signal switch retaining plate

9. Remove the upper bearing retainer screws.

10. Pull the switch gently from the column while guiding the wires through the column opening.

11. Installation is the reverse of removal. Tighten the mounting bracket to steering col-

umn bolts to 10 ft lbs and the bracket bolts to 9 ft lbs.

IGNITION SWITCH AND/OR IGNITION LOCK CYLINDER

Removal and Installation

STANDARD STEERING COLUMN

1. Disconnect the negative battery cable. Remove the steering wheel.

2. Remove the screw that attaches the turn signal lever to the steering column.

3. Remove the three screws that attach the upper bearing retainer to the turn signal switch.

4. Pull the turn signal switch as far upward as possible.

Snap ring removal

5. Using snap-ring pliers, remove the upper bearing housing snap-ring from the steering shaft.

6. Remove the screw that attaches the ignition key light assembly to the upper bearing housing.

7. Using care not to damage any components, pry the upper bearing housing off the steering shaft by lifting upward on alternate sides of the bearing housing with screwdrivers.

8. Lift upward as far as possible on the steering shaft lock plate and place a screwdriver or other object under it to hold it in the raised position. If this operation does not provide adequate working room under the lock plate, it will be necessary to press out the pin that attaches the lock plate to the steering shaft and remove the lock plate from the steering shaft. If the ignition switch is being replaced, the lock plate must be removed.

9. Using an offset screwdriver, remove

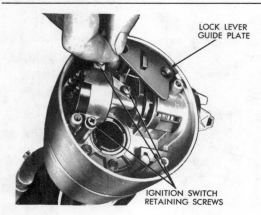

Lock lever guide plate

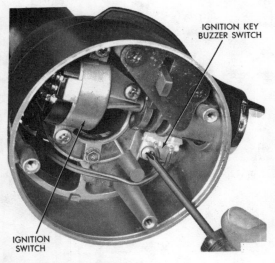

Ignition key buzzer switch

the two screws that attach the lock lever guide plate to the steering column.

10. With the ignition lock cylinder in the "Lock" position and the ignition key removed, insert a stiff wire into the lock cylinder release hole in the steering column. Push in on the

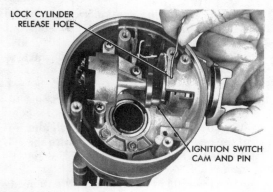

Lock cylinder removal

wire to release the spring-loaded lock retainer and pull the lock cylinder out of the steering column.

11. If the ignition switch is being replaced, remove the two screws that attach the ignition key buzzer switch to the steering column and the three screws that attach the ignition switch to the steering column. Lift off the ignition switch out of the housing.

12. Reverse the above procedure for installation.

Tilt Steering Column

1. Disconnect the negative battery cable.

2. Remove the steering wheel.

3. Remove the three attaching screws and remove the shaft lock cover.

4. Remove the screws that attach the tilt control lever and the turn signal lever to the steering column and then remove the levers.

5. Push in the hazard warning knob and unscrew the knob from the turn signal switch. Remove the ignition key lamp assembly.

6. Depress the lock plate to gain access to the lock plate retaining snap-ring. Remove the snap-ring from the steering shaft.

7. Remove the lock plate, cancelling cam, and spring.

8. Remove the three turn signal switch attaching screws, place the shift lever in the Low (L) position, and pull the switch and wires as far upward as possible.

9. With the ignition lock cylinder in the "Lock" position, insert a small screwdriver into the lock release slot in the housing cover.

Removing lock plate retaining ring

10. Press down with the screwdriver to release the spring latch at the bottom of the slot and pull the lock cylinder from the housing.

The following steps are for ignition switch replacement only.

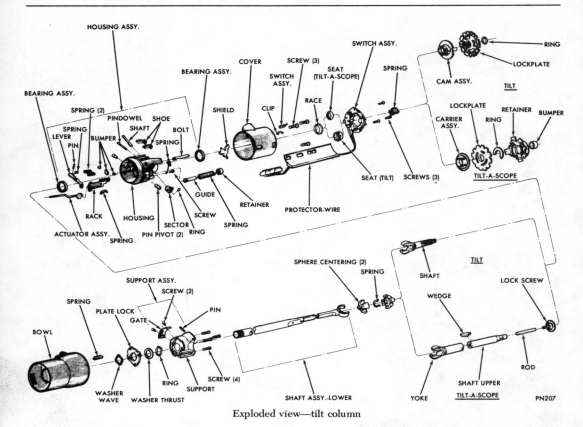

Exploded view—tilt column

11. Remove the three screws that attach the upper steering column housing to the steering column and remove the housing.

12. Install the column tilt control lever and move the column to the full "Up" position.

13. Insert a screwdriver into the slot in the spring retainer and press the retainer in approximately 3/16 in. Turn the retainer approximately 1/8 turn to the left until the ears align with the grooves in the housing. Remove the spring retainer, spring, and guide.

14. Push the steering shaft inward to enable removal of the inner race and seat. Remove the race and seat.

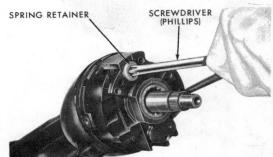

Tilt spring retainer

15. Make sure the ignition switch is in the "Lock" position, then remove the wire connector from the ignition switch and remove the screws that attach the ignition switch to the outside of the steering column.

16. Lift the ignition switch from the column and twist it to disengage the switch actuating rod from the rack. Remove the switch.

17. To install the ignition lock cylinder, insert the cylinder into the housing with the cylinder in the "Lock" position and the key *removed*.

18. Move the cylinder into the housing until it contacts the switch actuator. Move the

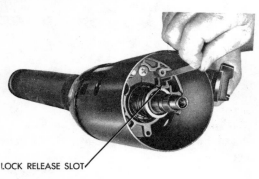

Lock cylinder removal

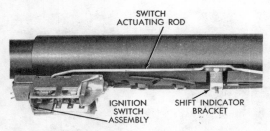

Ignition switch

Removing the tie-rod ends with a puller

switch actuator rod up and down to align the parts. When the parts are aligned, the cylinder will move inward and lock into place.

The following steps are for ignition switch installation only.

19. With the ignition switch in the "Lock" position, insert the actuating rod into the steering column.

20. Twist the switch and rod assembly as required to engage the actuating rod with the rack. Make sure the ignition lock cylinder is in the "Lock" position.

21. Install the ignition switch mounting screws but do not tighten them.

22. Move the ignition switch downward, away from the steering wheel, and tighten the switch mounting screws. Make sure that the ignition switch has not moved out of the lock detent.

23. Attach the switch wiring connector.

POWER STEERING PUMP

Removal and Installation

1. Loosen the pump mounting bolts and remove the power steering belt.

2. Disconnect the hoses at the pump. Be careful not to get any dirt in the hoses.

3. Remove the pump bolts and remove the pump with the bracket.

4. To install the pump, place it in position and install the mounting bolts. Tighten them to 30 ft lbs.

5. Install the belt and tighten the bolts.

6. Connect the pressure and return hoses. Replace the O-ring on the pressure hose, if so equipped.

7. Fill the pump with the power steering fluid specified in Chapter 1.

8. Start the engine and rotate the steering wheel from stop to stop several times to bleed the system. Check the pump fluid level and fill it as required. Make certain the hoses are away from the exhaust manifold and are not kinked.

TIE-ROD ENDS

Removal and Installation

1. Loosen the tie rod adjuster sleeve clamp nuts.

2. Remove the tie rod end stud nut and cotter pin.

3. If the outer tie rod end is being removed, remove the stud from the steering knuckle. If the inner tie rod end is being removed, remove the stud from the center link. The studs on all the tie rod ends fit in a tapered hole. They can be removed with a ball joint removal tool available at auto parts stores.

4. Unscrew the tie rod end from the threaded sleeve. The threads may be left or right-hand threads. Count the number of turns required to remove it.

5. To install, reverse the above. Turn the tie rod end in as many turns as was needed to remove it. This will give approximately correct toe-in.

6. Tighten the stud nuts to 40 ft lbs and install new cotter pins.

7. Set the toe-in as explained earlier in this chapter.

Chapter 9

Brakes

All Volaré and Aspen models are equipped with front disc brakes and rear drum brakes. A split hydraulic system is used, with independent circuits for the front and rear brakes. The brakes on all models are self-adjusting.

Hydraulic System

MASTER CYLINDER

Removal and Installation

1. Disconnect the brake lines from the master cylinder. Plug the outlets in the master cylinder.

2. Remove the nuts that attach the master cylinder to the firewall or power brake booster.

3. On models with standard brakes, disconnect the pushrod from the brake pedal.

4. Slide the master cylinder straight out and off the firewall or brake booster.

5. Reverse the procedure to install the master cylinder. When reconnecting the brake lines, start the fitting with your fingers and turn the fitting in several threads before using a wrench. This will prevent cross threading. If difficulty is encountered with threading the fittings, bend the brake line slightly so that the fitting enters the hole squarely. If a fluid leak occurs tighten the fit-

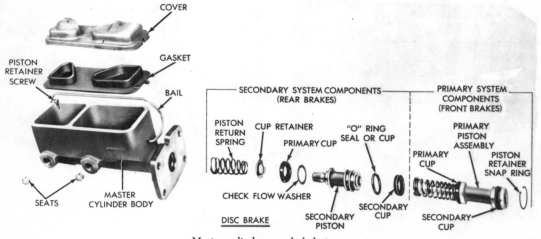

Master cylinder—exploded view

ting, check for a damaged seat or tubing end, or look for a hairline crack in the tubing.

6. Bleed the brake system after installation is complete.

Overhaul

If the master cylinder leaks externally, or if the pedal sinks while being held down, the master cylinder is probably worn. There are three possible solutions:

    a. Buy a new master cylinder.

    b. Trade the old one in on a rebuilt unit.

    c. Rebuild the old one with a rebuilding kit.

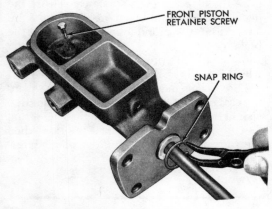

Snap ring and retainer screw removal

Overhaul is as follows:

NOTE: *Front and rear refer to the locations of the positions in the cylinder, not to the brakes they operate.*

1. Clean the outside of the cylinder. Remove the cover and drain the fluid. It should not be reused.

2. Remove the secondary (front) piston retainer screw from inside the reservoir. Remove the snap-ring from the end of the cylinder bore.

3. Remove the rear (primary) and front (secondary) pistons. If the front piston sticks in

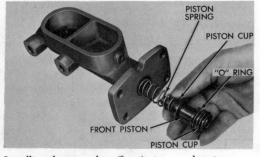

Installing the secondary (front) piston and spring

Primary piston installation

the cylinder, air pressure may be used to remove it. Always use new rubber cups if air pressure was used.

4. Note the position of the rubber cups and springs and remove them from the pistons and from the bore. Don't remove the primary (middle) cup of the primary (rear) piston. Replace the entire piston if the cup is worn.

5. Remove the tube seats, using an easy out or a screw threaded into the seat. Unless the seat is damaged it is not absolutely necessary to remove it.

6. Remove the residual pressure valves, if any, and springs found under the seats.

7. Clean the inside of the master cylinder with brake fluid or denatured alcohol.

8. Closely inspect the inside of the master cylinder. Polish the inside of the bore with crocus cloth. If there is rust or pit marks it will be necessary to use a hone. Discard the master cylinder if scores or pits cannot be eliminated by honing of 0.002 in. or less.

9. Do not reuse old rubber parts and be sure to use all the new parts supplied in the rebuilding kit.

10. Before assembly, thoroughly lubricate all parts (especially seals) with clean brake fluid.

11. Replace the primary cup on the front end of the secondary (front) piston with the lip away from the piston.

12. Carefully slide the O-ring over the rear of the piston and into the second land.

13. Slowly work the rear secondary cup over the piston and position it in the rear land. The lip must face to the rear.

14. Slide the cup retainer over the front piston stem with the cup lip facing away from the piston.

15. Replace the small end of the pressure spring into the retainer.

16. Position the assembly in the bore. Be sure the cups are not canted.

17. Slowly work the secondary cup over

the back of the rear (primary) piston with the cup lip facing forward.

18. Position the spring retainer in the center of the rear piston assembly. It should be over the shoulder of the front piston. Position the piston assembly in the bore. Slowly work the cup lips into the bore, then seat the piston assembly.

19. Hold the pistons in the seated position. Install the snap-ring. Insert the piston retaining screw and tighten it securely.

20. Replace the residual pressure valves, if any, and spring. Position them in the outlet and install the tube seats.

21. Before installing a new or reconditioned master cylinder, it will be necessary to bleed it.

   a. Insert bleeding tubes from the tube seats into the reservoirs and fill both brake reservoirs with brake fluid.

   b. Insert a dowel pin into the depression in the piston or operate the pushrod and push in and release the piston. It will return under its own spring pressure. Repeat this operation until all of the air bubbles are expelled.

   c. Remove the bleeding tubes, and install the cover and the gasket.

22. Install the master cylinder on the car.

BRAKE WARNING SYSTEMS

Four-wheel drum brake models have a pressure differential switch to alert the driver when one of the two brake circuits loses pressure. On disc-drum models, this switch is combined with a pressure metering valve to limit pressure to the rear brakes and prevent rear wheel locking. Both types are located in the engine compartment, usually on the frame rail. These valves reset themselves automatically after the malfunction is corrected and the brakes used. They do not interfere with normal system bleeding; however, if pressure bleeding is attempted on disc brake cars, a spring clip must be used to hold the metering valve stem out.

CAUTION: *Never push the metering valve stem in. The valve will be damaged and the front brakes will be disabled.*

BLEEDING

The purpose of bleeding the brakes is to expel air trapped in the hydraulic system. The system must be bled whenever the pedal feels spongy, indicating that compressible air has entered the system. It must also be bled whenever the system has been opened or

leaking. You will need a helper for this job.

The customary procedure is to start with the wheel farthest away from the master cylinder and work in. In other words, right rear - left rear - right front - left front.

1. Clean the bleed screw at each wheel.

2. Attach a small rubber hose to one of the bleed screws and place the end in a container of brake fluid.

3. Fill the master cylinder with brake fluid. Check the level often during bleeding. Pump up the brake pedal and hold it.

4. Open the bleed screw about one-quarter turn, press the brake pedal down and hold it, close the bleed screw, and slowly release the pedal. Continue until no more air bubbles are forced from the cylinder on application of the brake pedal.

5. Repeat the procedure on the remaining wheel cylinders.

Disc brakes may be bled in the same manner as drum brakes, except that the disc should be rotated to make sure that the piston has returned to the unapplied position when bleeding is completed and the bleed screw closed.

Front Disc Brakes

A sliding caliper front disc brake is used on all models. A single hydraulic piston is used, this acts on the inboard brake shoe. When the brake pedal is depressed, the piston forces the inside brake shoe or pad into contact with the disc. Increasing force against the disc causes the caliper to slide towards the disc and bring the outboard shoe into contact. The caliper slides on machined grooves or "ways" in the adapter that is bolted to the steering knuckle. Retaining spring clips keep the caliper from moving vertically.

BRAKE PADS

Inspection

A visual inspection of the brake pads, calipers, and brake lines is recommended every several thousand miles.

1. Jack up the front of the car and support it on stands. Remove the front wheels.

2. Check the rubber brake lines to the calipers for breaks or cracks. Check the metal brake lines for rust or damage from rocks or other road debris.

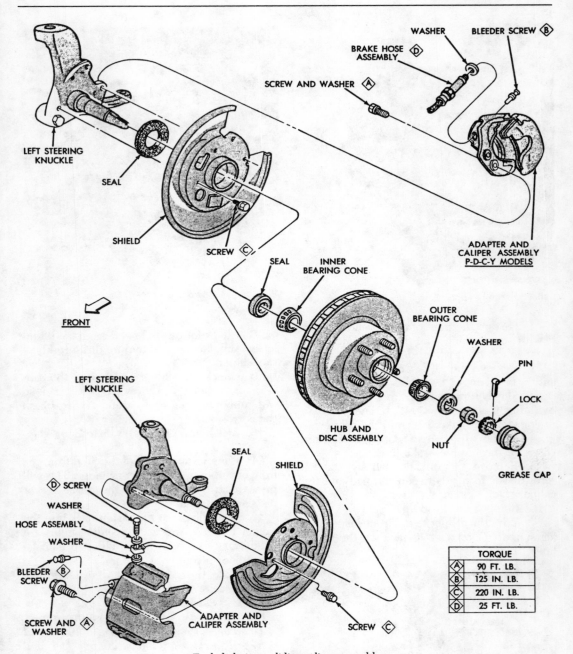

	TORQUE
Ⓐ	90 FT. LB.
Ⓑ	125 IN. LB.
Ⓒ	220 IN. LB.
Ⓓ	25 FT. LB.

Exploded view—sliding caliper assembly

3. Examine the surfaces of the disc for deep scoring or grooves.

4. Inspect the brake pads. The outside pads are normally thinner than the inside pads. Replace the brake pads if they are worn to within 1/32 in. of the disc.

5. Check the caliper for signs of brake fluid leakage. The caliper will have to be removed and rebuilt or replaced if any leakage is evident.

Removal and Installation

Brake pads should always be replaced in full axle sets, that is they should be renewed on both sides at the same time. Original equipment replacement sets contain four brake pads, new retainer clips, and O-rings. Always reinstall the anti-rattle springs under the retaining clip bolts, they prevent annoying brake squeaks and rattles.

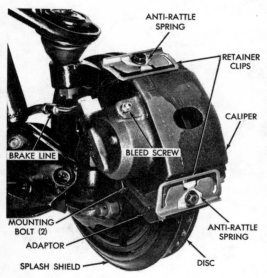

Caliper assembly—front view

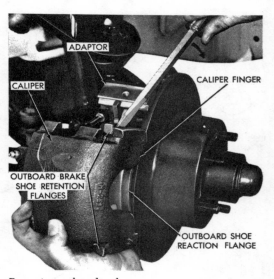

Removing outboard pad

1. Jack up the front of the car and support it with stands under the front crossmember. Remove the front wheels.

2. Remove the caliper retaining clips and anti-rattle springs.

3. Slowly remove the caliper from the disc by sliding it out and away. It's not necessary to disconnect the brake line from the caliper.

4. Support the caliper, so as not to put a strain on the flexible brake line.

5. Remove the outside pad by using a screwdriver to pry between the pad and the caliper. Don't gouge the disc.

6. Remove the inside pad.

7. Wire the caliper to the front suspension for support. Don't let it hang by the brake line.

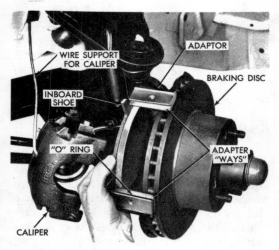

Removing inboard pad

8. Check for piston boot damage and fluid leaks. Any damage will require disassembly of the caliper.

9. Check the sliding surfaces on the caliper and the adaptor. If they are rusty, remove the rubber O-ring and carefully wire brush the corrosion.

10. Install new O-rings on the caliper adaptor.

11. Remove about half of the fluid from the front chamber of the master cylinder. This will prevent an overflow when the new, thicker pads are installed.

12. Carefully push the piston back into the caliper bore. A large pair of sliding pliers are handy for this job. Be careful not to damage the rubber piston boot.

13. Slide the new outboard pad into the caliper recess.

NOTE: *There should be no free-play between the brake pad flanges and the caliper. This can cause brake pad rattling. Should free-play exist as shown by vertical pad movement after installation, remove the pad from the caliper and tap the flanges down to make a slight interference fit.*

14. Install the outboard pad by snapping it into place with your hand. If it is necessary to use a C-clamp to install the pad, use the old pads to protect the new pad from damage.

15. Install new O-rings on the adapter. Put the inside pad in place by positioning the pad on the adaptor with its flanges in the adapter "ways."

16. Carefully slide the caliper assembly

into place in the adapter and over the disc. Align the caliper on the adapter.

CAUTION: *Don't pull the dust boot out of its groove when sliding the piston and boot over the inside pad.*

17. Install the anti-rattle springs and retaining clips and tighten the screws to 15 ft lbs. The springs go over the retaining clips.

18. Step on the brake pedal several times until you feel a firm pedal. Refill the master cylinder. Bleed the brakes if the pedal doesn't come up.

19. Install the wheels and tighten the lug nuts to 85 ft lbs in a criss-cross pattern.

20. Lower car and road test.

CALIPERS

Removal and Installation

Follow steps 1 through 6 of "Brake Pad Removal." Disconnect the brake line and remove the caliper. Installation is the reverse of removal. Bleed the brakes.

Overhaul

1. Remove the caliper assembly from the car *without* disconnecting the hydraulic line.

2. Support the caliper assembly on the upper control arm and surround it with shop towels to absorb any brake fluid. Slowly depress the brake pedal until the piston is pushed out of its bore.

CAUTION: *Do not use compressed air to force the piston from its bore; injury could result.*

3. Disconnect the brake line from the caliper and plug it to prevent fluid loss.

4. Mount the caliper in a soft-jawed vise and clamp lighty. Do not tighten the vise too much or the caliper will become distorted.

5. Work the dust boot out with your fingers.

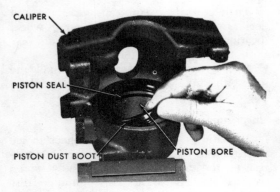

Removing dust boot

Removing piston seal

6. Use a small pointed *wooden* or *plastic* stick to work the piston seal out of the groove in the bore. Discard the seal.

CAUTION: *Using a screwdriver or other metal tool could scratch the piston bore.*

7. Using the same wooden or plastic stick, press the outer bushings out of the housing. Discard the old bushings. remove the inner bushings in the same manner. Discard them as well.

8. Clean all parts in denatured alcohol or brake fluid. Blow out all bores and passages with compressed air.

9. Inspect the piston and bore for scoring or pitting. Replace the piston if necessary. Bores with light scratches or corrosion may be cleaned with crocus cloth. Bores with deep scratches may be honed if you do not increase the bore diameter more than 0.002 in. Replace the housing if the bore must be enlarged beyond this.

NOTE: *Black stains are caused by piston seals and are harmless.*

10. If the bore had to be honed, clean its

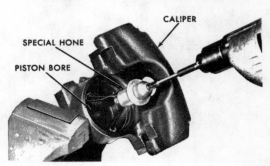

Honing piston bore

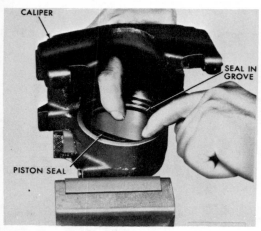

Installing piston seal

grooves with a stiff, non-metallic rotary brush. Clean the bore twice by flushing it out with brake fluid and drying it with a soft, lint-free cloth.

Caliper assembly is as follows:

1. Clamp the caliper in a soft-jawed vise; do not overtighten.

2. Dip a new piston seal in brake fluid or the lubricant supplied with the rebuilding kit. Position the new seal in one area of its groove and gently work it into place with clean fingers, so that it is correctly seated. Do not use an old seal.

3. Coat a new boot with brake fluid or lubricant (as above), leaving a generous amount inside.

4. Insert the boot in the caliper and work it into the groove, using your fingers only. The boot will snap into place once it is correctly positioned. Run your forefinger around the inside of the boot to make sure that it is correctly seated.

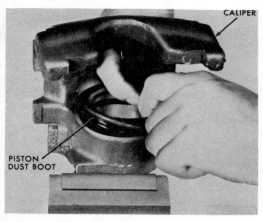

Installing piston dust boot

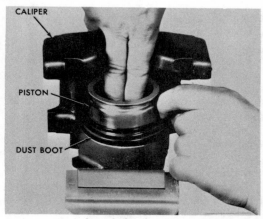

Inserting piston through dust boot

5. Install the bleed screw in its hole and plug the fluid inlet on the caliper.

6. Coat the piston with brake fluid or lubricant. Spread the boot with your fingers and work the piston into the boot.

7. Depress the piston; this will force the boot into its groove on the piston. Remove the plug and bottom the piston in the bore.

8. Compress the flanges of new guide pin bushings and work them into place by pressing *in* on the bushings with your fingertips, until they are seated. Make sure that the flanges cover the housing evenly on all sides.

9. Install the caliper on the car as previously outlined.

BRAKE DISC

Removal and Installation

The brake disc and hub are removed at the same time.

1. Raise and support the car and remove the tire and wheel.

2. Remove the caliper from the disc but do not disconnect the brake line. Support the caliper.

3. Remove the grease cap, cotter pin, nut lock, nut, thrust washer, and outer wheel bearing.

4. Slide the disc off the spindle.

5. Reverse the procedure to install the disc. Adjust the wheel bearing. Tighten wheel lug nuts to 85 ft lbs.

Inspection

1. With the wheel removed, check to see that there is no grease or other foreign material on the disc. If the disc is badly scored replace or refinish it. The minimum disc thickness is cast into the hub.

Brake disc showing minimum thickness

2. Measure the thickness of the disc with a micrometer at 12 points around the disc, 1 in. from the disc's edge. Any variation of more than 0.0005 in. means that the disc should be replaced.

3. Using a dial indicator, check the disc run out on both sides with the wheel bearing adjusted to zero endplay. Run out should be no greater than 0.004 in. If the run out exceeds this figure the disc should be refinished or replaced. Make sure the wheel bearing is properly adjusted when making this measurement.

WHEEL BEARINGS

Adjustment

1. Raise the front wheel off the floor.

2. Remove the grease cap. You can pry it off with a screw driver or grab it with a pair of water pump pliers.

3. Remove the cotter pin and the nut lock.

4. While turning the wheel, tighten the nut to 240–300 in. lbs.

5. Back the adjusting nut off completely,

Wheel bearing adjustment

then tighten it finger tight. Install the nut lock and the cotter pin.

6. Coat the inside of the cap with grease (don't fill it) and replace the cap.

NOTE: *Correct adjustment should result in 0.001–0.003 in. end-play.*

Removal, Packing, and Installation

1. Raise and support the car. Remove the wheel.

2. Remove the caliper.

3. Remove the disc and the outer bearing.

4. Remove the inner bearing.

5. To remove the bearing cone if necessary, drive the inner seal out of the hub and drive the cone out with a ¾ in. diameter nonmetallic rod. Install the new cone and install the new seal with the lip inward.

6. Clean the bearings thoroughly in a safe solvent. Check their condition, but don't spin them any more than is absolutely necessary.

7. Clean the spindle and apply a light coat of grease on all polished surfaces.

8. Pack both wheel bearings using wheel bearing grease made for disc brakes. Ordinary grease will melt and ooze out, ruining the pads. Place a healthy glob of grease in the palm of one hand and force the edge of the bearing into it so that the grease fills the bearing. Do this until the whole bearing is (ugh!) packed. Grease packing tools are available to make this job a lot less messy.

9. Fill the hub grease cavity with grease even with the inner diameter of the bearing cups. Replace the hub and adjust the bearings.

10. Replace the caliper.

11. Replace the wheel.

Rear Drum Brakes

BRAKE DRUMS

Removal and Installation

1. Remove the rear plug from the brake adjusting access hole on the inside of the wheel.

2. Slide a thin screwdriver through the hole and position the adjusting lever away from the adjusting notches on the star wheel.

3. Insert an adjusting tool or screwdriver into the brake adjusting hole and engage the star wheel. Pry downward with the tool to back off the brake adjustment.

4. Remove the rear wheel and tire. Re-

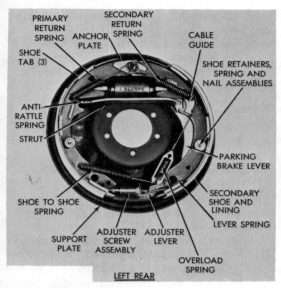

Drum brake assembly

Drum showing maximum diameter

move the clips (if any) from the wheel studs and discard them.

5. Remove the drum from the axle. The drum simply slips from the axle leaving the wheel studs in place in the axle. However, the drum will sometimes be rusted in place. To break the rust, strike the drum sharply several times with a soft hammer on the corner. Strike the drum in several places around its circumference. Do not strike the drum on the edge of the open side as this may cause cracks.

6. Installation is the reverse of the removal procedure.

Inspection

1. Drum run out (out of round) and diameter should be measured. Drum diameter should not vary more than 0.002 in. and run out should not exceed 0.006 in. Do not reface a drum more than 0.060 inches over its standard diameter.

NOTE: *The maximum safe inside diameter is marked on the drum.*

2. Check the drum for large cracks and scores. Replace the drum if necessary.

3. If the brake linings are wearing more on one edge than the other then the drum may be "bell" shaped and will have to be replaced or resurfaced.

BRAKE SHOES

Inspection

The brake drums must be removed to inspect the linings. If they are worn to $1/32$ in. or less at any point, the front linings must all be replaced.

NOTE: *This may not agree with your state's inspection specifications.*

Removal and Installation

NOTE: *If you are not thoroughly familiar with the procedures involved in brake replacement, disassemble and assemble one side at a time, leaving the other wheel intact, as a reference.*

Remove the wheel and brake drum and proceed as follows:

1. Remove the shoe return springs using a brake spring service tool. Detach the adjusting cable eye from the anchor and unhook the other end from the lever. Remove the cable, overload spring, guide and anchor plate.

2. Detach the adjusting lever from the spring, and separate the spring from the pivot. Remove the spring completely from the secondary shoe web and unfasten it from the primary shoe web.

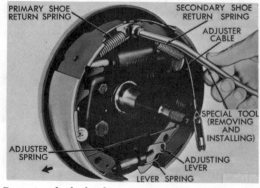

Removing the brake shoe return springs

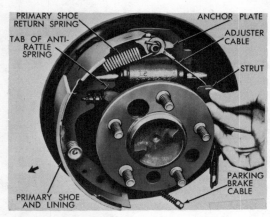

Removing the parking brake cable

3. With the anchor ends of both shoes spread apart, remove the parking brake lever strut, as well as the anti-rattle spring.

4. Detach the parking brake cable from the parking brake lever.

5. Remove the retainers, springs, and nails from the shoe. Extract both shoes from the pushrods, and lift them out. remove the star wheel assembly from the shoes.

6. Put a thin film of high temperature grease at the six shoe tab contact areas on the support plate.

7. Lubricate the pivot on the inner side of the secondary shoe web, and install the parking brake lever on it. Fasten the lever with its washer and horseshoe clip.

8. Connect the parking brake cable to the lever. Slip the secondary shoe next to the support plate, while engaging the shoe web with the pushrod, and push it against the anchor.

9. Position the parking brake strut behind the hub and slide it into the slot in the lever. Fit the anti-rattle spring over the free end of the strut.

10. Position the primary shoe, engage it in

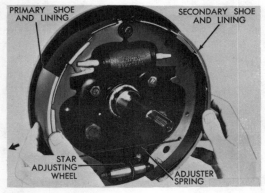

Shoe installation

the pushrod and with the free end of the parking brake strut. Place the anchor plate over the anchor and fit the eye of the adjustment cable over the anchor. Connect the primary shoe return spring to its web and fit its other end over the anchor.

11. Place the cable guide in the secondary shoe web. Hold it in this position while engaging the secondary shoe return spring, which goes through the guide and into the web. Put its other end over the anchor.

NOTE: *Be sure that the cable guide stays flat against the web, and that the secondary shoe return spring overlaps that of the primary.*

Squeeze the spring loops around the anchor, with pliers, until they are parallel.

12. Place the star wheel assembly between the shoes, with the star wheel assembly adjacent to the secondary shoe. The left rear star wheel is plated and marked with an "L."

13. Place the adjustment lever spring over the pivot pin on the shoe web and fit the lever under the spring, but over the pin. To lock the lever, push it toward the rear.

14. Install the shoe retaining nails, retainers, and spring. Thread the adjusting cable over the guide. Hook the end of the overload spring in the adjustment lever, making sure that the cable remains tight against the anchor and is aligned with the guide.

15. Install the brake drum and adjust the brakes. Initial adjustment is the same as for front drum brakes.

Initial Brake Adjustment

Although the brakes are self adjusting, it is best to make an initial adjustment after backing off the adjuster to remove the brake drum or after shoe replacement.

1. Raise the wheels to be adjusted so that they are free to spin.

2. Remove the rear adjusting hole cover from the backing plate.

3. Make sure the parking brake is fully released.

4. Insert an adjusting tool or screwdriver in the hole until it contacts the star wheel. Lift the handle of the tool upward, rotating the star wheel, until there is a slight drag felt when the tire is rotated.

5. Insert a piece of welding rod or a thin screwdriver into the adjustment hole. Push against the adjusting lever and hold it away from the star wheel. Back off on the star wheel

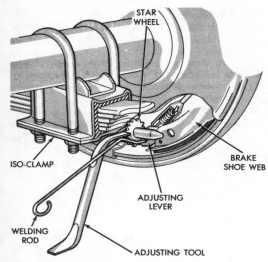

Brake adjustment

until no drag is felt. Replace the adjusting hole cover.

6. Repeat on the other wheel.

WHEEL CYLINDERS

Removal and Installation

1. Raise and support the car and remove the wheel and tire.

2. Remove the brake drum and brake shoes.

3. Remove the brake line from the cylinder.

4. Unfasten the wheel cylinder attaching bolts and remove the cylinder from its support.

5. Installation is the reverse of removal. Bleed the brakes after installing the cylinder.

Overhaul

1. Pry the boots off either end of the cylinder and remove the pushrods. Push in on one of the pistons to force out the other piston, its cup, the spring, and the piston itself.

2. Wash the pistons, the wheel cylinder housing, and the spring in fresh brake fluid. Dry them with compressed air.

3. Inspect the cylinder bore wall for signs of wear. If it is badly scored or pitted, the entire cylinder should be replaced. Light scratches or corrosion can be removed with crocus cloth or a hone.

4. Dip the pistons and new cups in clean brake fluid. Coat the cylinder wall with brake fluid.

5. Place the spring in the cylinder bore. Position the cups in either end of the cylinder with the open end of the cups facing inward (toward each other).

6. Place the pistons in either end of the cylinder bore with the recessed ends facing outward. Slide the pistons into the bore until the ends are flush with the end of the bore. Open the bleeder to relieve any pressure.

7. Fit the boots over the ends of the cylinder and push down until each boot is seated.

Parking Brake

CABLE

Adjustment

1. Rear brakes must be in adjustment before adjusting parking brakes. Raise and sup-

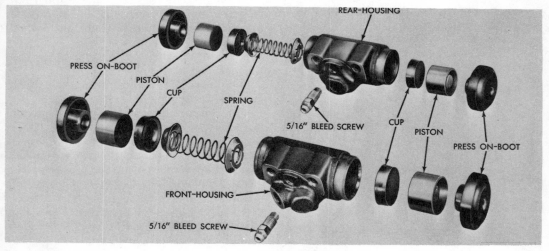

Wheel cylinder—exploded view

port the rear wheels. Release the parking brake lever and loosen the cable adjusting nut under the car.

2. Tighten the cable adjusting nut until a light drag is felt while rotating the wheel. Loosen the cable adjusting nut until both rear wheels can be rotated freely, then back off the cable adjusting nut two full turns.

3. Apply the parking brake several times and test to see that the rear wheels rotate freely.

Removal and Installation

1. Raise and support the car and remove the rear wheels.
2. Disconnect the brake cable from the adjuster connector.
3. Remove the retaining clip from the brake cable bracket at the end of the outer cable.
4. Remove the brake drum from the rear axle.
5. Remove the brake shoe retaining springs and return springs.

Removing brake cable

6. Remove the brake shoe strut and spring from the brake support and disconnect the brake cable from the operating arm.
7. Compress the retainers on the end of the brake cable housing and remove the cable from the support.
8. Installation is the reverse of removal.

Brake Specifications
(All measurements are given in inches)

Year	Master Cylinder Diameter	WHEEL CYLINDER DIAMETER		DISC OR DRUM DIAMETER	
		Disc	Drum	Front Disc	Rear Drum
All	1.03	2.75	$15/16$	10.98	10 (Sedan) 11 (Wagon)

Brake Diagnosis Chart

Condition	Possible Cause
Low Pedal	Brakes improperly adjusted (rear drum only), worn pads or linings, master cylinder worn or damaged, vacuum booster defective (power brakes only).
Spongy Pedal	Air in the hydraulic system, faulty check valve in the master cylinder, brake hoses expanding under pressure, incorrect brake fluid.
Hard Pedal	Pedal linkage binding, brakes improperly adjusted, pads or shoes worn or distorted, hoses or lines kinked or collapsed, master cylinder defective, vacuum booster or vacuum lines defective, engine vacuum low.
Fading Pedal	Air in hydraulic system, incorrect brake fluid (NOTE: *Repeated hard hard stops from high speed will cause pedal fade in all vehicles. The pedal will return to normal when the brakes cool down.*), defective or leaking master cylinder or wheel cylinders, hoses or lines leaking.
Grabbing or Pulling	Improper adjustment, pads or shoes greasy or otherwise contaminated, proportioning valve defective (both rear wheels grabbing only), loose or misaligned calipers, incorrect tire pressures, wheel bearings loose.

Brake Diagnosis Chart (cont.)

Condition	Possible Cause
Noise (squealing, clicking or scraping)	Improper adjustment, worn pads or shoes, scored or glazed drums or rotors, loose calipers.
Chatter or shudder	Rotor out of parallel, pads or shoes worn, drums out of round or hard-spotted.
Dragging Brakes	Parking brake sticking, brake shoes too tight, caliper pistons seized.

Chapter 10

Body

Doors

Removal and Installation

1. Open the door to the fully open position and place a jack or some other kind of support under the door. This will hold the weight of the door when the hinges are removed.

2. Scribe marks around the hinge plates on either the door or the body to aid in reinstallation.

3. The door can be removed from the hinges or the door and hinge assembly can be removed from the body as a unit. Remove the attaching screws from the door or the body and remove the door.

4. To install, first position the door on the

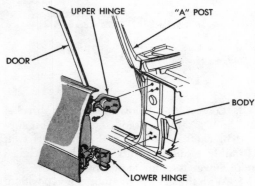

Door attachment

jack or support. Install the door attaching screws finger tight.

5. Adjust the door up or down with the jack until the alignment marks made earlier align with the hinges. Tighten the attaching screws.

DOOR PANELS

Removal and Installation

1. Remove the door lock knob. It's threaded on.

2. Remove the door handle attaching screws and remove the door handle.

3. Remove the two armrest attaching screws and remove the armrest.

4. Remove the screw attaching the window crank and remove the crank. If the car is equipped with electric windows, remove the switch asembly from the retaining cup on the trim panel and disconnect the switch from the connector.

5. If equipped with remote control mirror, remove the control assembly from the door panel.

6. Using a putty knife or other flat-bladed tool, unclip the door panel from the door.

7. To install, install the trim panel on the door. If so equipped, install the remote control mirror bezel.

8. Install the door handle and window crank. Install the armrest. Install the door lock knob.

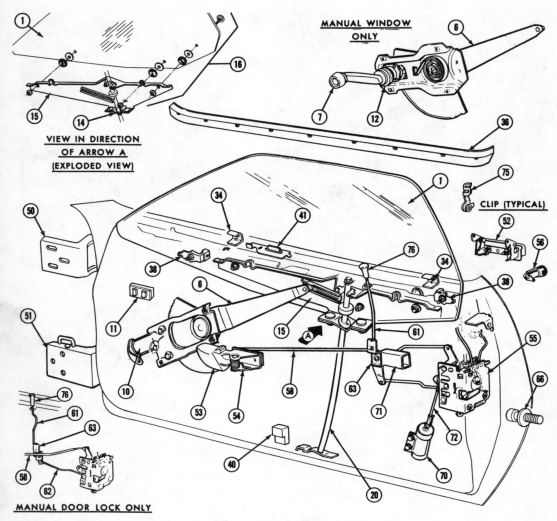

MANUAL WINDOW
ONLY

VIEW IN DIRECTION
OF ARROW A
(EXPLODED VIEW)

CLIP (TYPICAL)

MANUAL DOOR LOCK ONLY

Front door

1. Door glass	33. Bracket and liner assembly
6. Regulator	34. Glass stabilizer
7. Regulator handle	35. Trim support bracket
10. Motor	36. Outer belt
11. Switch	weatherstrip
12. Regulator handle	38. Up stop assembly
spacer	40. Down stop bumper
14. Glass track guide	41. Retainer assembly
15. Glass lift channel	50. Door hinge upper
16. Glass lift channel	51. Door hinge lower
fastener	52. Door handle outside
20. Track—tube type	53. Remote handle inside

54. Remote control	71. Locking switch
55. Door latch	assembly
56. Door lock cylinder	72. Link—solenoid
58. Link—remote control	to latch
to latch	73. Link—latch to
61. Link—pushrod to	locking
latch lock control	switch assembly
62. Link—latch lock	75. Linkage clips
control to latch	76. Locking knobs
63. Latch lock control	
66. Door latch striker	
70. Lock solenoid	

WINDOWS

Adjustment

1. Remove the trim panel as described earlier.

2. Remove the plastic air shield from the inner door panel.

3. Loosen the following screws: bracket and liner assembly, stabilizers, and trim support brackets. Also loosen the three glass lift assembly mounting nuts, and the two glass guide lower retainer mounting nuts.

4. With the glass in the fully down position, push the glass outboard until it contacts the

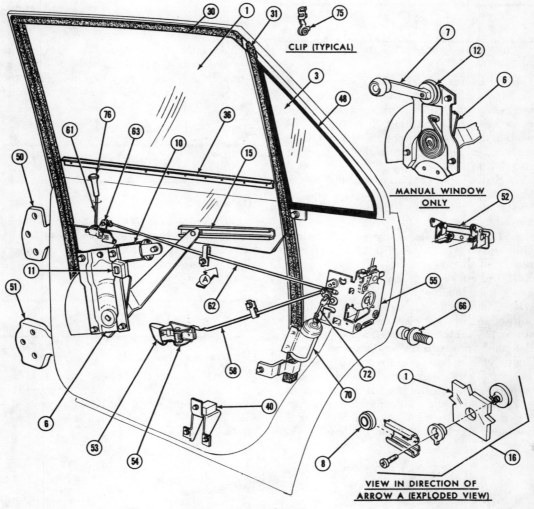

CLIP (TYPICAL)

MANUAL WINDOW
ONLY

VIEW IN DIRECTION OF
ARROW A (EXPLODED VIEW)

Rear door

1. Door glass	30. Door glass run	52. Door handle outside	62. Link—latch lock
6. Regulator	31. Door glass run	53. Remote handle inside	control to latch
7. Regulator handle	on division channel	54. Remote control	63. Latch lock control
8. Regulator slide	36. Outer Belt	55. Door latch	66. Door latch striker
10. Motor	weatherstrip	57. Link—outside	70. Lock solenoid
11. Switch	40. Down stop bumper	handle to latch	72. Link—solenoid
12. Regulator handle spacer	48. Stationary glass	58. Link—remote	to latch
15. Glass lift channel	weatherstrip	control to latch	75. Linkage clips
16. Glass lift channel	50. Door hinge upper	61. Link—pushrod to	76. Locking knob
fastener	51. Door hinge lower	latch lock control	

lower pad of the outer belt weatherstrip. Tighten the two stabilizer and trim support bracket screws.

5. Raise the glass to the full up position and make the necessary adjustments to seal the glass into the roof rail weatherstrip.

6. Tighten the three glass attaching nuts and the glass plate lower guide retainer mounting nuts.

7. Adjust the up stops until contact is made with the up stop flange on the glass lift plate. Tighten the up stop attaching nuts.

8. Pull the bracket and liner assembly inboard until it contacts the hook on the glass lift plate. Tighten the screw.

9. Reinstall the plastic shield and the door panel.

Hood

Alignment

Hood hinges on all models have slotted retaining bolt holes which allow adjusting the hinge-to-hood relationship. The hood-mounted end of the hinge is slotted for forward-and-backward motion. The body-mounted end of the hinge is slotted for an up-and-down motion.

1. Scribe the beginning position of the hinge in relation to the body. This will give you an idea of how much the hinges are being moved.

2. Loosen the necessary hinge retaining bolts and change the hinge positioning for correct hood alignment.

3. Tighten the bolts and close the hood to check the adjustment.

4. Remove the rubber bumpers from the adjustable screws at either end of the radiator support. Turn the screws as necessary to make the hood even with the fenders when closed. Tighten the locknut after the final adjustment. The rubber bumpers should just be slightly compressed when the hood is firmly closed.

5. The hood latch adjustment, if necessary, is performed after the hinges and bumpers are adjusted. The latch plate on the hood is slotted to provide forward-and-backward adjustment. The lock bolt may be adjusted up-or-down.

CAUTION: *Ensure that the rear of the hood is sealed at the cowl. This will prevent underhood fumes from being pulled into the passenger compartment through the cowl vent.*

Trunk Lid

Alignment

The trunk lid may be adjusted in the same manner as the hood. However, there is very little clearance and consequently only very slight adjustments can be made.

Fuel Tank

Removal and Installation

1. Disconnect the battery ground cable.

2. In order to relieve any pressure that may have built up in the tank, remove the filler cap before draining the tank or disconnecting any lines.

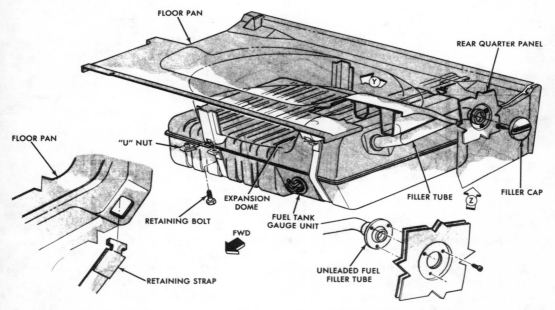

VIEW IN DIRECTION OF ARROW Y

VIEW IN DIRECTION OF ARROW Z

Fuel tank

3. There is no drain plug on the gas tank. The only way to drain the tank is to siphon the gas out. Needless to say, this job will be a lot easier if the gas tank is nearly empty to start with.

4. Remove the three screws that attach the filler tube to the body. Twist the filler tube carefully out of its rubber grommet.

5. Raise the car in the air and support it.

6. Place a jack or support of some type underneath the fuel tank. With the tank supported, loosen the nuts that hold the retaining straps to the "J" bolts. When the nuts are loose enough, remove the "J" bolts from the brackets.

7. Drop the straps to the ground and lower the tank far enough to remove the fuel line, ground strap, and fuel gauge wire. Remove the fuel tank.

8. To install the tank, first position the

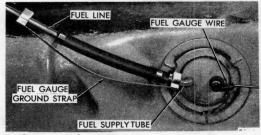

Fuel gauge sending unit

tank underneath the car. Connect the fuel line, ground strap, and gauge wire.

9. Raise the tank into position and install the retaining straps.

10. Lubricate the rubber filler tube grommet with a suitable rubber lubricant, then slide the filler tube into the grommet. Install the three attaching screws.

General Conversion Table

Multiply by	To convert	To	
2.54	Inches	Centimeters	.3937
30.48	Feet	Centimeters	.0328
.914	Yards	Meters	1.094
1.609	Miles	Kilometers	.621
.645	Square inches	Square cm.	.155
.836	Square yards	Square meters	1.196
16.39	Cubic inches	Cubic cm.	.061
28.3	Cubic feet	Liters	.0353
.4536	Pounds	Kilograms	2.2045
4.226	Gallons	Liters	.264
.068	Lbs./sq. in. (psi)	Atmospheres	14.7
.138	Foot pounds	Kg. m.	7.23
1.014	H.P. (DIN)	H.P. (SAE)	.9861
——	To obtain	From	Multiply by

Note: 1 cm. equals 10 mm.; 1 mm. equals .0394".

Conversion—Common Fractions to Decimals and Millimeters

INCHES			INCHES			INCHES		
Common Fractions	Decimal Fractions	Millimeters (approx.)	Common Fractions	Decimal Fractions	Millimeters (approx.)	Common Fractions	Decimal Fractions	Millimeters (approx.)
1/128	.008	0.20	11/32	.344	8.73	43/64	.672	17.07
1/64	.016	0.40	23/64	.359	9.13	11/16	.688	17.46
1/32	.031	0.79	3/8	.375	9.53	45/64	.703	17.86
3/64	.047	1.19	25/64	.391	9.92	23/32	.719	18.26
1/16	.063	1.59	13/32	.406	10.32	47/64	.734	18.65
5/64	.078	1.98	27/64	.422	10.72	3/4	.750	19.05
3/32	.094	2.38	7/16	.438	11.11	49/64	.766	19.45
7/64	.109	2.78	29/64	.453	11.51	25/32	.781	19.84
1/8	.125	3.18	15/32	.469	11.91	51/64	.797	20.24
9/64	.141	3.57	31/64	.484	12.30	13/16	.813	20.64
5/32	.156	3.97	1/2	.500	12.70	53/64	.828	21.03
11/64	.172	4.37	33/64	.516	13.10	27/32	.844	21.43
3/16	.188	4.76	17/32	.531	13.49	55/64	.859	21.83
13/64	.203	5.16	35/64	.547	13.89	7/8	.875	22.23
7/32	.219	5.56	9/16	.563	14.29	57/64	.891	22.62
15/64	.234	5.95	37/64	.578	14.68	29/32	.906	23.02
1/4	.250	6.35	19/32	.594	15.08	59/64	.922	23.42
17/64	.266	6.75	39/64	.609	15.48	15/16	.938	23.81
9/32	.281	7.14	5/8	.625	15.88	61/64	.953	24.21
19/64	.297	7.54	41/64	.641	16.27	31/32	.969	24.61
5/16	.313	7.94	21/32	.656	16.67	63/64	.984	25.00
21/64	.328	8.33						

Conversion—Millimeters to Decimal Inches

mm	inches	mm	inches	mm	inches	mm	inches	mm	inches
1	.039 370	31	1.220 470	61	2.401 570	91	3.582 670	210	8.267 700
2	.078 740	32	1.259 840	62	2.440 940	92	3.622 040	220	8.661 400
3	.118 110	33	1.299 210	63	2.480 310	93	3.661 410	230	9.055 100
4	.157 480	34	1.338 580	64	2.519 680	94	3.700 780	240	9.448 800
5	.196 850	35	1.377 949	65	2.559 050	95	3.740 150	250	9.842 500
6	.236 220	36	1.417 319	66	2.598 420	96	3.779 520	260	10.236 200
7	.275 590	37	1.456 689	67	2.637 790	97	3.818 890	270	10.629 900
8	.314 960	38	1.496 050	68	2.677 160	98	3.858 260	280	11.032 600
9	.354 330	39	1.535 430	69	2.716 530	99	3.897 630	290	11.417 300
10	.393 700	40	1.574 800	70	2.755 900	100	3.937 000	300	11.811 000
11	.433 070	41	1.614 170	71	2.795 270	105	4.133 848	310	12.204 700
12	.472 440	42	1.653 540	72	2.834 640	110	4.330 700	320	12.598 400
13	.511 810	43	1.692 910	73	2.874 010	115	4.527 550	330	12.992 100
14	.551 180	44	1.732 280	74	2.913 380	120	4.724 400	340	13.385 800
15	.590 550	45	1.771 650	75	2.952 750	125	4.921 250	350	13.779 500
16	.629 920	46	1.811 020	76	2.992 120	130	5.118 100	360	14.173 200
17	.669 290	47	1.850 390	77	3.031 490	135	5.314 950	370	14.566 900
18	.708 660	48	1.889 760	78	3.070 860	140	5.511 800	380	14.960 600
19	.748 030	49	1.929 130	79	3.110 230	145	5.708 650	390	15.354 300
20	.787 400	50	1.968 500	80	3.149 600	150	5.905 500	400	15.748 000
21	.826 770	51	2.007 870	81	3.188 970	155	6.102 350	500	19.685 000
22	.866 140	52	2.047 240	82	3.228 340	160	6.299 200	600	23.622 000
23	.905 510	53	2.086 610	83	3.267 710	165	6.496 050	700	27.559 000
24	.944 880	54	2.125 980	84	3.307 080	170	6.692 900	800	31.496 000
25	.984 250	55	2.165 350	85	3.346 450	175	6.889 750	900	35.433 000
26	1.023 620	56	2.204 720	86	3.385 820	180	7.086 600	1000	39.370 000
27	1.062 990	57	2.244 090	87	3.425 190	185	7.283 450	2000	78.740 000
28	1.102 360	58	2.283 460	88	3.464 560	190	7.480 300	3000	118.110 000
29	1.141 730	59	2.322 830	89	3.503 903	195	7.677 150	4000	157.480 000
30	1.181 100	60	2.362 200	90	3.543 300	200	7.874 000	5000	196.850 000

To change decimal millimeters to decimal inches, position the decimal point where desired on either side of the millimeter measurement shown and reset the inches decimal by the same number of digits in the same direction. For example, to convert 0.001 mm into decimal inches, reset the decimal behind the 1 mm (shown on the chart) to 0.001; change the decimal inch equivalent (0.039″ shown) to 0.000039″.

Tap Drill Sizes

National Fine or S.A.E.			National Coarse or U.S.S.		
Screw & Tap Size	Threads Per Inch	Use Drill Number	Screw & Tap Size	Threads Per Inch	Use Drill Number
No. 5	44	37	No. 5	40	39
No. 6	40	33	No. 6	32	36
No. 8	36	29	No. 8	32	29
No. 10	32	21	No. 10	24	25
No. 12	28	15	No. 12	24	17
1/4	28	3	1/4	20	8
5/16	24	1	5/16	18	F
3/8	24	Q	3/8	16	5/16
7/16	20	W	7/16	14	U
1/2	20	29/64	1/2	13	27/64
9/16	18	33/64	9/16	12	31/64
5/8	18	37/64	5/8	11	17/32
3/4	16	11/16	3/4	10	21/32
7/8	14	13/16	7/8	9	49/64
			1	8	7/8
1 1/8	12	1 3/64	1 1/8	7	63/64
1 1/4	12	1 11/64	1 1/4	7	1 7/64
1 1/2	12	1 27/64	1 1/2	6	1 11/32

Decimal Equivalent Size of the Number Drills

Drill No.	Decimal Equivalent	Drill No.	Decimal Equivalent	Drill No.	Decimal Equivalent
80	.0135	53	.0595	26	.1470
79	.0145	52	.0635	25	.1495
78	.0160	51	.0670	24	.1520
77	.0180	50	.0700	23	.1540
76	.0200	49	.0730	22	.1570
75	.0210	48	.0760	21	.1590
74	.0225	47	.0785	20	.1610
73	.0240	46	.0810	19	.1660
72	.0250	45	.0820	18	.1695
71	.0260	44	.0860	17	.1730
70	.0280	43	.0890	16	.1770
69	.0292	42	.0935	15	.1800
68	.0310	41	.0960	14	.1820
67	.0320	40	.0980	13	.1850
66	.0330	39	.0995	12	.1890
65	.0350	38	.1015	11	.1910
64	.0360	37	.1040	10	.1935
63	.0370	36	.1065	9	.1960
62	.0380	35	.1100	8	.1990
61	.0390	34	.1110	7	.2010
60	.0400	33	.1130	6	.2040
59	.0410	32	.1160	5	.2055
58	.0420	31	.1200	4	.2090
57	.0430	30	.1285	3	.2130
56	.0465	29	.1360	2	.2210
55	.0520	28	.1405	1	.2280
54	.0550	27	.1440		

Decimal Equivalent Size of the Letter Drills

Letter Drill	Decimal Equivalent	Letter Drill	Decimal Equivalent	Letter Drill	Decimal Equivalent
A	.234	J	.277	S	.348
B	.238	K	.281	T	.358
C	.242	L	.290	U	.368
D	.246	M	.295	V	.377
E	.250	N	.302	W	.386
F	.257	O	.316	X	.397
G	.261	P	.323	Y	.404
H	.266	Q	.332	Z	.413
I	.272	R	.339		

ANTI-FREEZE CHART

Temperatures Shown in Degrees Fahrenheit
+32 is Freezing

Cooling System Capacity Quarts	Quarts of ETHYLENE GLYCOL Needed for Protection to Temperatures Shown Below													
	1	2	3	4	5	6	7	8	9	10	11	12	13	14
10	+24°	+16°	+ 4°	−12°	−34°	−62°								
11	+25	+18	+ 8	− 6	−23	−47								
12	+26	+19	+10	0	−15	−34	−57°							
13	+27	+21	+13	+ 3	− 9	−25	−45							
14			+15	+ 6	− 5	−18	−34							
15			+16	+ 8	0	−12	−26							
16			+17	+10	+ 2	− 8	−19	−34	−52°					
17			+18	+12	+ 5	− 4	−14	−27	−42					
18			+19	+14	+ 7	0	−10	−21	−34	−50°				
19			+20	+15	+ 9	+ 2	− 7	−16	−28	−42				
20				+16	+10	+ 4	− 3	−12	−22	−34	−48°			
21				+17	+12	+ 6	0	− 9	−17	−28	−41			
22				+18	+13	+ 8	+ 2	− 6	−14	−23	−34	−47°		
23				+19	+14	+ 9	+ 4	− 3	−10	−19	−29	−40		
24				+19	+15	+10	+ 5	0	− 8	−15	−23	−34	−46°	
25				+20	+16	+12	+ 7	+ 1	− 5	−12	−20	−29	−40	−50°
26					+17	+13	+ 8	+ 3	− 3	− 9	−16	−25	−34	−44
27					+18	+14	+ 9	+ 5	− 1	− 7	−13	−21	−29	−39
28					+18	+15	+10	+ 6	+ 1	− 5	−11	−18	−25	−34
29					+19	+16	+12	+ 7	+ 2	− 3	− 8	−15	−22	−29
30					+20	+17	+13	+ 8	+ 4	− 1	− 6	−12	−18	−25

For capacities over 30 quarts divide true capacity by 3. Find quarts Anti-Freeze for the 1/3 and multiply by 3 for quarts to add.

For capacities under 10 quarts multiply true capacity by 3. Find quarts Anti-Freeze for the tripled volume and divide by 3 for quarts to add.

To Increase the Freezing Protection of Anti-Freeze Solutions Already Installed

Cooling System Capacity Quarts	Number of Quarts of ETHYLENE GLYCOL Anti-Freeze Required to Increase Protection													
	From +20°F. to					From +10°F. to					From 0°F. to			
	0°	−10°	−20°	−30°	−40°	0°	−10°	−20°	−30°	−40°	−10°	−20°	−30°	−40°
10	1 3/4	2 1/4	3	3 1/2	3 3/4	3/4	1 1/2	2 1/4	2 3/4	3 1/4	3/4	1 1/2	2	2 1/2
12	2	2 3/4	3 1/2	4	4 1/2	1	1 3/4	2 1/2	3 1/4	3 3/4	1	1 3/4	2 1/2	3 1/4
14	2 1/4	3 1/4	4	4 3/4	5 1/2	1 1/4	2	3	3 3/4	4 1/2	1	2	3	3 1/2
16	2 1/2	3 1/2	4 1/2	5 1/4	6	1 1/4	2 1/2	3 1/2	4 1/4	5 1/4	1 1/4	2 1/4	3 1/4	4
18	3	4	5	6	7	1 1/2	2 3/4	4	5	5 3/4	1 1/2	2 1/2	3 3/4	4 3/4
20	3 1/4	4 1/2	5 3/4	6 3/4	7 1/2	1 3/4	3	4 1/4	5 1/2	6 1/2	1 1/2	2 3/4	4 1/4	5 1/4
22	3 1/2	5	6 1/4	7 1/4	8 1/4	1 3/4	3 1/4	4 3/4	6	7 1/4	1 3/4	3 1/4	4 1/2	5 1/2
24	4	5 1/2	7	8	9	2	3 1/2	5	6 1/2	7 1/2	1 3/4	3 1/2	5	6
26	4 1/4	6	7 1/2	8 3/4	10	2	4	5 1/2	7	8 1/4	2	3 3/4	5 1/2	6 3/4
28	4 1/2	6 1/4	8	9 1/2	10 1/2	2 1/4	4 1/4	6	7 1/2	9	2	4	5 3/4	7 1/4
30	5	6 3/4	8 1/2	10	11 1/2	2 1/2	4 1/2	6 1/2	8	9 1/2	2 1/4	4 1/4	6 1/4	7 3/4

Test radiator solution with proper hydrometer. Determine from the table the number of quarts of solution to be drawn off from a full cooling system and replace with undiluted anti-freeze, to give the desired increased protection. For example, to increase protection of a 22-quart cooling system containing Ethylene Glycol (permanent type) anti-freeze, from +20°F. to −20°F. will require the replacement of 6 1/4 quarts of solution with undiluted anti-freeze.